MEDWIN'S
*CONVERSATIONS OF
LORD BYRON*

MEDWIN'S

CONVERSATIONS OF

LORD BYRON

Revised with a New Preface by the Author
for a New Edition and
Annotated by Lady Byron, John Cam Hobhouse,
Sir Walter Scott, Sir Charles Napier,
John Murray, John Galt, William Harness,
Robert Southey, Lady Caroline Lamb,
Leigh Hunt, Mary Shelley,
E. J. Trelawny, William Fletcher,
Countess Teresa Guiccioli,
and Others Who Knew the Poet Personally

EDITED BY

ERNEST J. LOVELL, JR.

PRINCETON, NEW JERSEY
PRINCETON UNIVERSITY PRESS
1966

Publication of this book
has been aided by
the Whitney Darrow Publication Reserve Fund
of Princeton University Press.
*
Printed in the United States of America
by Princeton University Press
Princeton, New Jersey

CONTENTS

INTRODUCTION

By Ernest J. Lovell, Jr.

THE STORY of Thomas Medwin and the background, birth, and violent aftermath of his *Conversations of Lord Byron* (1824) has been told in my *Captain Medwin: Friend of Byron and Shelley*, to which the reader is referred for details. It may be said briefly here, however, that even before he met Byron in late 1821, he was a man of some accomplishments. Son of a well-to-do Horsham solicitor, second cousin and boyhood friend of Shelley, he had preceded Shelley to Syon House Academy, had gone on to Oxford, leaving without a degree, and, not liking the law, he sailed in 1812 for India as an officer in His Majesty's 24th Light Dragoons.

Stationed chiefly at Cawnpore, he served without distinction during the Mahratta and Pindari War of 1817-1818 and saw little action, but in India he developed a rather remarkable variety of interests which would later recommend him to Byron. Aside from his military and hunting and fishing activities, he became a discriminating foreign observer, interested in the architecture, art, religion, literature, language, and customs of the people of India, which he described at length. In addition, he was writing tolerable verse, keeping a journal, studying Spanish and Portuguese. He was by no means just another hard-drinking, indolent cavalry officer.

When Byron first met him, Medwin, now attempting to live like a gentleman on the half-pay of a lieutenant, had two volumes of verse to his credit and a three-part article on the cave temples of Ellora; he had travelled in parts of the world as little known to most Englishmen as those Byron had visited; and he read with various degrees of skill Greek, Latin, Italian, French, and German, as well as those languages mentioned earlier. He was a broadly if carelessly educated man of the world and could thus serve in Pisa as a bridge for Byron between the unworldly literary genius of Shelley and the semiliteracy of Trelawny. His name would finally appear below the title of more than sixty publications—poems, tales, reminiscences, translations, articles on a variety of subjects, a novel, and a biography.

Byron received Medwin as a man of some connections and accomplishments, and, drawn together by their common interest in the more colorful forms of human life and in the literature and literary gossip of the day, they talked of everything from Shelley's *atheos* to a dose of Wordsworthian physic, which Byron told him he had received from Shelley in the summer of 1816. Surveying the topics of their conversation, one has the impression that Medwin was excluded from very few areas of Byron's life.

Medwin had in fact planted the seeds of the Pisan circle of Byron and Shelley, being chiefly responsible for its English membership—Edward E. Williams, his wife Jane, and Trelawny. Following the death of Shelley, he returned to Pisa shortly before Byron left, there meeting Leigh Hunt, and moved restlessly on to Geneva, London, Paris, Cheltenham, Wales, and again to Paris, where he saw a good deal of Washington Irving. Then, back once more in Geneva, without the aid of any English book of reference, in three weeks, he said, he wrote up the conversations of Byron, drawn from his diary. If true, here is the explanation of Medwin's more obvious errors. On May 15, 1824, the news of Byron's death had been publicly announced in London; Colburn had seen Medwin's manuscript and agreed before July 17 to publish.

The present edition is witness to the furor created by Medwin's book, which between 1824 and 1842 appeared in fifteen editions, in six countries, and was translated into French, German, and Italian. The enormous Continental influence of Byron, to which Bertrand Russell, Gilbert Highet, and others testify, was the product then, in significant part, of Medwin's Byron, an historical fact to be reckoned with and one which influenced the poet's public image greatly.

Many of Byron's friends and enemies and most of those mentioned in the *Conversations* commented upon the book, either privately or publicly, and their remarks supply the greater and more valuable part of the notes to this edition. The result is a continuing dialogue, amplified and enlarged, extending far beyond Pisa and the lifetime of Byron, as reality is passed from hand to hand down through the years and the portrait of Byron receives new dimensions. These footnotes to a significant chapter of literary history, often lighting up the moral and social assumptions of the age, also provide an exercise in evidence, as one witness debates with another.

Because Medwin was upon occasion careless, muddle-headed, dishonest, or insufficiently informed for his Boswellian task, his annotators and reviewers ran riot through his pages, pricked or goaded on by the knowledge that he knew the most intimate and secret details of Byron's life and theirs. Since they so often wrote, understandably, out of a sense of outrage, it may be well here, at the beginning, to hear some of the evidence in Medwin's favor, for his was the first of the many book-length reminiscences of Byron to be published, and thus it was especially vulnerable. John Galt, who in 1830 quoted extensively from the *Conversations* in his *Life of Byron*, clearly affirmed his belief in its authenticity: "The account given by Captain Medwin . . . has the raciness of his Lordship's own quaintness. . . . They [the conversations reported] have much of the poet's peculiar modes of thinking about them. . . ." Sir Walter Scott wrote on November 11, 1824, to Mrs. Hughes, who had sent him extracts from a review of Medwin, "from what I saw in the papers and from what I knew of Lord Byron I conceive Capt. Medwin to have been an accurate reporter." Robert Southey, in a letter addressed to the editor of the *Courier*, on December 8, 1824, stated, "that his lordship spoke to this effect, and in this temper, I have no doubt. . . . I take these Conversations to be authentic. . . ." Lady Caroline Lamb, about whom Byron had spoken heartlessly, wrote to Medwin in 1824 to defend herself but also to say, "your book . . . does you credit. . . . Parts of it are beautiful; and I can vouch for the truth of much, as I read his own Memoirs before Murray burnt them." Trelawny, if we may believe his *Records*, said to Byron, "Medwin has no design to lie about you; he is credulous and will note your idle words." Leigh Hunt, who had no reason to love Medwin, stated in 1828, "With the cautions here afforded the reader, a better idea of his Lordship may certainly be drawn from his account than from any other." William Parry, author of one of the best books on Byron written by those who knew him, affirmed in 1825, "I have heard him so often indulge in language similar to that which is reported by Mr. Medwin, that what he has stated appears to wear an air of truth." And John Wilson Croker wrote, in a review so favorable to Medwin that it was suppressed, "It is we think impossible to read his notes without seeing in them all the marks of general authenticity. No doubt he has been guilty of some inaccuracies of detail . . . but after all, we see no good reason to suppose that his inaccuracies are more frequent than the transmission of recollected conversations to paper is necessarily subject to, and the instances in which errors of any considerable importance have been detected are not many, nor such as to affect in any serious degree the credit of the reporter, nor in *any* degree the impression as to Lord Byron himself, which the general character of the work must excite."

In later times, James Fox, author of *Vindication of Lady Byron* (1871), concluded, "The conversations recorded by Captain Medwin, though inaccurate in some small circumstances, agree, in the main [concerning Byron's marriage and separation], with what was told afterwards by other authorities. . . ." When in 1913 H. Buxton Forman came to edit Medwin's revised *Life of Shelley* for the Oxford University Press, he could not decide "whether the Byron Conversations and the Life of Shelley should be called the two most valuable bad books of the century or the two worst valuable books of the century." It was a "hard point of casuistry," he wrote. Other scholars of this century have been more certain and less casuistical. Rowland E. Prothero (Lord Ernle) quotes from Medwin at great length in the notes to his magnificent edition of Byron's *Letters and Journals* and regards the *Conversations* as a "valuable . . . record of Byron's random talk." John Drinkwater, author of *The Pilgrim of Eternity* (1925), concludes that Medwin's volume is "one of the most justly abused and one of the best books in Byron literature. . . . There is scarcely a statement that can be trusted, and yet not one that does not contribute to a portrait of Byron that seen at a distance is strangely convincing." Samuel C. Chew, writing in 1956 in *The Major English Romantic Poets: A Review of Research*, describes Medwin's book as one of "the two principal records of the poet's conversation." Leslie A. Marchand, author of the definitive *Byron: A Biography*, seems to agree: Medwin's and Lady Blessington's *Conversations* are "in many respects the most interesting of all the contemporary records." Edmund Blunden, in an article on "Lord Byron: Some Early Biographies," concluded in 1956, "To sum up, Medwin is no mean Boswellian, and had he been more of a Boswell, his book on Byron—and Shelley—would have had less worth. The Byron in it is not stage-managed. It is a recording, with cracks."

Goethe read Medwin's *Conversations* twice: "I would not have missed them," he wrote, "but they leave a painful impression." He was distressed by the gossip and the trifles which Medwin recorded and by Byron's "disorderly life with dogs and monkeys and peacocks, everything without order or connection." Goethe resolved that no such book should ever be written about him. E. M. Butler explains, in *Byron and Goethe* (1956): "The irritation produced in Goethe by Medwin's *Conversations of Lord Byron* had one entirely unforeseen and unforeseeable result: a literary pearl in the shape of

Eckermann's *Conversations with Goethe*." But, alas, Eckermann's book "is neither art nor nature," Butler concludes, "this last gift of Goethe's to posterity, in which he himself consciously collaborated by sitting for his portrait in words; it is something between the two, and reads at times as if James Boswell were trying his hand at writing a *Symposium*." This sad fault, at least, Medwin avoided.

This edition is based on Medwin's copy (now in the Houghton Library) of his "New Edition" of 1824 (the third London edition), heavily annotated by the author, with a new preface, and intended for another new and last edition, which was never published. On the title page he struck out the damaging words (for which he had suffered), *Noted during a Residence with his Lordship at Pisa*, and explained elsewhere that the original title had been merely *The Conversations of Lord Byron* and that Colburn the publisher had "changed it, as more attractive, without my consent." Inasmuch as Medwin himself had not arrived at a final version of his text, his deletions and directions sometimes being contradictory, I have not hesitated at certain points, marked in the text, to restore passages deleted by Colburn. These restorations are supplied from the first edition of the *Conversations* and from a letter which Medwin wrote in 1825 to Edward Bulwer. At several points also I have allowed to stand passages seemingly marked by Medwin for deletion: notably, his long footnote-memoir of Shelley, details of which Medwin corrected (thus making it impossible to know his final intentions), and a "letter to a friend" near the end of the volume. Medwin's textual changes that are clearly revisions or expansions of existing matter are published as he intended them to be, in the body of the text or in his original footnotes, the latter marked by an asterisk or other printer's symbol, as in the early editions. Medwin's additions of new material are placed in footnotes introduced by a superscript numeral and his name, in italics. Unless otherwise specified, page references to the early editions of Medwin's *Conversations* have been changed to correspond to the pagination of the present edition.

Medwin's notes frequently take the form of quotations from Byron's letters as they appeared in Thomas Moore's *Letters and Journals of Lord Byron, With Notices of His Life* (1830). The sources of such quotations have regularly been translated into the page numbers of Prothero's edition of Byron's *Letters and Journals*, more easily accessible. Other references to Moore's *Life* have been given in terms of the pagination of the London edition of 1892, rather than the obscure four-volume edition used by Medwin. The symbol "(M)" at the close of a quotation indicates that Medwin copied out the passage in the margin of his book. Other notes by Medwin are taken from his long letter to the Editor of Galignani's *Weekly Register*, replying to John Murray in *The Gentleman's Magazine*, partly published in my *Captain Medwin*. The autograph letter is in the Pierpont Morgan Library, to the director of which my thanks are due.

Three other annotated copies of the *Conversations* supply comments from Lady Byron, Hobhouse, Trelawny, and Sir Charles Napier, who knew Byron in Cephalonia. The copy with marginal notes made by Lady Byron is now owned by the Earl of Lytton, as part of the famous Lovelace Collection. Mr. Malcolm Elwin, literary adviser to Lord Lytton and author of *Lord Byron's Wife* (1962), very generously supplied a transcript of these annotations. The copy annotated by Trelawny and Sir Charles Napier belonged to Dr. Henry Muir, for many years Medical Officer of Health at Argostoli. He introduced Byron to Dr. James Kennedy, and it was in Muir's house that their conversations on religion took place. This copy, now in the Houghton Library, seems to have been annotated by Trelawny and Napier before the close of 1826. Hobhouse's copy is now in the Yale University Library. My grateful appreciation is due to all those who made these copies available.

Other major sources of notes which were written by those who knew Byron and which comment explicitly on Medwin's book or reply directly to it include the following:

(1) Hobhouse's review in *The Westminster Review* for January, 1825; Hobhouse's suppressed pamphlet, *Exposure of the Misstatements in Captain Medwin's Pretended "Conversations of Lord Byron,"* a copy of which was kindly supplied to me by Sir John Murray; and unpublished passages from Hobhouse's diary, transcripts of which were kindly supplied by Mrs. Doris Langley Moore;

(2) John Murray's defense of himself in *The Gentleman's Magazine* for November, 1824;

(3) the review by John Galt, who knew Byron between 1810 and 1813, in *Blackwood's Edinburgh Magazine* for November, 1824;

(4) the review by William Harness, who knew Byron at Harrow and later, chiefly between 1802 and 1811, in *Blackwood's* for November, 1824;

(5) Robert Southey's letter to the Editor of the *Courier*, Decem-

ber 8, 1824, reprinted in Prothero's edition of Byron's *Letters and Journals*, VI, 395-399;

(6) Lady Caroline Lamb's long letter to Medwin, written probably in November, 1824, and published in Prothero's edition of Byron's *Letters and Journals*, II, 451-454;

(7) Leigh Hunt, chiefly in *Lord Byron and Some of His Contemporaries* (1828);

(8) Mary Shelley's letter to Hobhouse, November 10, 1824, published in my *Captain Medwin*, pp. 200-201;

(9) Sir Walter Scott, in various letters;

(10) William Fletcher's unpublished comments, now in the Pierpont Morgan Library;

(11) Teresa Guiccioli's comments in her unpublished "Vie de Lord Byron en Italie," photographic copies of which were kindly supplied by Professor Leslie A. Marchand;

(12) John Wilson Croker's suppressed review, set up in page proof for the *Quarterly Review* but so favorable to Medwin that it was never published. A copy is in the possession of Sir John Murray, to whose great generosity I am again indebted. The exact degree of intimacy which may have existed between Byron and Croker is difficult to estimate. Croker was a regular reviewer for the *Quarterly*, one of Murray's literary advisers, and Secretary to the Admiralty. Byron requested his aid on two occasions: once in 1813, seeking passage on a ship-of-war bound for the Mediterranean (passage was secured) and once again in 1819, through Murray, seeking a consulship for Count Guiccioli. In early 1816 Byron wrote a satiric poem on Croker, which he destroyed, but the *Morning Chronicle* announced its forthcoming publication, and Croker probably saw the announcement. This may help to explain why he is an unfriendly witness for Byron.

Inasmuch as this edition is intended as a supplement to *His Very Self and Voice: Collected Conversations of Lord Byron*, which excluded Medwin's *Conversations* as explained in the Introduction, quotations of others who reported Byron's conversation are often taken from that volume. My own comments are always enclosed within brackets. If no specific source follows a footnote, it is drawn from one of the unpublished sources listed above.

My grateful appreciation is due, once again, to the University of Texas Research Institute, for a leave of absence from teaching duties; to Miss Ruth Hale, Miss Kathleen Blow, and others of the University of Texas Library, for their unfailing courtesy and highly informed assistance; and to Mrs. Joan St. George Saunders, my friend and representative in London, for favors too numerous to mention. For helpful suggestions concerning the notes, I wish also to thank Professor Wilfred S. Dowden of Rice University, Professor William H. Marshall of the University of Pennsylvania, and Professor Leslie A. Marchand of Rutgers University.

AUSTIN, TEXAS
JANUARY 19, 1965

MEDWIN'S PREFACE TO THE
THIRD LONDON EDITION OF 1824

"A GREAT poet belongs to no country; his works are public property, and his Memoirs the inheritance of the public." Such were the sentiments of Lord Byron; and have they been attended to? Has not a manifest injustice been done to the world, and an injury to his memory, by the destruction of his Memoirs?[1] These are questions which it is now late, perhaps needless, to ask; but I will endeavour to lessen, if not to remedy, the evil.

I am aware that in publishing these reminiscences I shall have to contend with much obloquy from some parts of his family,—that I shall incur the animosity of many of his friends. There are authors, too, who will not be pleased to find their names in print,—to hear his real opinion of themselves, or of their works. There are others —— But I have the satisfaction of feeling that I have set about executing the task I have undertaken, conscientiously: I mean neither to throw a veil over his errors, nor a gloss over his virtues.

My sketch will be an imperfect and a rough one, it is true, but it will be from the life; and slight as it is, may prove more valuable, perhaps, than a finished drawing from memory. It will be any thing but a panegyric: my aim is to paint him as he was. That his passions were violent and impetuous, cannot be denied; but his feelings and affections were equally strong. Both demanded continual employment; and he had an impatience of repose, a "restlessness of rest," that kept them in constant activity. It is satisfactory too, at least it is some consolation, to reflect, that the last energies of his nature were consumed in the cause of liberty, and for the benefit of mankind.

[1] [For the most detailed account of the burning of Byron's famous Memoirs, see Doris L. Moore, *The Late Lord Byron* (Philadelphia, 1961, pp. 12-56.]

How I became acquainted with so many particulars of his history, so many incidents of his life, so many of his opinions, is easily explained. They were communicated during a period of many months' familiar intercourse,[2] without any injunctions to secrecy,[3] and committed to paper for the sake of reference only. They have not been shewn to any one individual,[4] and but for the fate of his MS. would never have appeared before the public.

I despise mere writing for the sake of book-making, and have disdained to swell out my materials into volumes. I have given his ideas as I noted them down at the time,—in his own words, as far as my recollection served.[5]

They are however, in many cases, the substance without the form. The brilliancy of his wit, the flow of his eloquence,

---

[2] [Medwin arrived in Pisa on November 14, 1821, met Byron, he states in his *Conversations*, on November 20, left Pisa for Rome about March 11, 1822, returned to Pisa on August 16, 1822, it seems, and left once more in the fourth week of August, never to see Byron again, although the two men exchanged letters. Thus Medwin's opportunities for talking with Byron extended over a total period of slightly more than four months.]

[3] *J. W. Croker*: Good God! can Mr. Medwin have deceived himself into a belief, that a man of honour is at liberty to publish, in print and to all the world, every thing which he has heard during any period of familiar and confidential intercourse, unless his friend shall have cautiously premised on each occasion an *injunction of secrecy*? . . . Unless Mr. Medwin can give some other and better explanation than he has done, no one can hesitate to pronounce his publication to be a most unjustifiable breach of private confidence, and an example which, if it were to prevail, would loosen all the bonds of social life, and destroy all confidence, friendship, and happiness amongst mankind.

[4] [Medwin's manuscript had been seen before publication by Sir Samuel Brydges, Washington Irving, Sir John St. Aubyn, and Thomas Colley Grattan.]

[5] [In February, 1832, in *The Literary Gazette*, Medwin publicly offered to show his original journal "to any person whom Mr. Murray may appoint." Medwin was back in England at the time.]

the sallies of his imagination, who could do justice to? His voice, his manner, which gave a charm to the whole, who could forget?

> "His subtle talk would cheer the winter night,
> And make me know myself; and the fire-light
> Would flash upon our faces, till the day
> Might dawn, and make me wonder at my stay."
>
> Shelley's *Julian and Maddalo*.

GENEVA, 1ST AUGUST, 1824.

MEDWIN'S NOTES
FOR A NEW PREFACE

MORE than 25 years have elapsed since the publication of these Conversations—which have past through half that number of Editions. A friend of mine many years ago told me that I had thrown them on the world like a bastard child; the period is arrived for patronizing [*i.e.*, defending] the offspring, and that parental Duty I now perform. To have done so before the appearance of Mr. Moore's *Notices* [*Letters and Journals of Lord Byron, with Notices of His Life*] would have been lost labour, for then the tide of detraction and calumny would have been too strong to stem; but as these Documents are now in all hands my task is easy, and on them I rest my defence.

That defence it may [be] thought comes late, but to a literary question Time is no bar. Though the wounds I have received no longer bleed, the scars remain [preceding sentence deleted]. The difference between my remorseless enemies and myself is, that they endeavoured by falsehood, falsehood that they thought could not be detected as such, through the medium of a venal press and the influence of the God Almighty of Publishers, to suppress a work which will last as long as the name of Byron endures and [to] injure the fame of one who stood single and was therefore a fair mark for vituperation and calumny. Even their critiques did not strike on the material objects of the book, and required the typographical genius of a reviewer to make a handle of, but they had their effects [preceding sentence deleted].

The real question before the World is, whether I had an opportunity of seeing Lord Byron and reporting his Conversation, whether I took notes of what passed between us, and whether the result is not a lively and faithful picture of the ordinary mode of passing his time, and habits of that very extraordinary man.

xix

If I had underrated his line of conversation, or given a false colour to his character, or misrepresented his estimate of contemporary talent, or taken away the life and spirit of an interesting anecdote by the way of telling it, the public would have had reason to complain. Nor would the work be in the repute it is abroad, have been translated into German, several times into French, and often reprinted in France and Belgium.

When I met Lord Byron in Pisa, I had just returned from India. Many of the topics of his Conversation were new to me, most of his Contemporaries unknown. It is monstrous to suppose that I could have had any Interest in libelling them. In that extraordinary Sketch Lord Byron is seen en Deshabille; with Messrs. Moore and Murray, knowing that all he wrote them would appear in print after his death, he was playing a part. The Reader will perceive by my Commentary within but how much I was really on the scent. It is indeed remarkable that many passages in Byron's Letters to Moore and others should be found almost in the identical words the great poet used to me. My work has no pretensions to another life. It occupied scarcely 3 Weeks and was taken literally from my Diary. Whilst employed in it, I swear, I had no means of consulting a single English book by way of reference.

Among the charges made against me is one that I had no right to divulge Conversations. My reply is that they were not of a private or confidential nature, that Lord Byron, whose favourite answer was that Every body hates every body, cared little what his friends said about him or what his friends thought of him or of his early escapades, which he had already detailed in his Autobiography; but among all the abuse (now forgotten) lavished on Boswell, it was never made a charge against him that he had published Dr. Johnson's Conversations, tho' his Journal was kept for that purpose, whilst mine was made with no such view, and but for the destruction of the Autograph Memoirs, as I said in the Original Preface, would never have seen the light [preceding twenty-two words deleted].

Like Boswell I was only a reporter or Editor. Not so Mr. Moore. It was his Duty as a Biographer and moralist to have portrayed Byron as he was—not to have chosen only the seamy side of his character and to have made his faults and vices low marks, that others might not have remembered in the same writer and firebrand [preceding two sentences deleted]. And as such [*i.e.*, as "reporter or Editor"], some allowances should have been [made] for a few exposures. My memory is fairly accurate, and it is marvelous that it should have been so retentive as it was. It is, however, to be supposed that Conversations set down sometimes after an interval of many hours should contain a few inaccuracies. Those few [?] I have corrected. [Remainder of paragraph is illegible.]

MEDWIN'S
CONVERSATIONS OF
LORD BYRON

PUBLISHER'S NOTE

The material in this book that would normally be treated as footnotes (the comments assembled by the editor and the editor's notes) is of such length in relation to the main text that placing the notes at the foot of each page in the usual way would make it impossible to keep the numbered references and the notes in reasonable proximity. To preserve the liveliness of this continuing debate between Medwin and his commentators, we have chosen to alternate brief passages of Medwin's text with sections of the comments and notes, which are in smaller type and set off by horizontal braces. The reader may prefer to read through an entire passage of Medwin's text before he goes on to the several notes pertinent to that passage. Medwin's original footnotes (marked by asterisks and daggers) are in the usual position, below the text reference.

CONVERSATIONS OF LORD BYRON

I WENT to Italy late in the Autumn of 1821, for the benefit of my health. Lord Byron, accompanied by Mr. Rogers as far as Florence, had passed on a few days before me, and was already at Pisa when I arrived.

His travelling equipage was rather a singular one, and afforded a strange catalogue for the *Dogana*: seven servants, five carriages, nine horses, a monkey, a bull-dog and a mastiff, two cats, three pea-fowls and some hens,[1] (I do not know whether I have classed them in order of rank,) formed part of his live stock; and all his books, consisting of a very large library of modern works, (for he bought all the best that came out,)[2] together with a vast quantity of furniture, might well be termed, with Cæsar, "impediments."

I had long formed a wish to see and be acquainted with Lord Byron; but his known refusal at that time to receive the visits of strangers, even of some who brought him letters of introduction from the most intimate friend he had,[3] and a prejudice excited against his own countrymen by a late insult,[4] would have deterred me from seeking an interview with him, had not the proposal come from himself, in consequence of his hearing Shelley speak of me.

---

[1] *Teresa Guiccioli*: These conversations are not imaginary, but they are . . . unstitched, undigested, light, exaggerated, indelicate, contradictory—as one part is proved false by another. . . . The personal impressions of Mr. Medwin may be true, but that which is not true is a multitude of things and words attributed to Lord Byron, since they are contradicted by the facts. . . . We will restrain ourselves and reveal several of them. For example, of that number [are] . . . the peacocks of Lord Byron's menagerie. [See also Medwin's "pea-fowls" on p. 10.]

Shelley to Thomas Love Peacock, August 10, 1821: I have

just met on the grand staircase [at Ravenna] five peacocks, two guinea hens, and an Egyptian crane. [*The Letters of Percy Bysshe Shelley*, ed. Frederick L. Jones (London, 1964), II, 331; hereafter referred to as *Letters*.]

Shelley to Mary Shelley, August 10, 1821: Here are two monkies, five cats, eight dogs, and ten horses. . . . [*Letters*, II, 324. On October 21, 1821, Byron owned only four carriages, not five (*LJ*, V, 395).]

[2] *Medwin*: His library was as I said mostly composed of modern works, for upon leaving London in 1814 [*sic*] he had been obliged in order to satisfy an execution on his House to sell his Library at Auction. [Byron's library was sold at public auction on April 8, 1816.]

[3] *Medwin*: He refused to see a Visitor who brought him a Letter of Introduction from Mr. Hobhouse. During our Drives we constantly met at the gate, through which past Englishmen who had come out to waylay and get a peep at him. Numbers came to Pisa expressly for that purpose.

[4] [Southey's insulting remarks on the "Satanic school" of writers, Byron chief among them, had been published on April 11, 1821, in the preface to *A Vision of Judgment*.]

⌣

20th NOVEMBER. "This is the Lung' Arno. He has hired the Lanfranchi palace for a year:—it is one of those marble piles that seem built for eternity, whilst the family whose name it bears no longer exists," said Shelley, as we entered a hall that seemed built for giants. "I remember the lines in the 'Inferno,'" said I: "a Lanfranchi was one of the persecutors of Ugolino."—"The same," answered Shelley; "you will see a picture of Ugolino and his sons in his room.[5] Fletcher, his valet, is as superstitious as his master, and says the house is haunted, so that he cannot sleep for rumbling noises overhead, which he compares to the rolling of bowls. No wonder; old Lanfranchi's ghost is unquiet, and walks at night."[6]

The palace was of such size, that Lord Byron only occupied the first floor; and at the top of the staircase leading to it was the English bull-dog, whose chain was long enough to guard the door, and prevent the entrance of strangers; he, however, knew Shelley, growled, and let us pass. In the ante-room we found several servants in livery, and Fletcher, (whom Shelley mentioned, and of whom I shall have occasion to speak,) who had been in his service from the time he left Harrow. "Like many old servants, he is a privileged person," whispered Shelley. "Don Juan had not a better Leporello, for imitating his master. He says that he is a Laurel struck by a *Metre*, (meteor) and when in Greece remarked upon one of the bas-reliefs of the Parthenon, 'La! what mantel-pieces these would make, my Lord!' " When we were announced, we found his Lordship writing. His reception was frank and kind; he took me cordially by the hand, and said:

"You are a relation and schoolfellow of Shelley's—we do not meet as strangers[7]—you must allow me to continue my letter on account of the post. Here's something for you to read, Shelley, (giving him part of his MS. of 'Heaven and Earth;')[8] tell me what you think of it."

---

[5] *Byron in his diary*, January 8, 1821: Mem.—received to-day a print, or etching, of the story of Ugolino, by an Italian painter. . . . [*LJ*, v, 160.]

[6] *Byron to Murray*, December 4, 1821: I have got here into a famous old feudal palazzo, on the Arno, large enough for a garrison, with dungeons below and cells in the walls, and so full of *Ghosts*, that the learned Fletcher (my valet) has begged leave to change his room, and then refused to occupy his *new* room, because there were more ghosts there than in the other. . . . The house belonged to the Lanfranchi family, (the same mentioned by Ugolino in his dream, as his persecutor with Sismondi,) and has had a fierce owner or two in its time. [*LJ*, v, 486-487 (M).]

[7] *Medwin*: My acquaintance with Lord Byron soon ripened into *intimacy* from the circumstance that we were nearly of the same age and mixed in London life in 1812—a life which he still clings to without any of those regrets which poisoned mine. Strangely enough we were never acquainted with each other at the period, though many of our mutual acquaintances were the

same, among which I might enumerate Martin Hawke, Captain [John] Hay, Captain Wallace—after of Paris celebrity—Lord Powerscourt, [?] Lord Blessington, and others. The [? best] or first of these many persons, with whom I was in a club at Brighton, [?] introduced me at Racquet's, of which Byron was also a member. *Martin Hawke* I was very fond of. He possessed so much bonhommie. From him Byron [? received] a story in his *Don Juan*.

Fletcher: Even myself when Batista was not in the way was told by his Lordship either to send him [Medwin] off by fair if not by foul means for he would not see him. . . . This will explain how much my Lord esteemed him as friend and said from the first he would not be bored to death with him for he saw there was no end with him for I see he will not be said no—and his Lordship said after those books being taken away by a person a stranger was an insult past bearing and they was sent for accordingly with a very severe reprimand.

Harness: None can doubt of the intimacy to which he was admitted, who has heard that he once presumed so far as to transgress the orders of the noble poet, and take a volume from the table of his study. The domestic [Fletcher], who had seen and remonstrated against the act, inquired of his master what course was to be adopted on the repetition of a similar offence. The reply was most laconic: "Kick his - - -." [*BEM*, xvi, 537.]

Augusta Leigh to Lady Holland, late November, 1824: I have received a letter from my Brother's Servant who had been in his service 20 years & who had come up from the country upon hearing of or reading this Book of Medwin's, & in the greatest despair at it, being much attached poor man!— He tells me that my Brother was in the habit of sending Mr Medwin from his door & saying he would never see him except out riding when others would be present. This proves *I* think sufficiently what an Impostor he must be. . . . [Unpublished; in the British Museum. See also Augusta Leigh to Hobhouse, quoted by Doris L. Moore, *The Late Lord Byron*, p. 123.]

[8] [Byron had sent a fair copy of *Heaven and Earth* to Murray on November 14, 1821.]

During the few minutes that Lord Byron was finishing his letter, I took an opportunity of narrowly observing him, and drawing his portrait in my mind.* Thorwaldsen's bust is too thin-necked and young[9] for Lord Byron. None of the engravings gave me the least idea of him. I saw a man about five feet eight,[10] apparently forty years of age: as was said of Milton, he barely escaped being short and thick. His face was fine, and the lower part symmetrically moulded; for the lips and chin had that curved and definite outline which distin-

* Being with him, day after day, some time afterwards, whilst he was sitting to Bartolini, the Florentine sculptor, for his bust, I had an opportunity of analyzing his features more critically; but found nothing to alter in my portrait. Bartolini's is an admirable likeness, at least was so in the clay model. I have not seen it since it was copied in marble, nor have I got a cast; he promised Bartolini should send me one. I think I see him now with that bull neck of his, on which he so much prided himself, and his noble and impressive curls were worthy of a poet; but he was I own fatigued with his sittings [?], for the sculptor destroyed his *ébauches* more than once before he could please himself. He came on his own accord.[11] When he had finished, Lord Byron said, "It is the last time I sit to sculptor or painter." This was on the 4th of January, 1822. He did not keep to this resolution, for he sate afterwards to West an American artist—at Leghorn—who made for me a replica of the Portrait.

While he was sitting to Bartolini, he dilated much on the English mania for busts. I remember his saying that portraits may be burnt— but what is to be done with busts? Now, said he, if a man were famous for *any* thing—for being a prize fighter or a cash fighter or a man fighter —or any thing in short to distinguish him from the herd—and carry him down to posterity—to [? little] good—that and all their traveling squires, Fox hunters and their ugly wives and Daughters—to think of immortalizing that [? crew] in marble. The idea is too ridiculous. Bartolini observed that [the] English did not make good busts, that he had no enthusiasm in all this fakery of a Grecian outline, that the fashion of our Compatriots [? which he liked] was not regular, that they made better portraits.

But what [said Byron] are they [to] do with busts, make lime of them?

Now if a man were a statesman or an orator, or a great general or better still a player like Kean or Kemble or a prize fighter like Gregson or a sparrer like Jackson—or even a cockfighter or famous for any thing, there might be some sense in his being handed down to posterity in marble—but these country squires with their commonplace wives and daughters—these most hand[some] Dandies—Portraits of their phizzes may be burnt or hung in effigy—or rot in attics—but of what use are these busts but to make lime of?[12]

{ 7 }

guishes Grecian beauty.[13] His forehead was high, and his temples broad; and he had a paleness in his complexion, almost to wanness. His hair thin and fine, had almost become grey, and waved in natural and graceful curls over his head, that was assimilating itself fast to the "bald first Cæsar's."

[9] [The word "ideal" is substituted for "young," then deleted.]

[10] [The words "seven or" are deleted; Medwin noted Moore's statement that Byron was five feet eight inches tall.]

[11] *Byron to Murray*, March 6 and September 23, 1822: It was done by *his own* [Bartolini's] particular request. . . . The bust does not turn out a very good one, . . . it exactly resembles a superannuated Jesuit. [*LJ*, VI, 37, 117.]

[12] [The relation between the three paragraphs immediately above is not wholly clear. The first of the three may be Medwin's first draft, parts of which he used in writing the second and third paragraphs.]

[13] *Moore*: By the somewhat increased roundness of the contours, the resemblance of his finely formed mouth and chin to those of the Belvidere Apollo had become still more striking. [In 1819 at La Mira; *Letters and Journals of Lord Byron: With Notices of His Life* (London, 1892), p. 410 (M); hereafter referred to as *Life*.]

Galt: His forehead was rather noble certainly, and the general cast of his physiognomy was genteel and Grecian. [*BEM*, XVI, 535 (M).]

He allowed it to grow longer behind than it is accustomed to be worn, and at that time had mustachios, which were not sufficiently dark to be becoming. In criticising his features it might, perhaps, be said that his eyes were placed too near his nose, and that one was rather smaller than the other;[14] they were of a greyish brown, but of a peculiar clearness, and when animated possessed a fire which seemed to look through and penetrate the thoughts of others, while they marked the inspirations of his own. His teeth were small, regular, and white; these, I afterwards found, he took great pains to preserve.*

I expected to discover that he had a club, perhaps a *cloven* foot; but it would have been difficult to distinguish one from the other, either in size or in form,[15] though it is true they were not the most symmetrical.

* For this purpose he used tobacco when he first went into the open air; and he told me he was in the habit of grinding his teeth in his sleep, to prevent which he was forced to put a napkin between them.

[14] [Augusta Leigh confirms the fact that one of Byron's eyes was smaller than the other. See Malcolm Elwin, *Lord Byron's Wife* (New York, 1962), p. 356.]

[15] *Medwin*: A schoolfellow of his told me that notwithstanding the deformity of *both* his feet he was active—and that he used to blame his mother's mock delicacy for his defect. In common with many Scotch ladies of that time she had a prejudice against *Accoucheurs*.

On the whole his figure was manly, and his countenance handsome and prepossessing, and very expressive; and the familiar ease of his conversation soon made me perfectly at home in his society. Our first interview was marked with a cordiality and confidence that flattered while it delighted me; and I felt anxious for the next day, in order that I might repeat my visit.

When I called on his Lordship at two o'clock, he had just left his bed-room, and was at breakfast, if it could be called one. It consisted of a cup of strong green tea, without milk or sugar, and an egg, of which he ate the yolk raw. I observed the abstemiousness of his meal.

"My digestion is weak; I am too bilious," said he, "to eat more than once a-day, and generally live on vegetables. To be sure I drink two bottles of wine at dinner, but they form only a vegetable diet. Just now I live on claret and soda-water. You are just come from Geneva, Shelley tells me. I passed the best part of the summer of 1816 at the Campagne Diodati, and was very nearly passing this last there. I went so far as to write to Hentsh the banker;[16] but Shelley, when he came to visit me at Ravenna, gave me such a flattering account of Pisa that I changed my mind. Then it is troublesome to travel so far with so much live and dead stock as I do; and I don't like to leave behind me any of my pets that have been accumulating since I came on the Continent.* One cannot trust to strangers to take care of them. You will see at the farmer's some of my pea-fowls *en pension*. Fletcher tells me that they are almost as bad fellow-travellers as the monkey†, which I will shew you."[17]

Here he led the way to a room, where, after playing with and caressing the creature for some time, he proposed a game of billiards.

I brought the conversation back on Switzerland and his travels, and asked him if he had been in Germany?

* He says afterwards in "Don Juan," Canto X, St. L.:
———— "He had a kind of inclination, or
Weakness, for what most people deem mere vermin,
Live animals."

† He afterwards bought another monkey in Pisa, in the street, because he saw it ill-used.

[16] *Byron to Hoppner*, July 23, 1821: I have written by this post to Mr. Hentsch, junior, the banker of Geneva, to provide (if possible) a house for me . . . on the *Jura* side of the lake of Geneva. . . . [*LJ*, v, 327.]
[17] *Medwin*: Mr. Monkey was brought every day into the Billiard room.

"No," said he, "not even at Trieste.[18] I hate despotism and the Goths too much.[19] I have travelled little on the Continent, at least never gone out of my way. This is partly owing to the indolence of my disposition, partly owing to my incumbrances. I had some idea, when at Rome, of visiting Naples, but was at that time anxious to get back to Venice. But Pæstum cannot surpass the ruins of Agrigentum,[20] which I saw by moonlight; nor Naples, Constantinople. You have no conception of the beauty of the twelve islands where the Turks have their country-houses, or of the blue Symplegades against which the Bosphorus beats with such restless violence.

"Switzerland is a country I have been satisfied with seeing once;[21] Turkey I could live in for ever. I never forget my predilections. I was in a wretched state of health, and worse spirits when I was at Geneva; but quiet and the lake, physicians better than Polidori, soon set me up. I never led so moral a life as during my residence in that country; but I gained no credit by it. Where there is a mortification, there ought to be reward.[22] On the contrary, there is no story so absurd that they did not invent at my cost. I was watched by glasses on the opposite side of the Lake, and by glasses too that must have had very distorted optics. I was waylaid in my evening drives—I was accused of corrupting all the *grisettes* in the Rue Basse. I believe that they looked upon me as a man-monster, worse than the *piqueur*.

[18] *Medwin*: It is singular that being at Venice nearby he should not have gone over to Trieste, but there were no Steamboats at that time.

[19] *Byron in his diary*, January 12, 1821: The Austrians, whom I abhor, loathe, and—I cannot find words for my hate of them. . . . [*LJ*, v, 172 (M).]

[20] [Byron and Hobhouse saw the ruins of Agrigentum (Girgenti) on August 30, 1809. The twelve islands of the next sentence may

refer to the Princes' Islands, a favorite summer resort, although there are in fact only nine of them.]

[21] *Byron to Moore*, September 19, 1821: Switzerland is a curst selfish, swinish country of brutes. . . . I never could bear the inhabitants, and still less their English visitors; for which reason, after writing for some information about houses, upon hearing that there was a colony of English all over the cantons of Geneva, etc., I immediately gave up the thought. . . . [*LJ*, v, 365-366 (M).]

[22] *Byron in his journal*, November 14, 1813: They say "Virtue is its own reward,"—it certainly should be paid well for its trouble. [*LJ*, ii, 313 (M).]

"Somebody possessed Madame de Staël with an opinion of my immorality.[23] I used occasionally to visit her at *Coppet*; and once she invited me to a family-dinner, and I found the room full of strangers, who had come to stare at me as at some outlandish beast in a raree-show. One of the ladies fainted,[24] and the rest looked as if his Satanic Majesty had been among them. Madame de Staël took the liberty to read me a lecture before this crowd; to which I only made her a low bow.

[23] *Elizabeth Hervey*: By the charms of his wit, his harmonious voice, and fascinating manner, he completely enchanted Madame de Stael without ever being able to change the bad opinion she has of his morals. [*HVSV*, p. 191.]

[24] *Byron to Murray*, May 15, 1819: It is true that Mrs. Hervey (she writes novels) fainted at my entrance into Coppet, and then came back again. [*LJ*, iv, 300-301 (M); Polidori had published the story in 1819, in his "Extract of a Letter from Geneva," which prefaces *The Vampyre*.]

"I knew very few of the Genevese. Hentsh was very civil to me; and I have a great respect for Sismondi.[25] I was forced to return the civilities of one of their Professors by asking him, and an old gentleman, a friend of Gray's, to dine with me.

I had gone out to sail early in the morning, and the wind prevented me from returning in time for dinner. I understand that I offended them mortally. Polidori did the honours.[26] Among our countrymen I made no new acquaintances; Shelley, Monk Lewis, and Hobhouse were almost the only English people I saw. No wonder I shewed a distaste for society at that time, and went little among the Genevese; besides, I could not speak French.[27] What is become of my boatman and boat?[28] I suppose she is rotten; she was never worth much. When I went the tour of the Lake in her with Shelley and Hobhouse,[29] she was nearly wrecked near the very spot where St. Preux and Julia were in danger of being drowned.[30] It would have been classical to have been lost there, but not so agreeable. Shelley was on the Lake much oftener than I, at all hours of the night and day: he almost lived on it; his great rage is a boat. We are both building now at Genoa, I a yacht, and he an open boat."[31]

------

[25] [It seems that Byron and Sismondi never met personally. See Jean-R. de Salis, *Sismondi, 1773-1842* (Paris, 1932), p. 335, note 1. Sismondi spent all of 1816 in Italy, could not have met Byron at Geneva.]

[26] *Hobhouse*: The invitation to the Genevese professor [M. Pictet] did not come from lord Byron; it was an imprudent liberty taken by his domestic physician [Polidori], and lord Byron was not detained from the dinner-table by the wind. He staid away on purpose, saying to the doctor, "as you asked these guests yourself, you may entertain them yourself." [*WR*, iii, 21.]

Medwin: Mr. Hobhouse says that the invitation of Professor Pictet was an "imprudent liberty" of Polidori. Lord Byron went to a soiree at Mr. Pictet's and thought himself bound to return the civility. This Dinner without Amphytrion gave great umbrage to the Savant, which would not have been the case if as stated by the Critic [Hobhouse]. I have this from one of the Professor's family.

Polidori: M. Pictet took him to the house of a lady to spend the evening. . . . Amongst other things they relate that, having invited M. Pictet and Bonstetten to dinner, he went on to the lake to Chillon, leaving a gentleman who travelled with him to receive them and make apologies. ["Extract of a Letter from Geneva."]

Byron to Murray, May 15, 1819: *He* [Polidori] asked Pictet, etc., to dinner, and of course was left to entertain them. [*LJ*, IV, 300.]

[27] [Polidori stated in 1816 that Byron did not speak French, but James Kennedy observed in 1823 that "he spoke French . . . well," and in his interview in 1823 with J. J. Coulmann he spoke French, although with a foreign accent (*HVSV*, pp. 182, 470, 343; see also pp. 209, 339, 352, 426, and *LJ*, VI, 229-230).]

[28] *Hobhouse*: Lord Byron had no boatman.

Medwin: Did he make the Tour of the Lake without one? The name of the man was Maurice. Mr. Hentsh the Banker says in a letter to me, "Je donnerai le tout en garde au Batelier Maurice, compagnon de notre célèbre ami." [Lady Blessington met Maurice in 1822; Benjamin Disraeli met him in 1826 (*HVSV*, pp. 183-184, 626, note 6). For several references to a boatman employed during the tour of the lake, see Shelley's letter of July 12, 1816 (*Letters*, I, 480, 483). It was in fact the stupidity of the boatman that nearly caused their boat to capsize.]

[29] *Hobhouse*: Mr. Hobhouse did not arrive at Diodati until after the tour alluded to. [*WR*, III, 21.]

Medwin: It seems that Lord Byron alluded to two different occasions of touring.

[30] *Shelley to Peacock*, July 12, 1816: My companion [Byron] remarked to me, that our danger from the storm took place precisely in the spot where Julie and her lover [in Rousseau's *La Nouvelle Héloïse*] were nearly overset, and where St. Preux was tempted to plunge with her into the lake. [*Letters*, I, 486.]

[31] [Here as elsewhere Medwin has telescoped two conversations: Byron's plans for building the *Bolivar* did not develop until late January or early February, 1822.]

We played at billiards till the carriage was announced, and I accompanied him in his drive. Soon after we got off the stones, we mounted our horses, which were waiting for us. Lord Byron[32] prides himself much on this exercise. He conducted us for some miles till we came to a farm-house, where he practises pistol-firing every evening. This is his favourite amusement, and may indeed be called almost a pursuit. He always has pistols in his holster, and eight or ten pair by the first makers in London carried by his courier.[33] We had each twelve rounds of ammunition, and in a diameter of four inches he put eleven out of twelve shots. I observed his hand shook exceedingly. He said that when he first began at Manton's he was the worst shot in the world, and Manton was perhaps the best.[34] The subject turned upon duelling, and he contended for its necessity, and quoted some strong arguments in favour of it.[35]

"I have been concerned," said he, "in many duels as second, but only in two as principal; one was with Hobhouse[36] before I became intimate with him. The best marksmen at a target are not the surest in the field. Cecil's and Stackpoole's affair proved this. They fought after a quarrel of three years, during which they were practising daily. Stackpoole was so good a shot that he used to cut off the heads of the fowls for dinner as they drank out of the coops. He had every wish to kill his antagonist, but he received his death-blow from Cecil, who fired rather first, or rather was the quickest shot of the two. All he said when falling was, 'D——n it, have I missed him?'[37] Shelley is a much better shot than I am, but he is thinking of metaphysics rather than of firing."

---

[32] [At this point Medwin deleted the words "is an admirable horseman, combining grace with the security of his seat. He" and joined the two original sentences.]

[33] *Hobhouse*: The first part of the statement is true—the second untrue—a courier carry *eight* or *ten* pair of pistols!! This courier did occasionally carry one pair of pistols. [*WR*, iii, 21.]

Medwin: Mr. Hobhouse with his word catching denies the possibility of a Courier carrying so many pairs of pistols. In fact the Pistols were always in the Carriage and only carried out of it by the Courier. The Reviewer was born to contradict.

[34] *Byron in his diary*, January 21, 1821: In 1809, 1810, 1811, 1812, 1813, 1814, it was my luck to split walking-sticks, wafers, half-crowns, shillings, and even the *eye* of a walking-stick, at twelve paces, with a single bullet—and all by *eye* and calculation; for my hand is not steady, and apt to change with the very weather. To the prowess which I here note, Joe Manton and others can bear testimony; for the former taught, and the latter has seen me do, these feats. [*LJ*, v, 180-181 (M).]

[35] *Goethe*: Properly speaking, he lived perpetually in a state of nature, and with his mode of existence the necessity for self-defense floated daily before his eyes. Hence his constant pistol shooting. Every moment he expected to be called out. [*Conversations with Eckermann*, ed. Oliver H. G. Leigh (Washington, 1901), p. 99.]

[36] *Hobhouse*: Lord Byron was never concerned in a duel in his life, either as second or principal. He was once *rather near* fighting a duel—and that was with an officer of the staff of general Oakes, at Malta. [*WR*, III, 21.]

J. W. Croker: This would be an answer *if* our credit in Lord Byron's entire and constant veracity was unshaken; but can we be certain that Lord Byron, (whose chief enjoyment was the noble and generous practice of pistol-firing at a target, on one of which occasions this conversation was held,) did not choose to swagger a little before the Lieutenant of Light Dragoons? He that could tell the Lieutenant all that we have just exposed, might easily have told him this, the most innocent rhodomontade of the whole batch: but Lord Byron does not quite say he *fought*—he says he was twice *concerned* as principal. Mr. Hobhouse mentions one case in which a *pistol-practicer* might take the latitude of representing himself as concerned; and we ourselves know another of the same kind—but be all this as it may, since falsehood must be imputed, why should it be to the party who had no interest in the falsehood; and who, if he had been inventing, can hardly be suspected of venturing to give dates and names and particulars, as Mr. Medwin has done?

Medwin: This Duel with Hobhouse appears to be a figment, and not less incorrect in its details is the Stackpoole and Cecil story. They are both specimens of his common habit of mystifying—or perhaps he had told these stories till he believed them. [It seems that Byron never fought a duel, but he had been "concerned" in at least four challenges, the best known being those of Moore and C. C. Cary on Malta. See Leslie A. Marchand, *Byron:*

A *Biography* (New York, 1957), I, 144-145; Thomas Moore, *Memoirs, Journal, and Correspondence*, ed. Lord John Russell (London, 1853-1856), I, 273; *HVSV*, p. 50; and *LJ*, II, 110, note; V, 428.]

[37] *An anonymous correspondent in The Gentleman's Magazine:* A correspondent . . . requests us to state from authority, that Captain Stacpoole [*sic*] was too well known, as a most honourable and gallant officer, for so unworthy an assertion to affect his memory . . . it is not fit that such a man should so falsely be held up . . . as a man capable of harbouring for three years a revengeful feeling, as one who had every wish to *kill* his antagonist. The fact was, simply, that three years previous to the lamented meeting, Lieut. Cecil had, as he declared, in joke and without intending the slightest imputation, called in question some assertion of Capt. Stacpoole, which having been repeated to him by one of his officers, upon their happening to arrive in the same port, in Jamaica, Captain Stacpoole required an apology for the words imputed to Mr. Cecil, which being refused, the parties met the next morning; but so far from enmity being entertained on either side, Captain Stacpoole had declared that he did not intend to injure him, and the deplorable event was lamented by Mr. Cecil as long as he lived. From another quarter we learn that Lieut. Cecil was considered by every one on the station to have acted so honourably, that within a very short time he was promoted to the rank of Captain by the Admiral, and died within a few months of a broken heart, in consequence, as he declared of having been the death of a fellow creature. [*GM*, CXXXVI, 450.]

I UNDERSTAND that Lord Byron is always in better spirits after having *culped* (as he calls it) the targe often, or hit a five-paul piece, the counterpart of which is always given to the farmer, who is making a little fortune. All the pieces struck, Lord Byron keeps to put, as he says, in his museum.[38]

We now continued our ride, and returned to Pisa by the Lucca gate.

"Pisa with its hanging tower and Sophia-like dome reminds me," said Lord Byron, "of an eastern place."

He then remarked the heavy smoke that rolled away from the city, spreading in the distance a vale of mist, through which the golden clouds of evening appeared.

"It is fine," said Lord Byron, "but no sunsets are to be compared with those of Venice. They are too gorgeous for any painter, and defy any poet. My rides, indeed, would have been nothing without the Venetian sunsets. Ask Shelley."[39]

"Stand on the marble bridge," said Shelley, "cast your eye, if you are not dazzled, on its river glowing as with fire, then follow the graceful curve of the palaces on the Lung' Arno till the arch is naved by the massy dungeon-tower (erroneously called Ugolino's), frowning in dark relief, and tell me if any thing can surpass a sunset at Pisa."

---

[38] *Medwin*: It was sometimes rather expensive practice for us, for we generally found [*i.e.*, provided] the *Museum* Coins.

They had invented a sort of macaronic language that was very droll. They called firing, *tiring*; hitting, *colping*; missing, *mancating*; riding, *cavalling*; walking, *a-spassing*, etc.

Goethe, I think erroneously, attributes Lord Byron's constant Pistol-shooting to the necessity of self-defence and the continual expectation of being called out. Practicing at a mark, as he says above, is of very little use as a preparation for an English Duel where the adversaries are placed back to back and fire at a signal. If Lord Byron had had such an object in view he would have adopted a different mode of practice. [Cf. Medwin's *Life of Shelley*, ed. H. Buxton Forman (London, 1913), pp. 328, 329. The original edition in two volumes (London, 1847) is distinguished in these notes by a reference to the volume number.]

There was a history attached to almost every pair of pistols in his possession, and he had names for several of them, because they were the pistols of victory and had been used in celebrated real actions. Among the rest was a Pistol which he called his best, &c., the one with which Best had killed his antagonist. Byron was very fond of hearing of Duels and telling them.

Edward E. Williams in his journal, February 20, 1822: Called on Lord B[yron]. . . . He told me that Best shot Lord Camelford [March 6, 1804] at 27 paces behind Holland House, and that two trees are now planted where they stood. [*Maria Gisborne & Edward E. Williams, Shelley's Friends: Their Journals and Letters*, ed. F. L. Jones (Norman, Okla., 1951), p. 131; hereafter referred to as *Journal*.]

[39] *Medwin: Vide* Shelley's gorgeous description of a Sunset from Lido in *Julian and Maddalo*.

The history of one, is that of almost every day. It is impossible to conceive a more unvaried life than Lord Byron led at this period. I continued to visit him at the same hour daily. Billiards, conversation, or reading, filled up the intervals till it was time to take our evening drive, ride, and pistol-practice. On our return, which was always in the same direction, we frequently met the Countess Guiccioli, in one of his Carriages, with whom he stopped to converse a few minutes.[40]

He dined at half an hour after sunset, (at twenty-four o'clock;) then drove to Count Gamba's, the Countess Guiccioli's father, passed several hours in her society, returned to his palace, and either read or wrote till two or three in the morning; occasionally drinking spirits diluted with water as a medicine, from a dread of a nephritic complaint, to which he was, or fancied himself, subject.[41] Such was his life at Pisa.

The Countess Guiccioli is twenty-three years of age, though she appears no more than seventeen or eighteen.[42] Unlike most of the Italian women, her complexion is delicately fair. Her eyes, large, dark, and languishing, are shaded by the longest eye-lashes in the world; and her hair, which is ungathered on her head, plays over her falling shoulders in a profusion of natural ringlets of the darkest auburn.[43] Her figure is, perhaps, too much *embonpoint* for her height, but her bust is perfect; her features want little of possessing a Grecian regularity of outline; and she has the most beautiful mouth and teeth imaginable. It is impossible to see without admiring—to hear the Guiccioli speak without being fascinated. Her amiability and gentleness shew themselves in every intonation of her voice, which, and the music of her perfect Italian, give a peculiar charm to every thing she utters. Grace and elegance seem component parts of her nature. Notwithstanding that she adores Lord Byron, it is evident that the exile and poverty of her aged father sometimes affect her spirits, and throw a shade of melancholy on her countenance, which adds to the deep interest this lovely girl creates.

[40] *Medwin*: One day he said, "I am very much obliged to Lady B[yron] hating so long, or she and I should have to marry again I suppose."

[41] *Medwin*: It seems that he had been once treated by his Physician for such a complaint in London. *Vide* Moore's *Notices*. [See *LJ*, II, 99, Byron to Hodgson, February 16, 1812: "Last week I was very ill and confined to bed with stone in the kidney. . . ."]

[42] [Teresa Guiccioli was born either in 1799 or at the beginning of 1800; her husband was born in 1761. See Iris Origo, *The Last Attachment* (New York, 1949), p. 493, note 2.]

[43] *Medwin*: Only Italian married women wear their hair down— hers was of a dark auburn—a golden colour.

"Extraordinary pains," said Lord Byron one day, "were taken with the education of Teresa. Her conversation is lively, without being frivolous; without being learned, she has read all the best authors of her own and the French language. She often conceals what she knows, from the fear of being thought to know too much; possibly because she knows I am not fond of blues.[44] To use an expression of Jeffrey's, 'If she has blue stockings, she contrives that her petticoat shall hide them.' "

Lord Byron is certainly very much attached to her, without being actually in love.[45] His description of the Giorgione in the Manfrini palace at Venice is meant for the Countess.[46] The sonnet prefixed to the 'Prophecy of Dante' was addressed to her; and some beautiful stanzas written when he was about to quit Venice to join her at Ravenna, describe the state of his feelings at that time.

---

[44] *Trelawny*: Nonsense. I deny this picture—tis no likeness [?] her face without expression small hazle eyes—lardge mouth—long bodyed & short limbed—[? cane] haired—in short a dumpy woman—spoke a provincial language like her brother & said Faliero the Doge of Venice was by far the best of Lord Byron writings.

Medwin: I passed every afternoon for many weeks with the Countess Guiccioli at Shelley's. She was then strikingly handsome, but when I saw her afterwards at Florence six or seven years afterwards at her Aunt's—Lamartine being of the party—her beauty had entirely faded. Sorrow—and who has suffered more—makes its ravages in the fairest most. [On Teresa's appearance, see also Bancroft's diary, May 22, 1822, in *Scribner's Magazine*, October, 1905, and *Mrs. Longfellow: Selected Letters and Journals*, ed. Edward Wagenknecht (New York, 1956), p. 37.]

[45] *Mary Shelley to Jane Williams*, February 19, 1823: Her [Teresa's] unamiable jealousies and falsehoods have destroyed what remained of affection in his [Byron's] heart, though he clings to her as two birds of opposite breed in one cage—there they are —and what is there better to do?

Mary Shelley to Jane Williams, May 31, 1823: L[ord] B[yron] is fixed on Greece—he gets rid of two burthens; the G[uiccioli] and the Liberal—the first is natural, though I pity her. [Both letters from the Abinger Collection, presumably unpublished. On Byron's cooling relations with Teresa, see also *HVSV*, pp. 348, 353.]

[46] *Hobhouse*: Lord Byron could not mean to represent the countess Guiccioli by his description [in *Beppo*, stanza 12] of the female in the celebrated picture by Giorgione [*Famiglia di Giorgione*]—for he had never seen the countess when he wrote the description. [*WR*, III, 21-22.]

CALLING on Lord Byron one evening after the opera, we happened to talk of *Cavalieri Serventi*, and Italian women; and he contended that much was to be said in excuse for them, and in defence of the system.

"We will put out of the question," said he, "a *Cavalier Serventeism*; that is only another term for prostitution, where the women get all the money they can, and have (as is the case in all such contracts) no love to give in exchange.—I speak of another, and of a different service."[47]

"Do you know how a girl is brought up here?" continued he. "Almost from infancy she is deprived of the endearments of home, and shut up in a convent till she has attained a marriageable or marketable age. The father now looks out for a suitable son-in-law. As a certain portion of his fortune is fixed by law for the dower of his children, his object is to find some needy man of equal rank, or a very rich one, the older the better, who will consent to take his daughter off his hands, under the market price. This, if she happen to be handsome, is not difficult of accomplishment. Objections are seldom made on the part of the young lady to the age, and personal or other defects of the intended, who perhaps visits her once in the parlour as a matter of form or curiosity. She is too happy to get her liberty on any terms, and he her money or her person. There is no love on either side. What happiness is to be expected, or constancy, from such a *liaison*? Is it not natural, that in her intercourse with a world, of which she knows and has seen nothing, and unrestrained mistress of her own time and actions, she should find somebody to like better, and who likes her better, than her husband?[48] The Count Guiccioli, for instance, who is the richest man in Romagna,[49] was sixty when he married Teresa; she sixteen.[50] From the first they had separate apartments, and she always used to call him *Sir*.[51] What could be expected from such a preposterous connexion? For some time she was an Angiolina, and he a Marino Faliero, a good old man; but young women, and your Italian

ones too, are not satisfied with your good old men. Love is
not the same dull, cold, calculating feeling here as in the
North. It is the business, the serious occupation of their lives;
it is a want, a necessity. Somebody properly defines a woman,
'a creature that loves.' They die of love; particularly the Romans: they begin to love earlier, and feel the passion later
than the Northern people. When I was at Venice, two dowagers of sixty made love to me.[52]—But to return to the Guiccioli. The old Count did not object to her availing herself of
the privileges of her country;[53] an *Italian* would have reconciled him to the thing: indeed for some time he winked at
our intimacy, but at length made an exception against me, as
a foreigner, a heretic, an Englishman, and, what was worse
than all, a liberal.[54]

---

[47] [Perhaps Byron meant to distinguish between the *cavalier
servente* and the *cicisbeo*; the latter term, he wrote in *Beppo*, xxxvii,
had "now grown vulgar and indecent."]

[48] *Byron to Murray*, February 21, 1820: In short, they transfer
marriage to adultery, and strike the *not* out of that commandment.
The reason is, that they marry for their parents, and love for
themselves. [*LJ*, iv, 409 (M).]

[49] *Byron to Murray*, June 29, 1819: Her husband . . . is the
richest noble of Ravenna, and almost of Romagna. . . . [*LJ*, iv,
320 (M).]

[50] *Hobhouse*: The countess Guiccioli was in her twentieth year.
[*WR*, iii, 22.]

Medwin: The alliteration of 60 and 16 does not satisfy this
microscopic gentleman. She is only 20. She was 17 when she
married. [The date of Teresa's birth is in doubt. Iris Origo, *The
Last Attachment*, p. 493, concludes that at the time of her marriage Teresa was 18 and her husband 57.]

[51] *Hobhouse*: They had not separate apartments, and she never
called her husband, Sir, but Alexander, his Christian name. [*WR*,
iii, 22. See Origo, pp. 119, 122, for letters of Teresa, written in
1819, when she was with Byron at Venice and La Mira, beginning
"My dear Alessandro" and "Dearest Alessandro."]

[52] *Medwin*: Italian ladies, when they once have the character for beauty, retain the *prestige* all their lives. [On Madame Benzoni's supposedly amorous interest in Byron, see Moore, *Life*, p. 415, and *HVSV*, p. 628, note 38.]

[53] *Medwin*: I remember her telling me that she was often closeted with him and that he was *a very bad man*.

[54] *Hobhouse*: The count Guiccioli was strongly and notoriously attached to the liberals himself. [*WR*, iii, 22.]

Medwin: How could it that if a notorious Carbonaro he was never indicted or exiled? [On Count Guiccioli as a "liberal," see Origo, pp. 25-26.]

"He insisted—the Guiccioli was as obstinate; her family took her part. Catholics cannot get divorces. But, to the scandal of all Romagna, the matter was at length referred to the Pope, who ordered her a separate maintenance, on condition that she should reside under her father's roof. All this was not agreeable, and at length I was forced to smuggle her out of Ravenna,[55] having disclosed a plot laid with the sanction of the Legate for shutting her up in a convent for life, which she narrowly escaped.[56]—Except Greece, I was never so attached to any place in my life as to Ravenna, and but for the failure of the Constitutionalists and this fracas, should probably never have left it. The peasantry are the best people in the world, and the beauty of their women is extraordinary. Those at Tivoli and Frescati,[57] who are so much vaunted, are mere Sabines, coarse creatures, compared to the Romagnese. You may talk of your English women, and it is true that out of one hundred Italians and English you will find thirty of the latter handsome; but then there will be one Italian on the other side of the scale, who will more than balance the deficit in numbers—one who, like the Florence Venus, has no rival, and can have none in the North. I have learnt more from the peasantry of the countries I have travelled in than from any other source, especially from the women: they are more intelligent, as well as communicative, than the men. I found also at Ravenna much education and liberality of thinking among the higher classes. The climate is delightful. I was unbroken in upon by society. Ravenna lies out of the way of travellers. I was never tired of my rides in the pine-forest: it breathes of the Decameron; it is poetical ground. Francesca lived, and Dante was exiled and died at Ravenna. There is something inspiring in such an air.*

* The following lines will shew the attachment Lord Byron had to the tranquil life he led at Ravenna:

"Sweet hour of twilight, in the solitude
  Of the pine-forest and the silent shore
Which bounds Ravenna's immemorial wood,
  Rooted where once the Adrian wave flow'd o'er
To where the last Cæsarean fortress stood,
  Evergreen forest! which Boccaccio's lore
And Dryden's lay made haunted ground to me,
  How have I loved the twilight hour and thee!
The shrill cicalas, people of the pine,
  Making their summer lives one ceaseless song,
Were the sole echoes save my steed's and mine,
  And vesper bell's that rose the boughs among."
                    Don Juan, Canto III. Stanza 105.

[55] *Teresa Guiccioli*: Countess G[uiccioli] was never abducted. *Hobhouse*: The countess openly followed her father, count Gamba, fifteen days after his banishment, to Florence. [*WR*, III, 22. Teresa, however, as she informed Byron, had been advised to talk to no one of her intentions, "but leave at night—for if my plan were known, they might stop it, and take away my passport" (Origo, p. 260).]

[56] *Shelley to Mary Shelley*, August 7, 1821: She was compelled to escape from the Papal territory in great haste, as measures had already been taken to place her in a Convent where she would have been unrelentingly confined for life. [*Letters*, II, 316.]

[57] [Properly spelled *Frascati*, a town twelve miles southeast of Rome.]

"The people liked me, as much as they hated the Government. It is not a little to say, I was popular with all the leaders of the Constitutional party. They knew that I came from a land of liberty, and wished well to their cause. I would have espoused it too, and assisted them to shake off their fetters. They knew my character, for I had been living two years at Venice, where many of the Ravennese have houses. I did not, however, take part in their intrigues, nor join in their political coteries;[58] but I had a magazine of one hundred stand of arms in the house,[59] when every thing was ripe for revolt. A curse on Carignan's imbecility![60] I could have pardoned him that too, if he had not impeached his partisans. The proscription was immense in Romagna, and embraced many of the first nobles: almost all my friends, among the rest the Gambas, who took no part in the affair, were included in it. They were exiled, and their possessions confiscated.[61] They knew that this must eventually drive me out of the country.[62] I did not follow them immediately; I was not to be bullied. I had myself fallen under the eye of the Government. If they could have got sufficient proof, they would have arrested me:[63] but no one betrayed me; indeed there was nothing to betray. I had received a very high degree, without passing through the intermediate ranks. In that corner you see papers of one of their societies.[64] Shortly after the plot was discovered, I received several anonymous letters, advising me to discontinue my forest rides;[65] but I entertained no apprehensions of treachery, and was more on horseback than ever. I never stir out without being well armed, and sleep with pistols. They knew that I never missed my aim; perhaps this saved me. An event occurred at this time at Ravenna that made a deep impression on me: I alluded to it in 'Don Juan.' The military Commandant of the place, who, though suspected of being secretly a Carbonaro, was too powerful a man to be arrested, was assassinated opposite to my palace; a spot perhaps selected by choice for the commission of the crime. The measures which were adopted to screen the murderer prove the assassination to have taken place by order of the police. I had my foot in the stirrup at my usual hour of exercise, when my horse started at the report of a gun. On looking up I perceived a man throw down a carbine and run away at full speed, and another stretched upon the pavement, a few yards from me. On hastening towards him, I found that it was the unhappy Commandant.[66] A crowd was soon collected, but no one ventured to offer the least assistance. I soon directed my servant to lift up the bleeding body and carry it into my palace; but it was represented to me that by so doing I should confirm the suspicion of my being of his party, and incur the displeasure of the Government. However, it was no time to calculate between humanity and danger. I assisted in bearing him into the house, and putting him on a bed. He was already dead from several wounds; he appeared to have breathed his last without a struggle. I never saw a countenance so calm. His adjutant followed the corpse into the house. I remember his lamentation over him:—'Povero diavolo! non aveva fatto male, anchè ad un cane.' "[67]

---

[58] *Medwin*: He means he did not attend the meetings of the Conspirators. [Medwin seems to be correct, although Byron was kept fully informed by the Counts Gamba and others, offered to contribute 1,000 louis to Carbonari headquarters at Naples, offered the use of his house at Ravenna in the event of open conflict, and was in fact an actual member of the movement.]

[59] *Hobhouse*: Lord Byron had five or six carbines or muskets, and five or six pair of pistols, ready for his travelling service [*WR*, iii, 23].

Byron in his diary, February 18, 1821: To-day I have had no communication with my Carbonari cronies; but, in the mean time, my lower apartments are full of their bayonets, fusils, cartridges, and what not. I suppose that they consider me as a depôt, to be sacrificed, in case of accidents. [*LJ*, v, 205 (M).]

[60] [The hopes of the Carbonari centered on the young Charles Albert (1798-1849), a prince of Carignano and later King of Sardinia (Piedmont), although he never became an actual member of the movement. When some of the leaders of the Neapolitan revolution of 1820 informed him that they needed his help, he

persuaded them to delay the outbreak briefly and informed the King, innocently asking that no one be punished. Following the uprising, the King abdicated, appointing Charles Albert as regent, and a constitution was granted. However, Charles Felix later repudiated the regent's acts, with Austrian aid easily put down the insurrection, and exiled Charles Albert to Florence. The young prince was regarded as a traitor by the liberals and as a dangerous revolutionary by the conservatives.]

[61] *Teresa Guiccioli*: The Confiscation of the property of the Counts Gamba . . . —unfortunately, imaginary.

Medwin: Count [Ruggero] Gamba was when this work was published a State Prisoner, and his Estates were under sequestration if not confiscated.

[62] *Teresa Guiccioli*: One of the principal causes of the exile of my relatives, was in reality the idea that Lord Byron would share the banishment of his friends. [Moore, *Life*, p. 518 (M).]

[63] *Hobhouse*: The papal government never evinced such an intention. Cardinal Gonsalvi was always extremely well-disposed towards lord Byron. [*WR*, iii, 23.]

Byron to Hoppner, July 23, 1821: They have arrested above a thousand of high and low throughout Romagna. . . . Every body says they would have done the same by me if they dared proceed openly. [*LJ*, v, 327.]

[64] *Medwin*: He added, "There lies the firebrand. Those bags contain all the Secrets of the Conspiracy in Romagna, all the names"—there he stopped and turned the subject.

[65] *Hobhouse*: Lord Byron did not receive any anonymous letter on this occasion. . . . [*WR*, iii, 23.]

Byron in his "Second Letter . . . on . . . Bowles's Strictures": Within the last month of this present writing (1821), I have had my life threatened . . . the anonymous denunciation was addressed to the Cardinal Legate of R[omagna]. . . . [*LJ*, v, 584 (M).]

[66] *Hobhouse*: The commandant was at the head of the police, and directed the police against the Carbonari.

The whole of what is put into lord Byron's mouth, as to lord Byron, is a romance—the truth is as follows:

It was eight o'clock in the evening—lord Byron was going into his bed-room to change his neck-cloth, in order to walk to an evening conversazione, accompanied by his servant, Battista Falsieri. He heard a musket shot, and he sent Battista to inquire the cause.

Battista went, and reported that the commandant had been killed at a little distance from the house. Lord Byron then went into the street himself, and ordered the wounded man to be carried into his house. . . . No one was seen to run away. . . . It may be mentioned also, that in *Don Juan* [V, xxxiii-xxxvii] the time of this accident is mentioned as being *"eight"* in the evening. [*WR*, iii, 23-24. Medwin was sadly confused about the details, but what is clear is that he did not have the *Don Juan* account before him when he wrote.]

[67] *Medwin*: He added that in Stiletto and Sword wounds the Countenance retained the peculiar passion impressed on it at the moment of death—not so with ball wounds. [Cf. *The Works of Lord Byron: Poetry*, ed. Rowland E. Prothero (London, 1898-1901), iii, 90, note 2 to *The Giaour*, where the observation, although not the phrasing, is suspiciously similar.]

"I AM SORRY," said he, "not to have a copy of my Memoirs to shew you; I gave them to Moore, or rather to Moore's little boy (at Venice). I remember saying, 'Here are 2000*l.* for you, my young friend.'[68] I made one reservation in the gift,—that they were not to be published till after my death.[69]

"I have not the least objection to their being circulated;[70] in fact they have been read by some of mine, and several of Moore's friends and acquaintances; among others, they were lent to Lady Burghersh. On returning the MS. her Ladyship told Moore that she had transcribed the whole work. This was *un peu fort*, and he suggested the propriety of her destroying the copy. She did so, by putting it into the fire in his presence.[71] Ever since this happened, Douglas Kinnaird has been recommending me to resume possession of the MS., thinking to frighten me by saying that a spurious or a real copy, surreptitiously obtained, may go forth to the world. I am quite indifferent about the world knowing all that they contain. There are very few licentious adventures of my own, or scandalous anecdotes that will affect others, in the book. It is taken up from my earliest recollections, almost from childhood,—very incoherent, written in a very loose and familiar style. The second part will prove a good lesson to young men; for it treats of the irregular life I led at one period, and the fatal consequences of dissipation. There are few parts that may not, and none that will not, be read by women."

[68] *Hobhouse*: Mr. Moore had no little boy with him at Venice. [*WR*, III, 24.]

Medwin: This passage should have been written, "to Moore, *for* his little boy."

Moore: In taking the [manuscript] bag, and thanking him most warmly, I added, "This will make a nice legacy for my little Tom. . . ." [*Life*, p. 422.]

[69] *Medwin*: The conflagration of the Autograph Memoirs was a fine piece of charlatanism. The reason of their transfer from Mr. Murray to Mr. Longman, and from Mr. Longman back to Mr.

Murray needs no comment. [See Doris Moore, *The Late Lord Byron*, p. 14.] Mr. Moore cannot deny that the substance of them is incorporated in his work, nor that the work itself is confessedly full of extracts from those very Memoirs. . . .

Well might they be committed to the flames, as it was their fate, instead of being quietly inurned to rise again from their ashes in the shape of five octavos or two prodigious quartos phoenix plumed like one of Mr. Moore's Angels—a rara avis destined to produce instead of £2,000, £6,000. . . .

After all it should be called Mr. Murray's Life of Byron, his Lordship styled Messrs. Moore's and Murray's Byron. Is it from such materials from a Bookseller that we are to judge and acquit, or from the Lintot of the age? Where is Lord Byron's Journal in Switzerland, where his Letters to Mrs. Leigh, his Correspondence with Lady Melbourne on the subject of his marriage, with Messrs. Hobhouse, D. Kinnaird, Scrope Davies, but more than all with his early and only friend, as he once confessed, Lord Clare?

[70] *Byron to Murray*, October 29, 1819: Neither [the Memoirs nor an 1814 journal also given to Moore] are for publication during my life. . . . In the mean time, if you like to read them you may, and show them to any body you like—I care not. [*LJ*, iv, 368. About two dozen persons, at the least, had read Byron's Memoirs. Moore had the original manuscript copied because he feared it would become worn out from passing through so many hands. See his diary, May 7, 1820. On the nature and content of the Memoirs, see Doris Moore, *The Late Lord Byron*, pp. 46-53, and *The Letters of Thomas Moore*, ed. Wilfred S. Dowden (London, 1964), ii, 479, 498, where Moore refers to a "passage about . . . an indecent circumstance alluded to" in Byron's "last interview with Lady Byron" and "a nameless person whom he calls 'love of loves,'" supposed by Lady Holland to be Augusta Leigh.]

[71] *Moore in his diary*, November 24, 1819: Went to Lady Burghersh's for the purpose of seeing her put her extracts from Lord Byron's Memoirs in the fire.

⌣

Another time he said: "A very full account of my marriage and separation is contained in my Memoirs. After they were completed, I wrote to Lady Byron, proposing to send them for her inspection, in order that any misstatement or inaccuracy (if any such existed, which I was not aware of,) might be pointed out and corrected. In her answer she declined the offer, without assigning any reason; but desiring, if not on her account, for the sake of her daughter, that they might never appear, and finishing with a threat.[72] My reply was the severest thing I ever wrote, and contained two quotations, one from Shakspeare, and another from Dante.* I told her that she knew all I had written was incontrovertible truth,[73] and that she did not wish to sanction the truth. I ended by saying, that she might depend on their being published. It was not till after this correspondence that I made Moore the depositary of the MS.[74]

"The first time of my seeing Miss Milbanke was at Lady Melbourne's.[75] It was a fatal day; and I remember that in going upstairs I stumbled,[76] and remarked to Moore, who accompanied me,[77] that it was a bad omen. I ought to have taken the warning. On entering the room I observed a young lady, more simply dressed than the rest of the assembly, sitting alone upon a sofa. I took her for a humble companion, and asked if I was right in my conjecture? 'She is a great heiress,'[78] said he in a whisper that became lower as he proceeded; 'you had better marry her, and repair the old place, Newstead.'

* I could not retain them.

[72] *Lady Byron*: A misrepresent[atio]n of the purport of the letter from Ly B.

Lady Byron to Lord Byron, March 10, 1820: I received your letter of January 1st offering to my perusal a Memoir of part of your life. I decline to inspect it. I consider the publication or circulation of such a composition at any time as prejudicial to Ada's future happiness. For my own sake I have no reason to shrink from publicity, but notwithstanding the injuries which I have suffered, I should lament some of the *consequences*. [Earl of Lovelace, *Astarte* (London, 1921), p. 108; Byron's letter appears on pp. 298-300.]

[73] *Lady Byron*: How, if not read?

[74] *Byron to Lady Byron*, April 3, 1820: I received yesterday your answer dated March 10. . . . To the mysterious menace of the last sentence . . . I could hardly be very sensible, even if I understood it, as before it could take place, I shall be where "nothing can touch him farther" [*Macbeth*, III, ii]. [Byron closes his letter, as Medwin stated, with a quotation from Dante, *Inferno*, xvi, 43-45, spoken by Rusticucci, who owed his place in hell to the temper of his wife. It is untrue that Byron gave the Memoirs to Moore only *after* writing to Lady Byron. Their gift was made in October, 1819.]

[75] [Byron first saw Annabella Milbanke on March 25, 1812, at Melbourne House, conversed for the first time with her on April 14, at Lady Cowper's.]

[76] *Caroline Lamb to Medwin*, November, 1824: What you say of his falling upstairs and of Miss Milbanke is all true. [*LJ*, ii, 451.]

[77] *Harness*: I am *quite certain* that the author of the Irish Melodies was not of the party. [*BEM*, xvi, 537.]

Medwin: I suppose that Moore the oracle of Holland House was not admissible into the Melbourne Set. [Moore, with Rogers, had introduced Lady Caroline Lamb to Byron, who had met Moore on November 4, 1811.]

Byron to Moore, March 25, 1812: Know all men by these presents, that you, Thomas Moore, stand indicted—no—invited, by special and particular solicitation, to Lady Caroline Lamb's tomorrow evening, at half-past nine o'clock. . . . Pray, come—I was so examined after you this morning, that I entreat you to answer in person. [*LJ*, ii, 113-115. It was at the morning party referred to that Annabella first saw Byron, although she was not then introduced to him.]

[78] *Lady Byron*: Lady Byron was not acquainted with Moore, & never became so. She saw some of his letters to Lord B. & thought favorably of them.

"There was something piquant, and what we term pretty, in Miss Milbanke. Her features were small and feminine, though not regular. She had the fairest skin imaginable. Her figure was perfect for her height, and there was a simplicity, a retired modesty about her, which was very characteristic, and formed a happy contrast to the cold artificial formality, and studied stiffness, which is called fashion.[79] She interested me exceedingly. It is unnecessary to detail the progress of our acquaintance. I became daily more attached to her, and it ended in my making her a proposal that was rejected. Her refusal was couched in terms that could not offend me. I was besides persuaded that, in declining my offer, she was governed by the influence of her mother;[80] and was the more confirmed in this opinion by her reviving our correspondence herself twelve months after.[81] The tenor of her letter was, that although she could not love me, she desired my friendship.[82] Friendship is a dangerous word for young ladies; it is Love full-fledged, and waiting for a fine day to fly.

"It had been predicted by Mrs. Williams, that twenty-seven was to be a dangerous age for me. The fortune-telling witch was right; it was destined to prove so.[83] I shall never forget the 2d of January! Lady Byron (Byrn, he pronounced it)[84] was the only unconcerned person present; Lady Noel, her mother, cried;[85] I trembled like a leaf, made the wrong responses, and after the ceremony called her Miss Milbanke.[86]

---

[79] *Harness*: Where has Captain Medwin lived? Is this the description of any woman of fashion in this country since the reign of long ruffles and hoop petticoats?—but, above all, is it possible to conceive any resemblance between this portrait and the individuals who have, at any period, mingled in the society of Melbourne House? [*BEM*, xvi, 537.]

Medwin: This description of Lady Byron tallies well with the Vignettes of her in Moore's and Murray's Life.

[80] *Lady Byron*: That Autumn the circumstance was kept secret by Lady B. Lady Milbanke (the Mother) objected but in vain to so positive a refusal.

[81] *Lady Byron*: In consequence of a message then sent to her by Lord Byron thro' Lady Melbourne, expressive of his remembrance of her (Ly B)—& in the prospect of [his] leaving England "for ever." [Lady Byron omits to say that it was she who first asked

Lady Melbourne to give a message to Byron, who then instructed Lady Melbourne to say to Annabella "what is proper," whereupon the latter renewed her correspondence with Byron, on August 22, 1813, under the guise of disinterested friendship.]

[82] *Lady Byron*: A misrepresentation. [See her letter, Elwin, *Lord Byron's Wife*, pp. 166-167: "that unreserved friendship which I wish to establish between us. . . ."]

[83] *Moore*: It was predestined [said the celebrated fortune-teller, Mrs. Williams] that . . . he should be twice married,—the second time to a foreign lady. About two years afterwards he himself mentioned these particulars. . . . [Moore, *Life*, p. 19 (M).]

[84] *Hunt*: Captain Medwin says, that in speaking of Lady Byron, he pronounced it "Byrn"; but this is a mistake. The Captain's ear might not have discerned the second vowel, but it was discernible to others. "Byrn" is *Byron*, pronounced shortly, with the northern burr [and a short *i*]. But he called himself Byron sometimes [with a long *i*]; and the Italians always called him so at least as nearly as they could. They made it *Bairon*, as I have noticed in Madame Guiccioli. [*HVSV*, p. 309.]

Medwin: Much dispute has arisen respecting Byron's pronunciation of his own name. Altho' he pronounced it as above written, being asked one day how it should be syllabled, he [said], "spell B y." [Compare *HVSV*, p. 96.]

[85] [For Lady Milbanke "on the verge of hysterics," see Marchand, ii, 505-506, and Elwin, p. 249.]

[86] *Moore*: When about to depart [on his honeymoon], Lord Byron said to the bride, "Miss Milbanke, are you ready?" [Moore, *Life*, p. 273 (M).]

"There is a singular history attached to the ring. The very day the match was concluded, a ring of my mother's, that had been lost, was dug up by the gardener at Newstead.[87] I thought it was sent on purpose for the wedding; but my mother's marriage had not been a fortunate one, and this ring was doomed to be the seal of an unhappier union still.*

*——————— "Save the *ring*,
Which, being the damned'st part of matrimony—"
Don Juan, Canto IX. Stanza 70.

"After the ordeal was over, we set off for a country-seat of Sir Ralph's; and I was surprised at the arrangements for the journey, and somewhat out of humour to find a lady's-maid stuck between me and my bride.[88] It was rather too early to assume the husband; so I was forced to submit, but it was not with a very good grace. Put yourself in a similar situation, and tell me if I had not some reason to be in the sulks. I have been accused of saying, on getting into the carriage, that I had married Lady Byron out of spite, and because she had refused me twice.[89] Though I was for a moment vexed at her prudery, or whatever you may choose to call it, if I had made so uncavalier, not to say brutal a speech, I am convinced Lady Byron would instantly have left the carriage to me and the maid (I mean the lady's). She had spirit enough to have done so, and would properly have resented the affront.

"Our honeymoon was not all sunshine; it had its clouds: and Hobhouse has some letters which would serve to explain the rise and fall in the barometer,—but it was never down at zero.

"You tell me the world says I married Miss Milbanke for her fortune, because she was a great heiress.[90] All I have ever received, or am likely to receive, (and that has been twice paid back too,) was 10,000*l*.[91] My own income at this period was small, and somewhat bespoken. Newstead was a very unprofitable estate, and brought me in a bare 1500*l*. a-year;[92] the Lancashire property was hampered with a law-suit, which has cost me 14,000*l*., and is not yet finished.[93]

---

[87] *Moore*: On the day of the arrival of the lady's answer, he was sitting at dinner, when his gardener came in and presented him with his mother's wedding ring, which she had lost many years before, and which the gardener had just found in digging up the mould under the window. Almost at the same moment, the letter from Miss Milbanke arrived; and Lord Byron exclaimed, "If it contains a consent, I will be married with this very ring." [Moore, *Life*, p. 264, note 2 (M).]

[88] *Lady Byron*: The Lady's Maid was on the Box outside. Sir J. Hobhouse handed Lady Byron into the Carriage and *knows this*.

Hobhouse: There was nobody in the carriage that conveyed lord and lady Byron from Seaham to Halnaby, on the day of their marriage, besides his lordship and his wife. [*WR*, III, 24.]

Mary Shelley to Hobhouse, November 10, 1824: Methinks I have heard Lord Byron complain of the presence of the lady's maid in the [honeymoon] carriage—but if you were there you must know best. [*Captain Medwin*, p. 200.]

Trelawny: Leporello's [Fletcher's] wife. Byron took the opportunity of the carragh [carriage] lurching to pummell her—Fletcher said "Oh my Lord what bad roads you have had, my Wife is black & blue all over."

Lady Byron's narrative: The stage before we reached S[ix] M[ile] B[ottom, in March, 1815,] he was in the most agitated state of spirits, & said, when within two or three miles of the house [Augusta Leigh's], "I feel as if I was just going to be married." My maid was in the carriage. . . . [Elwin, *Lord Byron's Wife*, p. 292. This was Ann Rood, later the wife of Fletcher, who had become Annabella's maid at Seaham in February, 1815, and "came up to London with Lord and Lady Byron in March 1815" (Elwin, p. 316, note 2; John Cam Hobhouse, *Recollections of a Long Life*, ed. Lady Dorchester, London, 1909-1911, II, 263). Ann Rood married Fletcher in January, 1816 (Elwin, p. 348). Byron's honeymoon may be understood as lasting until he and his wife took up residence in Piccadilly. Fletcher was with Byron at Six Mile Bottom (Marchand, II, 525).]

[89] *Lady Byron's narrative*: As soon as we got into the carriage [January 2, 1815] his countenance changed to gloom and defiance. . . . He called me to account in a revengeful manner for having so long withheld my consent to marry him, signifying I should suffer for it, and had better not have married him at all. [Elwin, p. 250. See also Moore, *Life*, p. 296, cited by Medwin.]

[90] *Lady Byron*: This was by no means certain at that time.

[91] [In the marriage settlement Sir Ralph Milbanke provided £16,000 and "entered into a Covenant to add £4,000 to it in three years, making £20,000." This last £4,000 was not in fact paid until 1828. The original £16,000 was placed in trust finally for Ada, but "of this not more than £6,000 had actually been made available before the Separation" (Doris Moore, pp. 128, 130). Medwin's £10,000 may be arrived at by adding the £4,000 se-

cured by Sir Ralph's covenant (of legal validity) and the £6,000 actually paid.

As for Byron's twice repaying the dowry, Byron "settled £60,-000 of his property on Lady Byron and her children." Hanson, Byron's lawyer, concluded, "Lord Byron did not possess a Shilling with Lady Byron" (Doris Moore, p. 128). For the complicated story of the financial relations of Byron and his wife, see Mrs. Moore's fourth chapter. See also below, p. 50 and note 136 to p. 51.]

[92] [Marchand, note to p. 584, l. 9, also arrives at £1,500 as the annual net income from Newstead.]

[93] [Hanson had kept the Lancashire estate in Chancery with a succession of lawsuits; it was not sold until after Byron's death (Marchand, p. 1159 and note to l. 24).]

"We had a house in town, gave dinner-parties, had separate carriages, and launched into every sort of extravagance.[94] This could not last long. The amount of my wife's 10,000*l.* soon melted away. I was beset by duns, and at length an execution was levied, and the bailiffs put in possession of the very beds we had to sleep on.[95] This was no very agreeable state of affairs, no very pleasant scene for Lady Byron to witness; and it was agreed she should pay her father a visit till the storm had blown over,[96] and some arrangements had been made with my creditors. You may suppose on what terms we parted,[97] from the style of a letter she wrote me on the road: you will think it began ridiculously enough,—'Dear Duck!'*[98]

"Imagine my astonishment to receive, immediately on her arrival in London, a few lines from her father,[99] of a very dry and unaffectionate nature, beginning 'Sir,'[100] and ending with saying that his daughter should never see me again.

"In my reply I disclaimed his authority, as a parent, over my wife,[101] and told him I was convinced the sentiments expressed were his, not hers. Another post, however, brought

* Shelley, who knew this story, used to say these two words would look odd in an Italian translation—*Anitra carissima.*

me a confirmation (under her own hand and seal) of her father's sentence.[102] I afterwards learnt from Fletcher's (my valet's) wife, who was at that time *femme-de-chambre* to Lady Byron,[103] that after her definite resolution was taken, and the fatal letter consigned to the post-office, she sent to withdraw it, and was in hysterics of joy that it was not too late.[104] It seems, however, that they did not last long, or that she was afterwards over-persuaded to forward it. There can be no doubt that the influence of her enemies prevailed over her affection for me. You ask me if no cause was assigned for this sudden resolution?—if I formed no conjecture about the cause? I will tell you.

———

[94] *Lady Byron: No* dinner parties were given— There was a London Carriage, & a Travelling Carriage, unfit for common use. He said he lived for less than as a single man. [But the town house in Piccadilly Terrace was] far too large. It was taken by Lord Byron inconsiderately at a high rent,—at the suggestion of Ly Melbourne. [Hobhouse, *WR*, III, 25, supports most of these statements.]

[95] *Lady Byron*: The beds were not removed nor the furniture deranged. [But immediately after Byron left London, bailiffs seized everything in the house, in late April, 1816.]

[96] *Lady Byron*: No such agreement was made, nor even proposed.

Byron to Sir Ralph Noel, February 2, 1816: It is true that . . . I had suggested to her the expediency of a temporary residence with her parents. My reason for this was very simple . . . the embarrassment of my circumstances, and my inability to maintain our present establishment. [Hobhouse, *Recollections*, II, 212.]

[97] *Lady Byron*: Lady Byron parted from Lord Byron with kindness. "Kindness"!—a weak word—but there is *not* one to express the truth.— Such conflicting feelings cannot be worded. See her letter to Moore. [*Life*, pp. 661-663.]

[98] *Hobhouse*: The letter did not begin "*Dear Duck.*" It began in terms very similar, but not the same put into Lord Byron's mouth, who, to be sure, knew them too well to make any blunder.

J. W. Croker: Now let us suppose that Mr. Medwin did not

quote the expression accurately,—let us suppose, for instance, (as the Italian translation given by Mr. Medwin of *anitra carissima* suggests,) that instead of *Dear Duck* the phrase really was *Dearest Duck*, how does that invalidate the truth of Mr. Medwin's story? Whatever the *terms* of the letter were, who but Lord Byron could have told Mr. Medwin that such a letter was written at all?—whatever was the little foolish term of domestic familiarity, who could have told Mr. Medwin that *any* term of familiarity was used? What matter is it whether the words were *dear* or *dearest*—*Duck* or *Pigeon*?—the charge against the lady is the same; and who but the profligate and shameless husband could have repeated any thing even *similar* to the commencement of his lady's letter? Mr. Hobhouse must excuse us if we say that his answer must be taken as a corroboration of *our* hypothesis, unless he can show how—except through Lord Byron—Thomas Medwin, Esq. of the 24th Light Dragoons could have known *any thing at all* of the matter. [Lady Byron's letter written "on the road," *i.e.*, at Woburn, opened with "Dearest B.," that written the next day, January 16, 1816, from Kirkby, is the "Dearest Duck" letter.]

[99] *Hobhouse*: It was not on lady Byron's arrival in London that Sir R. Noel wrote the letter to lord Byron. It was on lady Byron's arrival at Kirkby. . . . [*WR*, III, 25.]

Medwin: Mr. Hobhouse—*punctilious* critic and wordcatcher—owing to the want of the parenthesis from *immediately* to *arrival*, though it is already explained that Lady Byron had gone from London to her father's seat in Yorkshire [*sic*], wants to make it appear that I make the father write *from* London!! Candid Critic!

Lady Byron: These & other errors as to times & circumstances which Lord Byron himself could not possibly have committed, prove the Biographer to have erred so widely in some respects, that it is but fair to Lord Byron to suppose he Medwin did so in others.

[100] *Hobhouse*: Sir Ralph's letter was a long letter, not a few lines, and it began "My Lord," not "Sir." [*WR*, III, 25.]

J. W. Croker: Now the question raised by Lord Byron was not where Lady Byron arrived but whether Sir Ralph's letter was written immediately on her arrival from the same journey on which the before-mentioned affectionate letter was written. Nor was it Lord Byron's complaint that he addressed him as, Sir, instead of, My Lord; but that he had adopted the cold ceremonial of, Sir, or, My Lord, instead of, My *dear* Lord, or some similar style; but above all, the question is, was any such letter written, and who but Lord Byron could have told Mr. Medwin that Sir Ralph Noel had written to him about that time, and on that subject. Mr. Medwin may, no doubt, have been inaccurate in terms, but the main fact is true; and Lord Byron, who could betray confidences of this nature to a new and very casual acquaintance, cannot be suspected of being very nice in a strict and delicate adherence to the truth of the details.

[101] *Byron to Sir Ralph Noel*, February 2, 1816: There are parts of your letter which . . . arrogate a right which you do not now possess. For the present at least, your daughter is my wife. . . . [Elwin, *Lord Byron's Wife*, p. 391.]

[102] *Lady Byron*: By this letter the former ones were explained, but *it* was supprest. [Elwin, pp. 396-397, publishes the letter.]

[103] *Lady Byron*: And acted as a Spy on her. Her "deposition" was taken by Hanson, Lord B's solicitor.

[104] *Lady Byron*: It was sent for by me to make an alteration in it. [On Lady Byron's relief when informed by Augusta Leigh that Sir Ralph Noel's letter to Byron had not been delivered, see Mrs. Fletcher's statement, in Hobhouse, *Recollections*, II, 263-266. Augusta Leigh, not the post office, withheld delivery of Sir Ralph's letter; she eventually gave it to Byron. A similar but shorter statement by Mrs. Fletcher appears in *LJ*, III, 320-321.]

"I have prejudices about women: I do not like to see them eat. Rousseau makes Julie *un peu gourmande*; but that is not at all according to my taste. I do not like to be interrupted when I am writing. Lady Byron did not attend to these whims of mine.[105] The only harsh thing I ever remember saying to her was one evening shortly before our parting. I was standing before the fire, ruminating upon the embarrassment of my affairs, and other annoyances, when Lady Byron came up to me and said, 'Byron, am I in your way?'—to which I replied, 'Damnably!'[106] I was afterwards sorry, and reproached myself for the expression: but it escaped me unconsciously—involuntarily; I hardly knew what I said.

"I heard afterwards that Mrs. Charlment[107] had been the means of poisoning Lady Noel's mind against me;[108]—that she had employed herself and others in watching me in London, and had reported having traced me into a house in Portland-place. There was one act of which I might justly have complained, and which was unworthy of any one but such a confidante: I allude to the breaking open my writing-desk.[109] A book was found in it that did not do much credit to my taste in literature,[110] and some letters from a married woman with whom I had been intimate before my marriage. The use that was made of the latter was most unjustifiable, whatever may be thought of the breach of confidence that led to their discovery. Lady Byron sent them to the husband of the lady, who had the good sense to take no notice of their contents.[111] The gravest accusation that has been made against me is that of having intrigued with Mrs. Mardyn in my own house, introduced her to my own table, &c. There never was a more unfounded calumny.[112] Being on the Committee of Drury-lane Theatre, I have no doubt that several actresses called on me;[113] but as to Mrs. Mardyn, who was a beautiful woman, and might have been a dangerous visitress, I was scarcely acquainted (to speak) with her. I might even make a more serious charge against ———— than employing spies to watch suspected amours,

                  *   *   *   *

  *   *   *   *   *   *

  *   *   *   *   *   *

  *   *   *   *   *   *

---

[105] *Lady Byron*: Lord Byron was in the habit of dining *alone,*—in his own house,—& sometimes when at Seaham—Lady *Noel* having always made arrangements which left it optional with him to do so, & never taking it amiss.

[106] *Harness*: The answer was, "*That you are, indeed,*" as Byron told Tom Moore and others. The cold severity of the reply is in harmony with the general manners and character of the poet—the oath has a military raciness about it that smacks of the captain of dragoons. [*BEM*, xvi, 538 (M).]

Hobhouse: She [Augusta Leigh] recollected that Lady Byron had once asked Lord Byron if she was in his way before the fire, and that he had answered, "Yes, very much in his way." [Hobhouse, *Recollections*, II, 279.]

Byron in a memorandum: One day in the middle of my trouble I came into the room, and went up to the fire; she was standing before it, and said, "Am I in your way?" I answered, "Yes, you *are*," with emphasis. . . . That was the only time I spoke really harshly to her. [Marchand, II, 556.]

Lady Byron: No such words uttered by either, if the Survivor's Memory may be trusted.

[107] *Lady Byron*: Clermont. Total & entire Fabrication to the line drawn across p. 54 [*i.e.*, the first five sentences of Medwin's paragraph]. The word "afterwards" shews that Lord Byron had not any knowledge of this—but was duped by some one, subsequently to the Separation, if the belief were really entertained by him.

[108] *J. W. Croker*: Is not this *inaccuracy* as to the name a perfect proof of Mr. Medwin's veracity as to *facts*? How should he have ever heard of Mrs. Clermont?—how should he have thought of representing her as *poisoning Lady Byron's mind*? The variation of the name is so trifling that it may be a printer's error, but if he had wholly mistaken the name, would that be any evidence against the rest of the statement? How, except from the lips of Lord Byron, could Mr. Medwin have heard any part of the anecdote?

Byron to Moore, February 29, 1816: A Mrs. C[lermont] (now a kind of housekeeper and spy of Lady N[oel]'s), who, in her better days, was a washerwoman, is supposed to be—by the learned —very much the occult cause of our late domestic discrepancies. [*LJ*, III, 268 (M).]

[109] *Byron to Augusta Leigh*, September 14, 1816: You know I suppose that Lady B[n] *secretly opened my letter trunks before she left Town, and that* she *has also been* (*during* or since the separation) *in correspondence with* that self-avowed libeller & strumpet Wm. Lamb's wife [Lady Caroline]. [*Astarte*, p. 269.]

Lady Byron to Augusta Leigh, October 2, 1816: All that is said of C L[amb] appears to me nothing but the effect of apprehension—and the design to blacken me by association with her . . . is another effect of fear in order to invalidate any future disclosure which he may suspect or know it is in my power to make. . . . From this view his *adoption* (if not invention) of my being a *Picklock* is easily explained—for such a suspicion of my means of information would easily discredit my testimony— But there

also seems another disposition in parts of the letter—to alarm and
annoy *you*. . . . This is evident in . . . this very suggestion of my
having opened his papers—*letters of yours* probably— [*Astarte*,
pp. 270-271.]

[110] *Medwin*: He might very well say so. It was the one he afterwards named of Crébillon's, *The Sofa* [1740]. He was not however singular in his predilection for this witty and profligate
writer's novels.

Hobhouse: His *drawers* and *trunks* and *letter-cases*, were the
objects of research—in one place, which his Lordship certainly
did not intend for the inspection even of his wife, was found . . .
a few volumes of a work which as a curiosity might be kept, but
which was certainly not fit for an open library—*therefore* had it
been concealed by Lord Byron. [Hobhouse, *Recollections*, II, 250.
Hobhouse thought that the offending novel was the Marquis de
Sade's *Justine* (Marchand, II, 559, note 1).]

[111] *Lady Byron*: Lady NB. never sent any letters to any married man of that nature. The whole of this page is false. The
motive of such inventions has become plain to Lady NB.

[112] *Lady Byron*: This assertion of its being "an unfounded
calumny" is perfectly true, with whomever the story originated.

Mrs. Charlotte Mardyn: The nobleman alluded to never met
me but within the walls of Drury Lane Theatre; about twenty
sentences would comprise the total conversation with which I was
honored by him; and these sentences were delivered most probably within hearing and most certainly within view, of the whole
assembled green room. [*HVSV*, p. 142.]

[113] *Lady Byron*: No such *visits* to Lord Byron were known to
Lady Byron nor was she aware of any visits made *by* him *to* Actresses, except in one instance (not Mrs. M.) from his own information only. [Byron during his marriage had carried on some
kind of affair with the actress Susan Boyce.]

I had been shut up in a dark street[114] in London, writing (I
think he said) 'The Siege of Corinth,' and had refused myself
to every one till it was finished. I was surprised one day by a
Doctor and a Lawyer almost forcing themselves at the same
time into my room.[115] I did not know till afterwards the real
object of their visit. I thought their questions singular, frivo-

lous, and somewhat importunate, if not impertinent: but what should I have thought, if I had known that they were sent to provide proofs of my insanity? * * *
* * * * * *
* * * * * †

(†) "For Inez call'd some druggists and physicians,
 And tried to prove her loving lord was *mad*;
But as he had some lucid intermissions,
 She next decided he was only *bad*.
Yet when they ask'd her for her depositions,
 No sort of explanation could be had,
Save that her duty both to man and God
 Required this conduct,—which seem'd very odd.

She kept a journal where his faults were noted,
 And open'd certain trunks of books and letters,
All which might, if occasion served, be quoted:
 And then she had all Seville for abettors,
Besides her good old grandmother ————"
Don Juan, Canto I. Stanzas 27 and 28.

[114] *Hobhouse*: At the time here alluded to, lord Byron lived at No. 13, Piccadilly, looking into the Green Park. The conversation writer calls this a DARK street. [*WR*, III, 25.]

Medwin: Mr. Hobhouse says it was not a dark street. It is difficult in London in January to find a light one. He probably said "dark room." "Though breathing the thick atmosphere of Piccadilly when he wrote them [lines intended for but not used as the opening of *The Siege of Corinth*], it is plain that his fancy was far away, among the sunny hills and vales of Greece. . . ." [Moore, *Life*, p. 290.]

[115] *Lady Byron*: Nothing of this known by Lady NB. [Dr. Mathew Baillie did come to Byron's house, at Lady Byron's request, to discuss the poet's mental state with her, but he did not, it seems, speak to Byron. William Harness, however, asserted that "Dr. Bailey was [later] introduced to Lord Byron; and after some conversation, found that his surmise [of water on the brain] had been incorrect, and that there was no cause for alarm" (*BEM*, XVI, 538).

Dr. Stephen Lushington the lawyer was first consulted, by Lady Noel, *after* Lady Byron had gone home to her parents.]

"I have no doubt that my answers to these emissaries' interrogations were not very rational or consistent, for my imagination was heated by other things. But Dr. Baillie could not conscientiously make me out a certificate for Bedlam;[116] and perhaps the Lawyer gave a more favourable report to his employers. The Doctor said afterwards, he had been told that I always looked down when Lady Byron bent her eyes on me, and exhibited other symptoms equally infallible, particularly those that marked the late King's case so strongly.[117] I do not, however, tax Lady Byron with this transaction; probably she was not privy to it. She was the tool of others. Her mother always detested me; she had not even the decency to conceal it in her own house.[118] Dining one day at Sir Ralph's, (who was a good sort of man, and of whom you may form some idea, when I tell you that a leg of mutton was always served at his table, that he might cut the same joke upon it,) I broke a tooth, and was in great pain, which I could not avoid shewing.[119] 'It will do you good,' said Lady Noel; 'I am glad of it!' I gave her a look!

"You ask if Lady Byron were ever in love with me—I have answered that question already—No! I was the fashion when she first came out: I had the character of being a great rake, and was a great dandy—both of which young ladies like. She married me from vanity, and the hope of reforming and fixing me.[120] She was a spoiled child, and naturally of a jealous disposition; and this was increased by the infernal machinations of those in her confidence.[121]

"She was easily made the dupe of the designing, for she thought her knowledge of mankind infallible: she had got some foolish idea of Madame de Staël's into her head, that a person may be better known in the first hour than in ten years.[122] She had the habit of drawing people's characters after she had seen them once or twice. She wrote pages on pages about my character, but it was as unlike as possible.[123]

---

[116] *Lady Byron*: Dr. Baillie was consulted in private by Lady B. on Lord B's state of health at *Mrs. Leigh's* urgent request, &

owing chiefly to *her* professed Conviction of his *Insanity*, openly stated in her letters still preserved, & addressed to Lady B. After the 15th Feby. 1816 the reality of that Conviction was discredited by later circumstances.

[117] *Hobhouse*: Lady Byron answered [Hanson, Byron's lawyer], without the least hesitation, ". . . *my eye can always put down his*!!!" [Hanson then assured her that "he had never seen the least sign of insanity" in Byron. Hobhouse, *Recollections*, II, 253.]

[118] *Lady Byron*: Lady Noel's pride in her Son-in-law & affection for him were manifest to all. See page 102 [note 241, where Lady Byron observes that her mother sold some of her diamonds in order to purchase Phillips's portrait of Byron in Albanian costume.] Her letters to Ly B. after mar[e]. prove the same & are kept.

Medwin: Lord Byron, whether rightly or not, attributed much of his wife's conduct to him to the influence of her mother. [See *LJ*, IV, 49 (M); IV, 98.]

[119] *Lady Byron*: Pooh!

[120] *Lady Byron*: Ly NB. did not believe any reform[n] needed. She was ignorant. [For an excellent example of Annabella's reforming tendencies, see her letter to Byron, August 22, 1813 (Elwin, p. 167): "Observe more consistently the principles of unwearied benevolence. No longer suffer yourself to be the slave of the moment. . . . Have an object that will permanently occupy your feelings. . . . Do good. . . ."]

[121] *Lady Byron*: Lady Byron never received from *any one* such information or intimation as could give rise to Jealousy, with the exception of Lord Byron *himself*. [On Annabella as "a spoiled child," see Elwin's second chapter, "The Spoilt Child, 1792-1810."]

[122] *Lady Byron*: "Un jour ou dix ans"—M[e]. de Stael. [On August 25, 1813, after analysing Byron's character in her commonplace book, Annabella moved on (she thought) to define happiness, "which according to Mad[e] de Stael, consists in the concordance of our situation with our faculties.—Hence arise, in most instances, either Misanthropy or Despondency. . . ." (Marchand, I, 406).]

[123] *Lady Byron*: Whatever nonsense was written, it was never obtruded upon him— *During the whole time from the Marriage to the Sep[n]*. Lady Byron shewed but one thing she had written, beginning "Stranger on earth"—which he was anxious to add to the Hebrew Melodies,—but she declined. He *heard* of more of her MSS than he had seen, thro' an unfriendly Channel. I withhold the name.

"Lady Byron had good ideas, but could never express them; wrote poetry too, but it was only good by accident.[124] Her letters were always enigmatical, often unintelligible. She was governed by what she called fixed rules and principles, squared mathematically.*[125] She would have made an excellent wrangler at Cambridge. It must be confessed, however, that she gave no proof of her boasted consistency. First, she refused me, then she accepted me, then she separated herself from me:[126] —so much for consistency. I need not tell you of the obloquy and opprobrium that were cast upon my name when our separation was made public.[127] I once made a list from the Journals of the day, of the different worthies, ancient and modern, to whom I was compared. I remember a few: Nero, Apicius, Epicurus, Caligula, Heliogabalus, Henry the Eighth, and lastly the King.[128] All my former friends, even my cousin George Byron, who had been brought up with me, and whom I loved as a brother, took my wife's part. He followed the stream when it was strongest against me, and can never expect any thing from me; he shall never touch a sixpence of mine.[129] I was looked upon as the worst of husbands, the most abandoned and wicked of men, and my wife as a suffering angel—an incarnation of all the virtues and perfections of the sex. I was abused in the public prints, made the common talk of private companies, hissed as I went to the House of Lords, insulted in the streets, advised not to go to the theatre, whence the unfortunate Mrs. Mardyn had been driven with insult.[130] The Examiner was the only paper that dared say a word in my defence,[131] and Lady Jersey the only person in the fashionable world that did not look upon me as a monster.[132]

*   "I think that Dante's more abstruse ecstatics
          Meant to personify the mathematics."
             Don Juan, Canto III. Stanza 11.

[124] *Medwin*: See Madame Belloc's Life of Byron, which contains I think three of her effusions. Neither of these *was* "good by accident." They were of course furnished by Lady Byron herself— and this Life contains the first publication of Lord Byron's Journal during his Swiss tour, which is stamped with his genius and probably formed part of the Autobiography. It was given, it seems, to the keeping of Mrs. Leigh.

[125] *Lady Byron*: Very true. She never could acquire a clear style—but not owing to Mathematics—is still conscious of this deficiency.

[126] *Lady Byron*: Under such compulsion as could not be resisted.

[127] *Lady Byron*: The case was the reverse— The Press was with Lord Byron almost without exception [cf. p. 48 and p. 50, note 131]. Why was "the Separation made public"? Sir R. Milbanke had asked for "a private and amicable" arrangement—

[128] *Byron in his "Detached Thoughts,"* October 15, 1821: I have seen myself compared . . . within these nine years, to Rousseau . . . Henry the 8th . . . [and twenty-seven other persons; the name of Henry the Eighth is the only one common to both lists. *LJ*, v, 408 (M).]

[129] *Hobhouse*: The will, in which Captain George Byron was not bequeathed any of his cousin's property, was made in July 1815, long before the separation of lord and lady Byron. [*WR*, iii, 25.]

Lady Byron: All the present Lord Byron's expectations were then from his Cousin *the* Lord Byron but he *did* take part with Lady NB—as did the other Cousin also,—Sir Robert Wilmot Horton. [For very strong expressions of Byron's feelings on the conduct of George Byron (and Horton) during the time of the separation, see *Astarte*, pp. 285, 286.]

[130] *Hobhouse*: Lord Byron was never hissed as he went to the House of Lords nor insulted in the streets. [*WR*, iii, 25-26.]

Byron, "Reply to Blackwood's *Edinburgh Magazine*," March 15, 1820: I was advised not to go to the theatres, lest I should be hissed, nor to my duty in parliament, lest I should be insulted by the way. . . . [*LJ*, iv, 479 (M). On Byron's "ostracism," see Marchand, ii, 602, note 4. On Mrs. Mardyn, see *HVSV*, pp. 133, 141-142, 624, note 43. Hobhouse's diary notes that Kinnaird had received anonymous letters "stating that Mrs. Mardyn would be hissed on Byron's account" at Drury Lane (*Recollections*, I, 336).]

[131] *Hobhouse*: The Examiner was not the only paper that defended lord Byron. The Morning Chronicle was a zealous advocate of his lordship. . . . [*WR*, III, 26.]

[132] *Lady Byron*: Lady Jersey gave a party at which he appeared after the Sep[n].— She had invited Lady B. also, who did not go.

"I once addressed some lines to her that made her my friend ever after. The subject of them was suggested by her being excluded from a certain cabinet of the beauties of the day. I have the lines somewhere, and will shew them to you.[133]

"In addition to all these mortifications my affairs were irretrievably involved,[134] and almost so as to make me what they wished. I was compelled to part with Newstead, which I never could have ventured to sell in my mother's life-time.[135] As it is, I shall never forgive myself for having done so; though I am told that the estate would not now bring half as much as I got for it. This does not at all reconcile me to having parted with the old abbey.* I did not make up my mind to this step, but from the last necessity. I had my wife's portion to repay, and was determined to add 10,000*l.* more of my own to it; which I did.[136] I always hated being in debt, and do not owe a guinea. The moment I had put my affairs in train, and in little more than eighteen months after my marriage, I left England, an involuntary exile, intending it should be for ever†."[137]

* The regard which he entertained for it is proved by the passage in *Don Juan*, Canto XIII. Stanza 55, beginning thus:
  "To Norman Abbey whirl'd the noble pair," &c.
  † His feelings may be conceived by the two following passages:
  "I can't but say it is an awkward sight
  To see one's native land receding through
  The growing waters—it unmans one quite."
  Don Juan, Canto II. Stanza 12.
  "Self-exiled Harold wanders forth again,
  With nought of hope left."
  Childe Harold, Canto III. Stanza 16.

¹³³ *Medwin*: This proves my ignorance of his works, for they had been published long before. ["Condolatory Address to Sarah Countess of Jersey" was first published in the *Champion* in 1814.]

¹³⁴ *Lady Byron*: Ascertained not to have been the case when the M[arriage] Settlement was made.

¹³⁵ *Lady Byron*: Newstead had been sold first two years before the Mar^e. to Mr. Claughton, who paid the Forfeit for not completing the purchase. Another sale was soon effected, & had been concluded before the Marriage— [Newstead was "sold" in August 1812 to Thomas Claughton, who defaulted on the payment and thus forfeited it. It was again put up for auction on July 28, 1815, but was not finally sold until the end of 1817, to Wildman. Medwin correctly linked the sale of Newstead and Mrs. Byron. See Robert Charles Dallas, *Recollections of the Life of Lord Byron* (London, 1824), pp. 74, 249 (M).]

¹³⁶ *Lady Byron*: Perfectly groundless. Lord Byron received his Wife's Fortune £20,000, one half on the Marriage, the other half on the Separation—& never refunded any part of the Principal— In addition to her Pin-money, £300, which was settled, he allowed £200 for Separate Maintenance, by the Deed of Separation. The interest was paid on the unpaid half, till that £10,000 was paid. For the verification of these facts reference should be made to the Books of Messrs. Coutts (on Lady B's side) & Kinnairds Bankers (on Lord B's side). [Lady Byron was sadly confused; see above, p. 37, note 91.]

¹³⁷ [Byron left England about sixteen months after he had married, but not "intending it should be forever."]

SPEAKING of the multitude of strangers, whose visits of curiosity or impertinence he was harassed by for some years after he came abroad, particularly at Venice, he said:

"Who would wish to make a show-bear of himself, and dance to any tune any fool likes to play? Madame de Staël said, I think of Goethe, that people who did not wish to be judged by what they said, did not deserve that the world should trouble itself about what they thought. She had herself a most unconscionable insatiability of talking and shining. If she had talked less, it would have given her time to have written more, and would have been better. For my part, it is indifferent to me what the world says or thinks of me. Let them know me in my books. My conversation is never brilliant.

"Americans are the only people to whom I never refused to shew myself.[138] The Yankees individually are great friends of mine. I wish to be well thought of on the other side of the Atlantic; not that I am better appreciated there, than on this; perhaps worse. Some American Reviewer has been persevering in his abuse and personality, but he should have minded his ledger; he never excited my spleen.* I was confirmed in my resolution of shutting my door against all the travelling English by the impertinence of an anonymous scribbler, who said he might have known me, but would not."

I interrupted him by telling him he need not have been so angry on that occasion,—that it was an authoress who had been guilty of that remark. "I don't wonder," added I, "that a spinster should have avoided associating with so dangerous an acquaintance as you had the character of being at Venice."

* The taste and critical acumen of the American magazine will appear from the following extract:

"The verses (it is of 'The Prisoner of Chillon' that it speaks) are in the eight syllable measure, and occasionally display some pretty poetry; at all events, there is little in them to offend.

"We do not find any passage of sufficient beauty or originality to warrant extract."

Am. Critical Review, 1817.

"Well, I did not know that these 'Sketches of Italy' were the production of a woman;[139] but whether it was a Mr., Mrs., or Miss, the remark was equally uncalled for. To be sure, the life I led at Venice was not the most saintlike in the world."

"Yes," said I, "if you were to be canonized, it must be as San Ciappelletto."

"Not so bad as that either," said he somewhat seriously.[140]

[138] *Byron in his "Detached Thoughts"*: Whenever an American requests to see me (which is *not* unfrequently), I comply. . . . [*LJ*, v, 416.]

Medwin: And yet he did refuse a few days after this to allow Mr. Paterson—now called Bonaparte, the son of Jerome [Bonaparte] and Mrs. Paterson, his divorced wife—to be introduced to him. He made a detour to Pisa for the purpose. [On Mrs. Paterson, the American first wife of Jerome Bonaparte, see Origo, *The Last Attachment*, pp. 395 and 519, note 41.]

[139] *Medwin*: It is singular proof of mystification that he in this Dialogue pretends not to have known that this work [*Sketches Descriptive of Italy*, 1820, by Jane Waldie] *was* author[ed] by a Lady, for at Ravenna he says, "I open my letter to say, that on reading *more* of the 4 volumes on Italy, where the Author says 'declined an introduction,' I perceive (*horresco referens*) that it is written by a WOMAN!!!" [*LJ*, v, 84. Before Byron knew that the writer was a woman, he had replied in a fiery note at the end of *Marino Faliero*, where he wrote, ". . . I invariably refused to receive any English with whom I was not previously acquainted, even when they had letters from England." Byron's words, as originally reported by Medwin, are not proof, of course, of "mystification."]

[140] [A reference to the first story of the *Decameron*: "Master Ciappelletto dupeth a holy friar with a false confession and dieth; and having been in his lifetime the worst of men, he is, after his death, reputed a saint and called Saint Ciappelletto" (M).]

"Venice," resumed he, "is a melancholy place to reside in: —to see a city die daily as she does, is a sad contemplation. I sought to distract my mind from a sense of her desolation, and my own solitude, by plunging into a vortex that was any thing but pleasure. When one gets into a mill-stream, it is difficult to swim against it, and keep out of the wheels. The consequences of being carried down by it would furnish an excellent lesson for youth. You are too old to profit by it. But, who ever profited by the experience of others, or his own? When you read my Memoirs, you will learn the evils, moral and physical, of true dissipation. I assure you my life is very entertaining, and very instructive."

I said, "I suppose, when you left England, you were a Childe Harold, and at Venice a Don Giovanni, and Fletcher your Leporello." He laughed at the remark. I asked him, in what way his life would prove a good lesson? and he gave me several anecdotes of himself, which I have thrown into a sort of narrative.

"ALMOST all the friends of my youth are dead;[141] (some shot in duels,) ruined,[142] or in the galleys:" (mentioning the names of several.)

"Among those I lost in the early part of my career, was Lord Falkland,—poor fellow! our fathers' fathers were friends. He lost his life for a joke,[143] and one too he did not make himself. The present race is more steady than the last. They have less constitution, and not so much money;—that accounts for the change in their morals.

"I am now tamed; but before I married, shewed some of the blood of my ancestors. It is ridiculous to say that we do not inherit our passions, as well as the gout, or any other disorder.

"I was not so young when my father died, but that I perfectly remember him;[144] and had very early a horror of matrimony, from the sight of domestic broils: this feeling came over me very strongly at my wedding. Something whispered me that I was sealing my own death-warrant. I am a great believer in presentiments. Socrates' dæmon was no fiction; Monk Lewis had his monitor, and Napoleon many warnings. At the last moment I would have retreated, if I could have done so.[145] I called to mind a friend of mine, who had married a young, beautiful, and rich girl, and yet was miserable. He had strongly urged me against putting my neck in the same yoke: and to shew you how firmly I was resolved to attend to his advice, I betted Hay fifty guineas to one that I should always remain single.[146] Six years afterwards I sent him the money. The day before I proposed to Lady Byron, I had no idea of doing so."[147]

---

[141] *Moore*: In a letter, written between two and three months after his mother's death, he states no less a number than six persons, all friends or relatives, who have been snatched away from him by death between May and the end of August. [Moore, *Life*,

p. 129, note 1 (M). These six included Matthews, Wingfield, Hargreaves Hanson, and Edleston.]

[142] *Medwin*: Among them were Parson Andrews, Scrope Davies [these names deleted], Martin Hawke, Captain Hay, Captain Wallace of Parisian celebrity—a strange circle for a young Nobleman.

[143] [Charles John Cary, Viscount Falkland, twenty years Byron's senior, was killed in a duel on March 7, 1809, with his friend Mr. Powell. At Stephenson's Hotel in Bond Street, Falkland said to Powell, neither man being sober, "What, drunk again to-night, Pogey?" Following Powell's reply, Falkland thrashed him with a cane, next morning offered his apology privately but refused to apologize publicly at Stephenson's. The duel followed. See *GM*, cv, 273.]

Lady Byron: Lord Byron gave £1000 to relieve the Mother of Lord Falkland. [Byron gave £500 to Falkland's widow, who had fallen ludicrously in love with him. She was the mother of five children.]

[144] [Byron's father died in France on August 2, 1791, but he left Aberdeen on or shortly after September 8, 1790, when Byron was two years and seven months old, and did not see his son again. See Marchand, pp. 30-31.]

[145] [Byron told Annabella that in December 1814 he had written from Six Mile Bottom withdrawing from the engagement, but that Augusta Leigh had persuaded him from sending the letter. See Ethel C. Mayne, *The Life and Letters of Lady Byron* (London, 1929), p. 154.]

[146] *Byron to Captain John Hay*, January 26, 1815: Enclosed is my draft for your hundred guineas. . . . [*LJ*, iii, 173.]

[147] *Lady Byron*: True, as proved by letters he afterwards disclosed to me.

Medwin: He had through a friend proposed to and been refused by another lady [Lady Charlotte Leveson Gower]—and on the very day of such refusal made the offer. [See Moore, *Life*, p. 264.]

After this digression he continued: "I lost my father when I was only six years of age.[148] My mother, when she was in a rage with me, (and I gave her cause enough,)[149] used to say, 'Ah, you little dog, you are a Byron all over; you are as bad as your father!' It was very different from Mrs. Malaprop's saying, 'Ah! good dear Mr. Malaprop, I never loved him till he was dead.'[150] But, in fact, my father was, in his youth, any thing but a 'Cœlebs in search of a wife.' He would have made a bad hero for Hannah More. He ran out three fortunes, and married or ran away with three women,[151] and once wanted a guinea, that he wrote for; I have the note. He seemed born for his own ruin, and that of the other sex. He began by seducing Lady Carmarthen, and spent for her 4,000*l.* a-year; and not content with one adventure of this kind, afterwards eloped with Miss Gordon.[152] This marriage was not destined to be a very fortunate one either, and I don't wonder at her differing from Sheridan's widow in the play. They certainly could not have claimed the flitch.[153]

[148] *Hobhouse*: Lord Byron was only three years and a half old when his father died. [*WR*, III, 26.]

[149] *Lady Byron*: From some letters of his Mother's in the possession of Lady B. it would appear that she felt much affection for him.

[150] *Hobhouse*: Mrs. Malaprop's words are very different; and lord Byron was singularly accurate as well as apposite in his quotations. The pretended conversation makes him neither one nor the other. [*WR*, III, 26.]

Mrs. Malaprop: 'Tis safest in matrimony to begin with a little aversion. I am sure I hated your poor dear uncle before marriage as if he'd been a blackamoor—and yet, miss, you are sensible what a wife I made!—and when it pleased Heaven to release me from him, 'tis unknown what tears I shed! [*The Rivals*, I, ii.]

[151] *Hobhouse*: Lord Byron's father did not run out *three* fortunes, nor marry or run away with *three* women. [*WR*, III, 26. Byron's father was notorious, and the correct number of his amours is no longer to be arrived at. Disinherited by his father, he ran through the fortunes of both his wives, and, it is said, accepted

contributions from other ladies who favored him. See Marchand,
I, 12.]

¹⁵² [Lady Carmarthen, mother of Augusta Leigh, had inherited
from her father for life an estate that returned £4,000 a year
(Marchand, I, 13). It seems that she and Captain Byron went to
France only after their marriage. Properly speaking, Captain
Byron did not elope with Catherine Gordon, for they were married
in Bath, where she was visiting.]

¹⁵³ [Until the latter part of the eighteenth century a flitch of
bacon was given by the lord of the manor of Little Dunmow, in
Essex, to any married couple who lived for a year without quarrels
or regrets.]

"The phrenologists tell me that other lines besides that
of thought" (the middle of three horizontal lines on his forehead, on which he prided himself,) "are strongly developed
in the hinder part of my cranium; particularly that called
philoprogenitiveness.¹⁵⁴ I suppose, too, the pugnacious bump
might be found somewhere, because my uncle had it.

"You have heard the unfortunate story of his duel with his
relation and neighbour. After that melancholy event, he shut
himself up at Newstead, and was in the habit of feeding
crickets, which were his only companions. He had made them
so tame as to crawl over him, and used to whip them with a
wisp of straw, if too familiar. When he died, tradition says
that they left the house in a body.¹⁵⁵ I suppose I derive my
superstition from this branch of the family; but though I attend to none of these new-fangled theories, I am inclined to
think that there is more in the chart of the skull than the
Edinburgh Reviewers suppose.* However that may be, I was
a wayward youth, and gave my mother a world of trouble,—
as I fear Ada will hers, for I am told she is a little termagant.
I had an ancestor too that expired laughing, (I suppose that
my good spirits came from him;) and two whose affection was
such for each other, that they died almost at the same time.¹⁵⁶

* He had probably been reading the article on Gall and Spurzheim.¹⁵⁷

There seems to have been a flaw in my escutcheon there, or that loving couple have monopolized all the connubial bliss of the family.

"I passed my boyhood at Mar Lodge near Aberdeen, occasionally visiting the Highlands; and long retained an affection for Scotland*;—that, I suppose, I imbibed from my mother. My love for it, however, was at one time much shaken by the critique in 'The Edinburgh Review' on 'The Hours of Idleness,' and I transferred a portion of my dislike to the country; but my affection for it soon flowed back into its old channel.[158]

* He came to England in 1798.

[154] *Lady Byron*: Spurzheim said in 1815 that the head was "full of Antithesis"— He (B) mentioned this himself. [Spurzheim the phrenologist examined Byron, it seems, on September 16, 1814 (*LJ*, III, 137).]

[155] *Moore*: During his latter years, the only companions of his solitude—besides that colony of crickets, which he is said to have amused himself with rearing and feeding—were [two servants]. To this Lord Byron used to add, on the authority of old servants of the family, that on the day of their patron's death, these crickets all left the house simultaneously. . . . [Moore, *Life*, p. 11 and note 2 (M).]

[156] *Medwin*: Lord Byron alludes to the Deaths of Capt. George Byron [father of the 7th Lord Byron] and his wife [sister of R. C. Dallas]. Dallas says [p. 195, note], "In England he lived above twelve months; during which he suffered the misery of witnessing the dissolution of a beautiful . . . and beloved wife, who died at Bath, on the 26th of February, 1793, at the age of twenty-nine years; upon which he fled with his children to Dawlish, and there closed his eyes upon them, just three months and a fortnight after they had lost their mother." A plain stone at the entrance of the Church at Dawlish of fine marble [? draws] attention merely [to] the dates of his birth and death.

[157] [A review-article in the *Edinburgh Review*, XXV (June, 1815), 227-268, "The Doctrines of Gall and Spurzheim," damned both phrenologists as quacks.]

¹⁵⁸ *Moore*: Cordial, however, and deep as were the impressions which he retained of Scotland, he would sometimes in this, as in all his other amiable feelings, endeavour perversely to belie his own better nature. . . . The abuse with which, in his anger against the Edinburgh Review, he overwhelmed every thing Scotch, is an instance of this temporary triumph of wilfulness. . . . [Moore, *Life*, p. 12 (M).]

"I don't know from whom I inherited verse-making; probably the wild scenery of Morven and Loch-na-gar, and the banks of the Dee, were the parents of my poetical vein, and the developers of my poetical *boss*. If it was so, it was dormant; at least, I never wrote any thing worth mentioning till I was in love. Dante dates his passion for Beatrice at twelve: I was almost as young when I fell over head and ears in love; but I anticipate. I was sent to Harrow at twelve,¹⁵⁹ and spent my vacations at Newstead. It was there that I first saw Mary Chaworth.* She was several years older than myself: but, at my age, boys like something older than themselves, as they do younger, later in life.¹⁶⁰ Our estates adjoined; but, owing

*   ———— "It was a name
Which pleased him, and yet pleased him not;—and why?
Time taught him a deep answer."
                                        The Dream.

"I have a passion for the name of 'Mary,'
For once it was a magic sound to me;
And still it half calls up the realms of fairy,
Where I beheld what never was to be.
All feelings changed, but this was last to vary—
A spell from which even yet I am not quite free.
But I grow sad!"————
                                Don Juan, Canto V. Stanza 4.

———— "Yet still, to pay my court, I
Gave what I had—a heart:—as the world went, I
Gave what was worth a world,—for worlds could never
Restore me the pure feelings gone for ever!
'Twas the boy's 'mite,' and, like the 'widow's,' may,
Perhaps, be weigh'd hereafter, if not now."
                                Don Juan, Canto VI. Stanza 5, &c,

to the unhappy circumstance of the feud to which I before alluded, our families (as is generally the case with neighbours who happen to be relations)[161] were never on terms of more than common civility,—scarcely those. I passed the summer vacation of this year among the Malvern hills: those were days of romance! She was the *beau idéal* of all that my youthful fancy could paint of beautiful; and I have taken all my fables about the celestial nature of women from the perfection my imagination created in her—I say created, for I found her, like the rest of the sex, any thing but angelic.[162]

"I returned to Harrow, after my trip to Cheltenham,[163] more deeply enamoured than ever, and passed the next holidays at Newstead. I now began to fancy myself a man, and to make love in earnest. Our meetings were stolen ones, and my letters passed through the medium of a confidante. A gate leading from Mr. Chaworth's grounds to those of my mother, was the place of our interviews. But the ardour was all on my side. I was serious; she was volatile. She liked me as a younger brother, and treated and laughed at me as a boy.[164] She, however, gave me her picture, and that was something to make verses upon.*

* He had always a black ribbon round his neck, to which was attached a locket containing hair and a picture.[165] We had been playing at billiards one night till the balls appeared double, when all at once he searched hastily for something under his waistcoat, and said, in great alarm, "Good God! I have lost my ————!" but before he had finished the sentence, he discovered the hidden treasure.

[159] *Medwin*: He was 13.

[160] *Medwin*: This observation he illustrated by saying, "Rogers used to say"—and here he mimicked his toothless way of muttering—"when you're as old as I am, you'll like youth."

[161] *Medwin*: There had been, I think, some intermarriage between the Byron and Chaworth families. [The 3rd Lord Byron (died 1695) married Elizabeth Chaworth, daughter of George, Viscount Chaworth. See *LJ*, i, 17, note.]

[162] [In 1814, separated from her husband, Mary Chaworth Musters actively pursued Byron, writing to him fifty letters in six months. See Marchand, i, 456.]

[163] [Professor Leslie A. Marchand has pointed out to me that Medwin has here telescoped Byron's early love for his first cousin Margaret Parker and his later affair with his distant cousin Mary Chaworth, as the references to Cheltenham and the Malvern Hills, which he visited in 1801, indicate. He fell desperately in love with Mary Chaworth in 1803.]

[164] *Medwin*: She called him the lame boy. [See Moore, *Life*, p. 28.]

[165] *Harness*: The locket . . . , if it be the same he wore in 1813, containing a lock of fair soft hair, with a golden skull and cross-bones placed upon it, was not a memorial of this attachment. The hair was of a fair girl, who died before his passion had departed, and whose name I could never prevail on him to mention. [*BEM*, xvi, 540. Was this Edleston's hair? See Marchand, i, 296, note 3.]

Medwin: The one I saw was not the same. There was no skull and crossbones—but a portrait and not of a fair girl. Nor was the portrait that of Miss Chaworth. He had long forgotten her! [In May, 1823, Byron wore a large brooch containing Augusta's hair. See Mayne, *Life of Lady Byron*, p. 258, note.]

"During the last year that I was at Harrow, all my thoughts were occupied on this love-affair. I had, besides, a spirit that ill brooked the restraints of school-discipline; for I had been encouraged by servants in all my violence of temper, and was used to command. Every thing like a task was repugnant to my nature; and I came away a very indifferent classic, and read in nothing that was useful. That subordination, which is the soul of all discipline, I submitted to with great difficulty; yet I did submit to it; and I have always retained a sense of Drury's* kindness,[166] which enabled me to bear it and fagging too. The Duke of Dorset was my fag.[167] I was not a very hard task-master. There were times in which, if I had not considered it as a school, I should have been happy at Harrow.

* See Lines addressed to him in the 'Hours of Idleness.'

There is one spot I should like to see again: I was particularly delighted with the view from the Church-yard, and used to sit for hours on the stile leading into the fields;—even then I formed a wish to be buried there.[168] Of all my schoolfellows I know no one for whom I have retained so much friendship as for Lord Clare.[169] I have been constantly corresponding with him ever since I knew he was in Italy; and look forward to seeing him, and talking over with him our old Harrow stories, with infinite delight. There is no pleasure in life equal to that of meeting an old friend. You know how glad I was to see Hay. Why did not Scrope Davies come to see me? Some one told me that he was at Florence, but it is impossible.

---

[166] *Byron in a manuscript journal*: Dr. Drury, whom I plagued sufficiently too, was the best, the kindest, (and yet strict, too,) friend I ever had—and I look upon him still as a father. [Moore, *Life*, p. 21 (M).]

[167] *Harness*: This is not the case; they were in different houses, and Malton was Byron's fag, to whom he was extremely kind. [*BEM*, xvi, 539. I find no other reference to Malton. Byron recalled in 1808 (*LJ*, iii, 171, note), "Wingfield and Kemmis were both my fags at Harrow. . . ."]

Lady Byron: The Duke of D[orset] died in 1815 deeply regretted by Lord Byron. He was quite overwhelmed by the news. [See also *LJ*, iii, 181.]

[168] *Moore*: They show a tomb in the churchyard at Harrow, commanding a view over Windsor, which was so well known to be his favourite resting-place, that the boys called it "Byron's tomb"; and here, they say, he used to sit for hours wrapt up in thought. . . . [Moore, *Life*, p. 26 (M); see also *LJ*, vi, 69-70.]

[169] *Byron in his "Detached Thoughts"*: My School friendships were with *me passions*. . . . That with Lord Clare began one of the earliest and lasted longest. . . . I never hear the word "*Clare*" without a beating of the heart even *now*. . . . [*LJ*, v, 455 (M).]

"There are two things that strike me at this moment, which I did at Harrow: I fought Lord Calthorpe for writing 'D—d

Atheist!' under my name;[170] and prevented the school-room from being burnt during a rebellion, by pointing out to the boys the names of their fathers and grandfathers on the walls.[171]

"Had I married Miss C——, perhaps the whole tenor of my life would have been different.* She jilted me, however; but her marriage proved any thing but a happy one.† She was at length separated from Mr. Musters, and proposed an interview with me, but by the advice of my sister I declined it.[172] I remember meeting her after my return from Greece,[173] but pride had conquered my love; and yet it was not with perfect indifference I saw her.‡

"For a man to become a poet (witness Petrarch and Dante) he must be in love, or miserable. I was both when I wrote 'The Hours of Idleness:' some of those poems, in spite of what the reviewers say, are as good as any I ever produced.

"For some years after the event that had so much influence on my fate, I tried to drown the remembrance of it and her in the most depraving dissipation;§ but the poison was in the cup.   *   *   *   *   *

   *   *   *   *   *   *

"There had been found by the gardener, in digging, a skull that had probably belonged to some jolly friar or monk of the Abbey about the time it was dismonasteried."

* Perhaps in his lyrical pieces, even those 'To Thyrza,' he never surpassed those exquisitely feeling Stanzas, beginning—

"O had my fate been join'd to thine," &c.

† ——————————— "the one
To end in madness; both in misery."
                                            The Dream.

‡ "Yet I was calm. I knew the time
    My heart would swell but at thy look;
But now to tremble were a crime.
    We met, and not a nerve was shook!"

§ "And monks might deem their time was come agen,
    If ancient tales say true, nor wrong the holy men."
                        Childe Harold, Canto I. Stanza 7.

"I heard at the Countess Suwaloff's[174] the other evening," said I, interrupting him, "that you drink out of a skull now." He took no notice of my observation, but continued:

"Observing it to be of giant size, and in a perfect state of preservation, a strange fancy seized me of having it set and mounted as a drinking-cup. I accordingly sent it to town, and it returned with a very high polish, and of a mottled colour like tortoiseshell; (Colonel Wildman now has it.)[175] I remember scribbling some lines about it; but that was not all: I afterwards established at the Abbey a new order. The members consisted of twelve, and I elected myself grand master, or Abbot of the Skull, a grand heraldic title. A set of black gowns, mine distinguished from the rest, was ordered, and from time to time, when a particular hard day was expected, a chapter was held; the *crane* was filled with claret, and, in imitation of the Goths of old, passed about to the gods of the Consistory, whilst many a grim joke was cut at its expense."[176]

---

[170] *Harness*: We have an oath attributed to the amiable and excellent Lord Calthorpe, whose manners and conversation, we can assure Captain Medwin, are, and always have been, those of a gentleman, and, even as a school-boy, were untainted by the low-bred vice of swearing. [*BEM*, xvi, 538.]

Byron to James Kennedy, August, 1823: Lord Calthorpe was the first who called me an atheist when we were at school at Harrow, for which I gave him as good a drubbing as ever he got in his life. [*HVSV*, p. 430.]

[171] *Medwin*: Byron's own name would now act as a spell against a similar attempt. I saw his name carved at Harrow in three places in very large characters. [On Byron's part in the Harrow rebellion against Dr. Butler, see Marchand, i, 95.]

[172] *Lady Byron*: On the contrary *she* declined the Interview as Ly B heard from Ld B & Mrs. Leigh, when together.

Byron to J. J. Coulmann, July 12, 1823: When an occasion offered, I was upon the point, with her [Mary Chaworth's] consent, of paying her a visit, when my sister, who has always had more influence over me than anyone else, persuaded me not to do it. [*LJ*, vi, 234.]

Byron to Lady Melbourne, February 6, 1814: You will very probably say that I ought to have gone over [to see Mary Chaworth] at all events, and Augusta has also been trying her rhetoric to the same purpose, and urging me repeatedly to call before I left the country. [*Lord Byron's Correspondence*, ed. John Murray (London, 1922), I, 241.]

[173] [Byron talked with Mary Chaworth for the last time in 1809, before his trip to Greece, not after his return. See Moore, *Life*, p. 85 (M) and *LJ*, I, 198.]

[174] [Medwin's Countess Suwaloff is perhaps the same Princess Suwarrow (Suwarof) that Claire Clairmont in her unpublished diary recorded seeing on January 1, 1822, at the Casa Boutourlin, in Florence. The great Russian general, who figures in *Don Juan*, bore both the title of Prince and of Count.]

[175] *Moore*: Another use to which he appropriated one of the skulls found in digging at Newstead was the having it mounted in silver, and converted into a drinking cup . . . [now] in the possession of . . . Colonel Wildman. [Moore, *Life*, p. 87, note 3 (M).]

[176] *Hobhouse*: This story was told in a magazine or newspaper of the day [1809] on some slight foundation—but the details here put into lord Byron's mouth are all untrue. . . .

Those who knew lord Byron will detect at once the vulgarisms of the pretended conversation. The story as dressed up for sale is a fiction. [*WR*, III, 27.]

C. S. Matthews to his sister, May 22, 1809: I must not omit the custom of handing round, after dinner, on the removal of the cloth, a human skull filled with burgundy. After revelling on choice viands, and the finest wines of France, we adjourned to tea. . . . A set of monkish dresses, which had been provided, with all the proper apparatus of crosses, beads, tonsures, etc., often gave a variety to our appearance, and to our pursuits. [Moore, *Life*, p. 83 (M).]

Byron to Murray, November 19, 1820: We went down to Newstead together, where I had got a famous cellar, and *Monks'* dresses from a masquerade warehouse. We were a company of some seven or eight, with an occasional neighbour or so for visitors, and used to sit up late in our friars' dresses, drinking burgundy, claret, champagne, and what not, out of the *skull-cup*, and all sorts of glasses, and buffooning all round the house in our conventual garments. Matthews always denominated me "the Abbot." . . . [*LJ*, I, 153-155.]

"You seem," said I, "to have had a particular predilection for skulls and cross-bones: a friend of mine, Mr. ———, told me he took some home for you from Switzerland."

"They were from the field of Morat,"[177] said he; "a single bone of one of those heroes is worth all the skulls of all the priests that ever existed."

"Talking of Morat," said I, "where did you find the story of Julia Alpinula? M——— and I searched among its archives in vain."[178]

"I took the inscription," said he, "from an old chronicle; the stone has no existence.—But to continue. You know the story of the bear that I brought up for a degree when I was at Trinity.[179] I had a great hatred of College rules, and contempt for academical honours. How many of their wranglers have ever distinguished themselves in the world? There was, by the bye, rather a witty satire founded on my bear. A friend of Shelley's made an Ourang Outang (Oran Hauton, Esq.) the hero of a novel, had him created a baronet, and returned for the borough of One Vote—I forget the name of the novel*. I believe they were as glad to get rid of me at Cambridge† as they were at Harrow.

"Another of the wild freaks I played during my mother's life-time, was to dress up Mrs. ———, and to pass her off as my brother Gordon, in order that my mother might not hear of my having such a female acquaintance.[180] You would not think me a Scipio in those days, but I can safely say I never seduced any woman. I will give you an instance of great forbearance: Mrs. L. G——— wrote and offered to let me have her daughter for 100*l.* Can you fancy such depravity? The old lady's *P. S.* was excellent. 'With *dilicaci* every thing may be made *asy.*' But the same post brought me a letter from the young one deprecating my taking advantage of their

* Melincourt. [It was Lord Monboddo's orang-outang, described in two of his works, that suggested to Peacock the character of Sir Oran Haut-ton.]

† He remained at Cambridge till nineteen.

necessities, and ending with saying that she prized her virtue. I respected it too,[181] and sent her some money.

[177] [The bones from the field of Morat, which are now in the possession of Sir John Murray, were taken to England by William John St. Aubyn, identified by Medwin in an unpublished marginal note to his *Life of Shelley* (facing 1, 250, which is p. 152 of Forman's edition) as the "friend . . . who occasionally made a morning call at Diodati" in 1816. See also *LJ*, iv, 39 (note 1) and 45.]

[178] [Medwin's "M———" may well be a typographical error for "W———," either E. E. Williams or William John St. Aubyn. On Julia Alpinula, see Byron's note to *Childe Harold*, iii, 66.]

[179] *Byron to Elizabeth Bridget Pigot*, October 26, 1807: I have got a new friend, the finest in the world, a *tame bear*. When I brought him here [Trinity College], they asked me what I meant to do with him, and my reply was, "he should *sit for a fellowship*." [*LJ*, i, 147.]

[180] *Medwin*: He was confined then to the great scandal of the House, and drove all the people out of it, two Bishops and a Dean —words expunged from my manuscript by Mr. Colburn. *Blackwood* says [xvi, 532], ". . . keeping a girl in boy's clothes, and passing her off for his cousin, lest his mother should hear of it, Lord Byron has had abundant cause to repent; but the affair itself had a most ludicrous conclusion, for the young gentleman miscarried in a certain family hotel in Bond Street, to the inexpressible horror of the chambermaids, and the consternation of all the house." Here Mr. Hobhouse [*i.e.*, Galt] was wrong—the child died. [See Moore, *Life*, p. 70, for a similar account, presumably of the same girl.]

[181] *Medwin*: By the aid of Fletcher how much he was changed in Italy. [Cf. Byron's story of the French *entremetteuse*, who wrote in the postscript of her letter to Byron, "Remember, Milor, that *delicaci ensure everi succés*" (Byron's "Second Letter . . . on Bowles's Strictures," dated March 25, 1821, but not published until 1835, *LJ*, v, 575). Peter Quennell, *Byron: The Years of Fame* (New York, 1935), pp. 121-122, believes that the daughter of Mrs. L. G—— was Isabella Lancaster, whose letter of May 6, 1812, he quotes.]

"There are few Josephs in the world, and many Potiphar's wives. A curious thing happened to me shortly after the honeymoon, which was very awkward at the time, but has since amused me much. It so happened that three married women were on a wedding visit to my wife, (and in the same room, at the same time,) whom I had known to be all birds of the same nest. Fancy the scene of confusion that ensued![182]

"I have seen a great deal of Italian society, and swum in a gondola,[183] but nothing could equal the profligacy of high life in England, especially that of ——— when I knew it.[184]

---

[182] *Lady Byron*: Some months after the Marᵉ. in Piccadilly. Every one knew the secret of every other—but it passed without any "*Confusion*"—that a bystander would have remarked. The visitors were admitted with Lady Byron's consent. He acknowledged to Lady B the moment after their departure, that she had succeeded perfectly in preventing embarrassment.

Lady Caroline Lamb to Medwin, November, 1824: Shortly after he married, once, Lady Melbourne took me to see his Wife in Piccadilly. It was a cruel request, but Lord Byron himself made it. It is to this wedding visit he alludes. Mrs. Leigh, myself, Lady Melbourne, Lady Noel, & Lady Byron, were in the room. I never looked up. Annabella was very cold to me. Lord Byron came in & seemed agitated—his hand was cold, but he seemed kind. This was the last time upon this earth I ever met him. [*LJ*, II, 453. Lady Noel, then Milbanke, was in London briefly in mid-April, 1815.]

[183] [Cf. the motto to *Beppo*, from *As You Like It*: ". . . swam in a *Gondola*."]

[184] *Galt*: As far, perhaps, as Lord Byron spoke from his own experience, and from the report of his associates, we are not inclined to dispute the accusation; but is it not perfectly well-known, that, in England, society in high life is divided into two classes, as distinct and separate from each other as any two *castes* can well be? With the one, both manners and minds are cherished in the most graceful excellence—domestic virtue combined with all that is elegant, gentle, and beneficent, as fair and free from stain as habitual honour in its highest acceptation can imply. To this class Lord Byron had NOT access. [*BEM*, XVI, 532.]

Medwin: What does Mr. Hobhouse [*i.e.*, Galt] mean by this?

Did he not frequent Lady Melbourne's and Lady Jersey's circles? [To illustrate Byron's awareness of "the profligacy of high life in England," Medwin quotes Byron's account of seeing at Covent Garden "the most distinguished old and young Babylonians of quality . . . your public and your *understood* courtesans" (*LJ*, II, 378). Byron told Annabella that in 1813 he had had sexual intercourse with Lady Melbourne and with her daughter-in-law, Lady Caroline Lamb (Elwin, pp. 387, 401).]

———————————

"There was a lady at that time, double my own age, the mother of several children who were perfect angels, with whom I had formed a *liaison* that continued without interruption for eight months. The autumn of a beauty like her's is preferable to the spring in others. She told me she was never in love till she was thirty; and I thought myself so with her when she was forty. I never felt a stronger passion; which she returned with equal ardour. I was as fond of, indeed more attached than I ought to have been, to one who had bestowed her favours on many; but I was flattered at a preference that had led her to discard another, who in personal attractions and fashion was far my superior. She had been sacrificed, almost before she was a woman, to one whose mind and body were equally contemptible in the scale of creation; and on whom she bestowed a numerous family, to which the law gave him the right to be called father. Strange as it may seem, she gained (as all women do) an influence over me so strong, that I had great difficulty in breaking with her, even when I knew she had been inconstant to me; and once was on the point of going abroad with her,—and narrowly escaped this folly.[185] I was at this time a mere Bond-street lounger—a great man at lobbies, coffee and gambling-houses:[186] my afternoons were passed in visits, luncheons, lounging and boxing—not to mention drinking! If I had known you in early life, you would not have been alive now. I remember Scrope Davies, Hobhouse, and myself, clubbing 19*l.*, all we had in our pockets, and losing it at a hell in St. James's-street, at chicken-hazard,

which may be called *fowl* (foul); and afterwards getting
drunk together till H. and S. D. quarrelled. Scrope afterwards
wrote to me for my pistols to shoot himself; but I declined
lending them, on the plea that they would be forfeited as a
deodand.[187] I knew my answer would have more effect than
four sides of prosing.

[185] *Galt*: His affair with Lady [Oxford, wife of Edward Harley,
Earl of Oxford] . . . was truly absurd. The folly of it lost him a
sincere friend [Galt]. At no time could he bear the slightest ad-
monition. . . . In that affair, the gentleman alluded to . . . said,
"By the by, my Lord, it is reported you have become a contributor
to the Harleian Miscellany." The result was a sullen answer, which
ended in an estrangement, that broke up their intercourse. [*BEM*,
xvi, 533. Galt told this same story in his *Literary Life and Mis-
cellanies*; see *HVSV*, pp. 73-74 and 618, note 68. Byron's immediate predecessor seems to have been Lord Archibald Hamilton
(Marchand, i, 352). It was Medwin's intent to delete this entire
account of Lady Oxford.]

[186] *Medwin*: Lord Byron often talked with me of those times.
He says [*LJ*, v, 425] that he was once "fond" of dice and threw
in "fourteen mains." He was too fond of them, for it seems he lost
to Scrope Davies £4800 [the sum lent by Davies to Byron in
1809]. Martin Hawke, Hay, etc. picked him fairly clean—I
suspect.

[187] *Byron in his "Detached Thoughts"*: We had, I say, twenty
guineas or so, and we lost them [at Brighthelmstone, in 1808],
returning home in bad humour. . . . We emerged in our dressing-
gowns to discuss a bottle or two of Champaigne and Hock. . . . In
course of this discussion, words arose; Scrope seized H[obhouse]
by the throat; H. seized a knife in self-defence, and stabbed Scrope
in the shoulder to avoid being throttled. . . . Scrope was furious:
first he wanted to fight, then to go away in a post-chaise, and then
to *shoot* himself, which latter intention I offered to forward, provided that he did not use *my pistols*, which, in case of suicide,
would become a deo-dand to the King. [*LJ*, v, 448.]

Galt: The answer to Scroope Davis, when he wanted to borrow
Byron's pistols to shoot himself, is one of the few characteristic
things in Captain Medwin's Journal. In such, his Lordship ex-
celled. [*BEM*, xvi, 533.]

"Don't suppose, however, that I took any pleasure in all these excesses, or that parson A. H. or W—— were associates to my taste.[188] The miserable consequences of such a life are detailed at length in my Memoirs. My own master at an age when I most required a guide, and left to the dominion of my passions when they were the strongest, with a fortune anticipated before I came into possession of it, and a constitution impaired by early excesses, I commenced my travels in 1809, with a joyless indifference to a world that was all before me.*

"Well might you say, speaking feelingly," said I:
   "There is no sterner moralist than pleasure†."

*   "I wish they knew the life of a young noble;

.   .   .   .

They're young, but know not youth; it is anticipated;
Handsome but wasted, rich without a sou;
Their vigour in a thousand arms is dissipated,
Their cash comes *from*, their wealth goes *to* a Jew."
         Don Juan, Canto XI. Stanzas 74 and 75.

† He used to say there were three great men ruined in one year, Brummell, himself, and Napoleon!

[188] [Medwin altered "A. K. or W—" to "A. H. or W—" and in the bottom margin wrote "Parson Andrews, Hay, Wallace." "Andrews" is then deleted and an illegible name beginning with "A" (perhaps Ainley or Austin) is substituted. The same series, with the same illegible substitution, appears in note 142, p. 56. For Byron on Captain Wallace, see *LJ*, v, 419.]

I asked him about Venice: "Venice!" said he, "I detest every recollection of the place, the people, and my pursuits. I there mixed again in society, trod again the old round of conversaziones, balls, and concerts, was every night at the opera, a constant frequenter of the Ridotto[189] during the Carnival, and, in short, entered into all the dissipation of that luxurious place. Every thing in a Venetian life,—its gondolas, its effeminating indolence, its Siroccos,—tend to enervate the mind and body. My rides were a resource and a stimulus; but the deep sands of Lido broke my horses down, and I got tired of that monotonous sea-shore;—to be sure, I passed the Villeg-giatura on the Brenta*.

"I wrote little at Venice, and was forced into the search of pleasure,—an employment I was soon jaded with the pursuit of.

"Women were there, as they have ever been fated to be, my bane. Like Napoleon, I have always had a great contempt for women; and formed this opinion of them not hastily, but from my own fatal experience. My writings, indeed, tend to exalt the sex; and my imagination has always delighted in giving them a *beau idéal* likeness, but I only drew them as a painter or statuary would do,—as they should be.† Perhaps my prejudices, and keeping them at a distance, contributed to prevent the illusion from altogether being worn out and destroyed as to their celestialities.

"They are in an unnatural state of society. The Turks and Eastern people manage these matters better than we do. They lock them up, and they are much happier. Give a woman a looking-glass and a few sugar-plums, and she will be satisfied.

"I have suffered from the other sex ever since I can remember any thing. I began by being jilted, and ended by being unwived. Those are wisest who make no connexion of wife or mistress. The *k*night-service of the Continent, with or with-

---

* To give the reader an idea of the stories circulated and believed about Lord Byron, I will state one as a specimen of the rest, which I heard the other day:

"Lord Byron, who is an execrably bad horseman, was riding one evening in the Brenta, spouting 'Metastasio.' A Venetian, passing in a close carriage at the time, laughed at his bad Italian; upon which his Lordship horsewhipped him, and threw a card in at the window. The nobleman took no notice of the insult."—Answer. Lord Byron was an excellent horseman, never read a line of 'Metastasio,' and pronounced Italian like a native. He must have been remarkably ingenious to horsewhip in a *close carriage*, and find a nobleman who pocketed the affront! But "*ex uno disce omnes.*"[190]

† His 'Medora, Gulnare (Kaled), Zuleika, Thyrza, Angiolina, Myrrha, Adah,—and Haidee,' in Don Juan, are beautiful creations of gentleness, sensibility, firmness, and constancy. If, as a reviewer has sagely discovered, all his male characters, from Childe Harold down to Lucifer, are the same, he cannot be denied the dramatic faculty in his women,—in whom there is little family likeness.

out the *k*, is perhaps a slavery as bad, or worse, than either. An intrigue with a married woman at home, though more secret, is equally difficult to break. I had no tie of any kind at Venice, yet I was not without my annoyances. You may remember seeing the portrait of a female which Murray got engraved, and dubbed my 'Fornarina.'[191]

"Harlowe, the poor fellow who died soon after his return from Rome, and who used to copy pictures from memory, took my likeness when he was at Venice:[192] and one day this frail one, who was a casual acquaintance of mine, happened to be at my palace, and to be seen by the painter, who was struck with her, and begged she might sit to him. She did so, and I sent the drawing home as a specimen of the Venetians, and not a bad one either; for the jade was handsome, though the most troublesome shrew and termagant I ever met with. To give you an idea of the lady, she used to call me the *Gran Cane della Madonna*. When once she obtained a footing inside my door, she took a dislike to the outside of it, and I had great difficulty in uncolonizing her. She forced her way back one day when I was at dinner, and snatching a knife from the table, offered to stab herself if I did not consent to her stay. Seeing I took no notice of her threat, as knowing it to be only a feint, she ran into the balcony and threw herself into the canal. As it was only knee-deep and there were plenty of gondolas, one of them picked her up. This affair made a great noise at the time. Some said that I had thrown her into the water, others that she had drowned herself for love; but this is the real story.[193]

---

189 [On the ridotto, see *Beppo*, lviii, and *LJ*, iv, 49, note.]

190 [Byron tells the story of the "fellow in a carriage," whom he slapped in the face, in a letter from La Mira (*LJ*, iv, 149-150).]

191 *Moore*: The most distinguished and, at last, the reigning favourite of all this unworthy Harem was a woman named Mar-

garita Cogni, . . . who, from the trade of her husband, was known by the title of the Fornarina. A portrait of this handsome virago [was] drawn by Harlowe when at Venice. . . . [Moore, *Life*, p. 383 (M).]

[192] *Medwin*: He alluded to a Copy of the *Transfiguration* made by that brilliant and promising artist. This likeness of Lord Byron was truly an ideal one. It is as unlike as possible, and yet it furnishes the frontispiece to most of the foreign Editions of his Works. [Harlow's portrait of Margarita must also be quite unlike her; in no way does it suggest Byron's fiery "Medea alighted from her chariot, or the sibyl of the tempest."]

[193] *Byron to Murray*, August 1, 1819: On seeing me safe [from the storm], she did not wait to greet me, as might be expected, but calling out to me—*Ah! can' della Madonna, xe esto il tempo per andar' al' Lido?* (Ah! Dog of the Virgin, is this a time to go to Lido?) ran into the house. . . .

But her reign drew near a close. . . . I told her quietly that she must return home. . . . The next day, while I was at dinner, she walked in (having broke open a glass door that led from the hall below to the staircase, by way of prologue,) and, advancing strait up to the table, snatched the knife from my hand. . . . Whether she meant to use this against herself or me, I know not. . . . I then called my boatmen, and desired them to get the Gondola ready, and conduct her to her own house again. . . . I resumed my dinner.

We heard a great noise: I went out, and met them on the staircase, carrying her up stairs. She had thrown herself into the Canal. [*LJ*, IV, 333-334 (M).]

"I got into nearly as great a scrape by making my court to a spinster. As many Dowagers as you please at Venice, but beware of flirting with *Raggazzas*. I had been one night under her window serenading, and the next morning who should be announced at the same time but a priest and a police-officer, come, as I thought, either to shoot or marry me again,—I did not care which.[194] I was disgusted and tired with the life I led at Venice, and was glad to turn my back on it. The Austrian Government, too, partly contributed to drive me away. They intercepted my books and papers, opened my letters, and proscribed my works. I was not sorry for this last arbitrary act, as a very bad translation of 'Childe Harold' had just appeared, which I was not at all pleased with. I did not like my old friend in his new loose dress; it was a deshabille that did not at all become him,—those *sciolti versi* that they put him into."[195]

[194] *Byron to Murray*, May 18, 1819: I have undergone some trouble on her account, for last winter the truculent tyrant her flinty-hearted father . . . sent a priest to me, and a Commissary of police, and they locked the Girl up. . . . The fair one is eighteen; her name, Angelina. . . . [*LJ*, IV, 302.]

[195] *Byron to Murray*: May 8, 1820: The other day they confiscated the whole translation of the 4th Canto of *Childe Harold*, and have persecuted Leoni, the translator. . . . [*LJ*, V, 21.]

IT is difficult to judge, from the contradictory nature of his writings, what the religious opinions of Lord Byron really were. Perhaps the conversations I held with him may throw some light upon a subject that cannot fail to excite curiosity. On the whole, I am inclined to think that if he were occasionally sceptical, and thought it, as he says,

———— "A pleasant voyage, perhaps, to float,
Like Pyrrho, on a sea of speculation,"*

yet his wavering never amounted to a disbelief in the divine Founder of Christianity.[196]

"I always took great delight," observed he, "in the English Cathedral service. It cannot fail to inspire every man, who feels at all, with devotion. Notwithstanding which, Christianity is not the best source of inspiration for a poet. No poet should be tied down to a direct profession of faith. Metaphysics open a vast field; Nature, and anti-Mosaical speculations on the origin of the world, a wide range, and sources of poetry that are shut out by Christianity."

I advanced Tasso and Milton.

"Tasso and Milton," replied he, "wrote on Christian subjects, it is true; but how did they treat them? The 'Jerusalem Delivered' deals little in Christian doctrines, and the 'Paradise Lost' makes use of the heathen mythology, which is surely scarcely allowable. Milton discarded papacy, and adopted no creed in its room; he never attended divine worship.

"His great epics, that nobody reads, prove nothing. He took his text from the Old and New Testaments. He shocks the severe apprehensions of the Catholics, as he did those of the divines of his day, by too great a familiarity with Heaven, and the introduction of the Divinity himself; and, more than all, by making the Devil his hero, and deifying the dæmons.

"He certainly excites compassion for Satan, and endeavours to make him out an injured personage—he gives him human passions too, makes him pity Adam and Eve, and justify him-

* *Don Juan*, Canto IX. Stanza 18.

self much as Prometheus does. Yet Milton was never blamed for all this. I should be very curious to know what his real belief was.* The 'Paradise Lost' and 'Regained' do not satisfy me on this point. One might as well say that Moore is a fire-worshipper, or a follower of Mokanna, because he chose those subjects from the East; or that I am a Cainist."

Another time he said: "One mode of worship yields to another; no religion has lasted more than two thousand years. Out of the eight hundred millions that the globe contains, only two hundred millions are Christians. Query,—What is to become of the six hundred millions that do not believe, and of those incalculable millions that lived before Christ?

"People at home are mad about Missionary Societies, and missions to the East. I have been applied to, to subscribe, several times since, and once before I left England. The Catholic priests have been labouring hard for nearly a century; but what have they done? Out of eighty millions of Hindoos, how many proselytes have been made? Sir J. Malcolm[197] said at Murray's before several persons, that the Padres, as he called them, had only made six converts at Bombay during his time, and that even this black little flock forsook their shepherds when the rum was out. Their faith evaporated with the fumes of the arrack. Besides, the Hindoos believe that they have had nine incarnations: the Missionaries preach, that a people whom the Indians only know to despise, have had one. It is nine to one against them, by their own shewing.

"Another doctrine can never be in repute among the Solomons of the East. It cannot be easy to persuade men who have had as many wives as they pleased, to be content with one; besides, a woman is old at twenty in that country. What are men to do? They are not all St. Anthonies.—I will tell you a story. A certain Signior Antonio of my acquaintance married a very little round fat wife,[198] very fond of waltzing, who went

* A religious work of Milton's has since been discovered, and will throw light on this interesting subject.[199]

by the name of the *Tentazione di Sant' Antonio*. There is a picture, a celebrated one, in which a little woman not unresem-
bling my description plays the principal *rôle*, and is most troublesome to the Saint, most trying to his virtue. Very few of the
modern saints will have his forbearance, though they may
imitate him in his martyrdom.

"I have been reading," said he one day, "Tacitus' account
of the siege of Jerusalem, under Titus. What a sovereign contempt the Romans had for the Jews! Their country seems to
have been little better than themselves.

"Priestley denied the original sin, and that any would be
damned. Wesley, the object of Southey's panegyric, preached
the doctrines of election and faith, and, like all the sectarians,
does not want texts to prove both.[200]

---

[196] *Lady Byron*: Lady Byron can attest this.
Medwin: He had always an evident fear of confessing to himself
his own infidelity [preceding word substituted for "disbelief,"
crossed out].
[197] [Byron met Sir John Malcolm, whose *History of Persia* appeared in 1815, in or before July, 1814. See *LJ*, III, 113 and
note.]
[198] *Medwin*: Count St. Antonio, afterwards Duca di Canazzori
[? Covazzori], who married Miss Johnstone or Johnsone—I don't
know with or without a *t* or *e*.
[199] [Milton's *Treatise on Christian Doctrine*, discovered in 1823,
was first published in 1825.]
[200] [Priestley, once a Unitarian, became a Socinian. Southey's
Life of Wesley appeared in 1820.]

"The best Christians can never be satisfied of their own sal-
vation. Dr. Johnson died like a coward, and Cowper was near
shooting himself; Hume went off the stage like a brave man,
and Voltaire's last moments do not seem to have been clouded
by any fears of what was to come. A man may study any thing
till he believes in it. Creech died a Lucretian, Burckhardt and

Browne were Mohammedans. Sale, the translator of the Koran, was suspected of being an Islamite, but a very different one from you, Shiloh*, (as he sometimes used to call Shelley.)[201]

"You are a Protestant—you protest against all religions. There is Taaffe will traduce Dante till he becomes a Dantist.[202] I am called a Manichæan: I may rather be called an Anychæan, or Anything-arian.[203] How do you like my sect? The sect of Anything-arians sounds well, does it not?"

Calling on him the next day, we found him, as was sometimes the case, silent, dull, and sombre. At length he said:

"Here is a little book somebody has sent me about Christianity, that has made me very uncomfortable: the reasoning seems to me very strong, the proofs are very staggering. I don't think you can answer it, Shelley; at least I am sure I can't, and what is more, I don't wish it."

Speaking of Gibbon, he said: "Long Baillie thought the question set at rest in the 'History of the Decline and Fall,' but I am not so easily convinced. It is not a matter of volition to unbelieve. Who likes to own that he has been a fool all his life,—to unlearn all that he has been taught in his youth? or can think that some of the best men that ever lived have been fools? I have often wished I had been born a Catholic. That purgatory of theirs is a comfortable doctrine; I wonder the reformers gave it up, or did not substitute something as consolatory in its room. It is an improvement on the transmigration, Shelley, which all your wiseacre philosophers taught.

"You believe in Plato's three principles;—[204] why not in the Trinity? One is not more mystical than the other. I don't know why I am considered an enemy to religion, and an unbeliever. I disowned the other day that I was of Shelley's school in metaphysics, though I admired his poetry; not but what he has changed his mode of thinking very much since he wrote the Notes to 'Queen Mab,' which I was accused of having a hand in. I know, however, that I am considered an

* Alluding to 'The Revolt of Islam.'

infidel. My wife and sister, when they joined parties, sent me prayer-books.²⁰⁵ There was a Mr. Mulock, who went about the Continent preaching orthodoxy in politics and religion, a writer of bad sonnets, and a lecturer in worse prose,—he tried to convert me to some new sect of Christianity.²⁰⁶ He was a great anti-materialist, and abused Locke."

---

²⁰¹ [Dr. Johnson was increasingly fearful of death, although one account states that he died devoutly and calmly. Cooper was insane from 1796 until his death in 1800. Hume, as death approached, showed no fear and had no recourse to religion. Voltaire motioned the priests away from his deathbed and died without their attentions. Thomas Creech, who hanged himself in 1700, translated Lucretius into heroic couplets. John Lewis Burckhardt (1784-1817), who bequeathed 800 volumes of Oriental manuscripts to Cambridge University, was so learned in Moslem lore and law and so competent in Arabic that he passed himself off successfully in the Levant as a doctor of Moslem law. In 1799 William George Browne (1768-1813) published his *Travels in Africa, Egypt and Syria, from the year 1792 to 1798*. George Sale (*c.* 1697-1736) translated the Koran in 1734.]

²⁰² [Murray acted as distributor of Taaffe's *Comment on Dante*.]

²⁰³ [On the charge of Manicheism brought against Byron, see his "Letter on Bowles's Strictures," published March, 1821 (*LJ*, v, 563).]

²⁰⁴ [Perhaps a reference to Plato's concept of justice in the *Republic*: a right division of labor among the three social classes and among the three corresponding faculties of the individual soul.]

²⁰⁵ [Although Annabella in 1816 was "committed to saving Byron's soul through reforming Augusta" (Marchand, p. 650), it seems improbable that the two women sent him prayerbooks. Shortly before he left England, Augusta presented him with a small Bible, which he kept at his bedside.]

²⁰⁶ *Byron to Murray*, March 1, 1820: The editor of the *Bologna Telegraph* has sent me a paper with extracts from Mr. Mulock's . . . *Atheism Answered*, in which there is a long eulogium of my poesy, and a great *compatimento* for my misery. I never could understand what they mean by accusing me of irreligion. . . . [*LJ*, IV, 416. For the extracts from Mulock, see *LJ*, IV, 496-497.]

On another occasion he said: "I am always getting new correspondents. Here are three letters just arrived, from strangers all of them. One is from a French woman, who has been writing to me off and on for the last three years.[207] She is not only a blue-bottle, but a poetess, I suspect. Her object in addressing me now, she says, is to get me to write on the loss of a slave-ship, the particulars of which she details.

"The second epistle is short, and in a hand I know very well: it is anonymous too.[208] Hear what she says: 'I cannot longer exist without acknowledging the tumultuous and agonizing delight with which my soul burns at the glowing beauties of yours.'

"A third is of a very different character from the last; it is from a Mr. Sheppard,[209] inclosing a prayer made for my welfare by his wife a few days before her death. The letter states that he has had the misfortune to lose this amiable woman, who had seen me at Ramsgate, many years ago, rambling among the cliffs; that she had been impressed with a sense of my irreligion from the tenor of my works, and had often prayed fervently for my conversion, particularly in her last moments. The prayer is beautifully written. I like devotion in women. She must have been a divine creature. I pity the man who has lost her! I shall write to him by return of the courier, to console with him, and tell him that Mrs. Sheppard need not have entertained any concern for my spiritual affairs, for that no man is more of a Christian than I am, whatever my writings may have led her and others to suspect."

---

[207] *Medwin*: Madame [Sophie Nichault de la Valette] Gay, the "mother of the celebrated poetess" Delphine Gay—now Madame de Girardin. I met them often at Mr. De Lamartine's at Florence. [The quoted phrase is from Moore's *Life,* p. 460, note. See also *LJ*, v, 104, note.]

[208] *Medwin*: Harriette Wilson. [See her *Memoirs* (1825) and Peter Quennell, *To Lord Byron*, pp. 142-161. She seems to have

exchanged a few words with Byron at a masked ball in London, later wrote him numerous letters.]

[209] *Medwin*: Sheppard. See this letter in Moore's *Life*, p. [542 and p. 543. John Sheppard wrote on November 21, 1821; Byron replied on December 8, 1821. The correspondence was published in 1823, in Sheppard's *Thoughts Preparative or Persuasive to Private Devotion*. Harriette Wilson wrote on December 20, 1821, a letter which he would have received in early January, 1822 (see Marchand, note to l. 5 of p. 960). In Ravenna, October 17, 1820, Byron was trying to discover the identity of Sophie Gay (*LJ*, v, 104); there may well have been further correspondence, now lost.]

"A CIRCUMSTANCE took place in Greece that impressed itself lastingly on my memory. I had once thought of founding a tale on it; but the subject is too harrowing for any nerves,—too terrible for any pen! An order was issued at Yanina by its sanguinary Rajah, that any Turkish woman convicted of incontinence with a Christian should be stoned to death! Love is slow at calculating dangers, and defies tyrants and their edicts; and many were the victims to the savage barbarity of this of Ali's. Among others a girl of sixteen, of a beauty such as that country only produces, fell under the vigilant eye of the police. She was suspected, and not without reason, of carrying on a secret intrigue with a Neapolitan of some rank, whose long stay in the city could be attributed to no other cause than this attachment. Her crime (if crime it be to love as they loved) was too fully proved; they were torn from each other's arms, never to meet again: and yet both might have escaped,—she by abjuring her religion, or he by adopting hers. They resolutely refused to become apostates from their faith. Ali Pacha was never known to pardon. She was stoned by those dæmons, although in the fourth month of her pregnancy! He was sent to a town where the plague was raging, and died happy in not having long outlived the object of his affections![210]

---

[210] *Galt*: [The account] is one continued bundle of errors; besides making Byron use terms and speak of things, which, from his Lordship's knowledge of Turkey, he would never have done. The story alluded to is the fate of Phrosyné, the elegy on whose death is one of the most popular and pathetic breathings of the modern Grecian muse. Lord Byron often used to sing the melody. . . . We shall relate the real story, remarking, in the first place, that the affair happened long before Lord Byron's first voyage to Greece, although, as it is reported in the Notes of his Conversations, it might be thought his Lordship was in that country at the time.

The girl, as we said, was called Phrosyné; she was the wife of a Neapolitan. Muctar Pashaw, son of Ali, fell in love with her, and seduced her. Among other presents with which he won her favour was a diamond ring, that he himself had been accustomed to wear. One day, in the baths, a wife of Muctar met Phrosyné there, and recognizing the ring, was at no loss to guess for what purpose it had been given. Fired with revenge and jealousy, she went to the vizier, (who ever heard of Rajah being applied to designate Ali Pashaw,) her father-in-law, and told what she had discovered. The justice and vengeance of that stern old tyrant were alike speedy. Phrosyné was seized, and with several other young women—twelve, we believe, being tied in a sack—was thrown into the lake, and her husband banished the city. Admitting, however, that Lord Byron had spoken of some other story—which we are persuaded he did not—even the one Captain Medwin repeats was not at all likely to have had the catastrophe he describes. The Mahomedan girl, for her transgression with a Christian, would have been drowned, and the Christian decapitated. Nor was Ali Pashaw of a temper to resort to such refinement of punishment, as merely to expose a criminal to the chance of taking the plague. [*BEM*, xvi, 534. See the story of Phrosine as related by Byron in his note to *The Giaour*, l. 1328 and by Hobhouse in *Travels in Albania*, the latter quoted in *Poetry*, iii, 145, note.]

Sir Charles Napier: The real Story is this. Ali Pasha wanted to secure the residence of Joseph Caretto (a relation of the famous La Cherette the Vendeean chief) in his Capital as an Engineer—he found out that a beautiful Turkish woman who was married had seen and fallen in love with the Piedmontese Caretto—he therefore sent a Corfu jew to her, who so wrought upon her that she resolved to go to Caretto. The jew told Caretto that there was a beautiful woman in love with him, and w^d come to him that night—she came—she remained 3 days and at last told him who she was. Caretto saw his danger but it was too late. After some time the jew told her husband (who had been at Constantinople) where she was. They were arrested & separated. She was tried—no proof existed as to crim. con. The Turkish law demands *three* witnesses of the act. The judge, tho a Turk, tried to save her—& told her that 3 witnesses were required and she had only to deny the fact. She was desperately in love with Caretto. She thought he *had been killed at once* by Turkish fury and the law (which is merciless to a Christian). She therefore resolved to die and *distinctly asserted* her adulterous intercourse in full court—she was remanded to the next day to try and save her. The next day she repeated her avowal and to show her resolution detailed the facts—she was of course condemned and executed—a hole was dug as deep as her waist—she was placed in it. The troops took small stones the size of walnuts and pelted her head. She never uttered a groan & only turned her head when struck. This continued for a long time, when a dervish, actuated by religious zeal against her or by an *antireligious* feeling of compassion, took a large stone in both hands and dashed out her brains and so ended this scene of horror, as far as she was concerned—as to Caretto, Ali told the turkish family to whom this poor victim of religion belonged that Caretto was necessary to his Service and therefore should not be hurt by them but that if he attempted to go away they might kill him—after this he told Caretto he had no chance but to live at Joannina—and whenever Ali sent him on duty he was always attended by some males of the poor girl's family, who always amused him by accounts of the tortures they w^d inflict on him if Ali died, and Caretto always kept on his hat to hide his hair which he always kept cut in the albanian form in order to escape in that dress at any moment; he always kept an albanian dress ready in his room and spoke Romaic perfectly. All this *I heard from himself*, and an Italian blackguard who called himself Captain of Ali's Cavalry his name began with a Q but I cannot remember it. This fellow *commanded the party who executed the woman.* I heard the Same also from Colovò and others at Joannina. Caretto is a clever man. he afterwards defended Joannina for Ali and lost his eye—finding his master treated him ill, he dropped one night from the Walls and escaped wounded to the turks and at this moment is I believe at [?Revefia] from which place I had a letter from him nearly five years ago.

"One of the principal incidents in 'The Giaour' is derived from a real occurrence, and one too in which I myself was nearly and deeply interested; but an unwillingness to have it considered a traveller's tale made me suppress the fact of its genuineness. The Marquis of Sligo, who knew the particulars of the story, reminded me of them in England, and wondered I had not authenticated them in the Preface:—[211]

"When I was at Athens, there was an edict in force similar to that of Ali's, except that the mode of punishment was different. It was necessary, therefore, that all love-affairs should be carried on with the greatest privacy. I was very fond at that time of a Turkish girl,—ay, fond of her as I have been of few women. All went on very well till the Ramazan. For forty days, which is rather a long fast for lovers, all intercourse between the sexes is forbidden by law, as well as by religion. During this Lent of the Mussulmans, the women are not allowed to quit their apartments. I was in despair, and could hardly contrive to get a cinder, or a token-flower sent to express it. We had not met for several days, and all my thoughts were occupied in planning an assignation, when, as ill fate would have it, the means I took to effect it led to the discovery of our secret. The penalty was death,—death without reprieve,—a horrible death, at which one cannot think without shuddering! An order was issued for the law being put into immediate effect. In the mean time I knew nothing of what had happened, and it was determined that I should be kept in ignorance of the whole affair till it was too late to interfere. A mere accident only enabled me to prevent the completion of the sentence. I was taking one of my usual evening rides by the sea-side, when I observed a crowd of people moving down to the shore, and the arms of the soldiers glittering among them. They were not so far off, but that I thought I could now and then distinguish a faint and stifled shriek. My curiosity was forcibly excited, and I dispatched one of my followers to enquire the cause of the procession. What was my horror to learn that they were carrying an unfortunate girl, sewn up in a sack, to be thrown into the sea! I did not hesitate as to what was to be done. I knew I could depend on my faithful Albanians, and rode up to the officer commanding the party, threatening, in case of his refusal to give up his prisoner, that I would adopt means to compel him. He did not like the business he was on, or perhaps the determined look of my body-guard, and consented to accompany me back to the city with the girl, whom I soon discovered to be my Turkish favourite. Suffice it to say, that my interference with the chief magistrate, backed by a heavy bribe, saved her; but it was only on condition that I should break off all intercourse with her, and that she should immediately quit Athens, and be sent to her friends in Thebes. There she died, a few days after her arrival, of a fever—perhaps of love."²¹²

²¹¹ *Medwin*: He [Sligo] not only reminded Lord Byron of the story in England but wrote, for the very purpose of screening him, the following letter, which he need not have wondered that Lord Byron did not put into the preface. The letter was [? evidently] fabricated at his desire: "The new governor, unaccustomed to have the same intercourse with the Christians as his predecessor, had of course the barbarous Turkish ideas with regard to women. In consequence, and in compliance with the strict letter of the Mahommedan law, he ordered this girl to be sewed up in a sack, and thrown into the sea,—as is, indeed, quite customary at Constantinople. As you were returning from bathing in the Piræus, you met the procession going down to execute the sentence of the Waywode on this unfortunate girl. Report continues to say that on finding out what the object of their journey was, and who was the miserable sufferer, you immediately interfered: and on some delay in obeying your orders, you were obliged to inform the leader of the escort, that force should make him comply;—that, on farther hesitation, you drew a pistol, and told him, that if he did not immediately obey your orders, and come back with you to the Aga's house, you would shoot him dead. On this the man turned about and went with you to the governor's house; here you succeeded, partly by personal threats, and partly by bribery and entreaty, in procuring her pardon, on condition of her leaving Athens. I was told that you then conveyed her in safety to the convent, and despatched her off at night to Thebes, where she found a safe asylum. Such is the story I heard, as nearly as I can recollect it at present." [Moore, *Life*, p. 178.]

The most innocent critic, when he reads the following passages from Moore's *Notices*, must perceive that the real facts of the case are here given, as indeed he [Byron] seems to have himself detailed them to his friends, but hear his own confession.

"I showed him [Galt] Sligo's letter on the reports of the Turkish girl's *aventure* at Athens soon after it happened. He and Lord Holland, Lewis, and Moore, and Rogers, and Lady Melbourne have seen it. Murray has a copy. I thought it had been *unknown*, and wish it were; but Sligo arrived only some days after, and the *rumours* are the subject of his letter. That I shall preserve,—*it is as well.* Lewis and Galt were both *horrified*; and L. wondered I did not introduce the situation into *The Giaour*. He *may* wonder;—he might wonder more at that production's being written at all. But to describe the *feelings* of *that situation* were impossible—it is *icy* even to recollect them." [*LJ*, ii, 361. Byron rendered illegible ten lines of Sligo's letter (Marchand, p. 409, note 5).]

²¹² *Hobhouse*: No other contradiction is necessary than to mention, that the girl whose life lord Byron saved at Athens, was not an object of his lordship's attachment—but that of his lordship's Turkish servant. [*WR*, iii, 27.]

Fletcher: Medwin makes another tale up equally untrue . . . where he says . . . my Lord was very much attached to a Turkish Girl even so much so M says that his Lordship has been of few women. I remember the Circumstances very well. It happened to be Dervise one of his Lordship's Guards and attendants whom Ali Pacha presented my Lord with in Albanian Turkey—had it been a Christian no powers nor bribe could have saved her.

Galt: The girl in question was . . . common . . . and the probability is, that her general incontinence with all sorts of travellers, and not her particular *liaison* with him, was the cause of the *customary* doom, from which she was rescued by his Lordship. [*BEM*, xvi, 534.]

Lady Hester Stanhope: I think he was a strange character. . . . One time he was mopish, and nobody was to speak to him; another, he was for being jocular with everybody. Then he was a sort of Don Quixote, fighting with the police for a woman of the town. [*HVSV*, p. 36.]

Mary Shelley, reported by Moore: Spoke of the story of the girl in the *Giaour*. Founded (as B. has often told me) on the circumstance of a young girl, whom he knew himself in Greece, and whom he supposed to be a Greek, but who proved to be a Turk; and who underwent on his account the punishment mentioned in the poem [drowning]. [Moore's diary for July 17, 1824.]

Edward E. Williams in his diary, March 13, 1822: Called on Lord B— When in Greece he had been in the habit of associating with a young lady whom he imagined to be a Greek, but having missed her for some days, to his surprise and horror he heard that she was a young Turk whose amour having been discovered Ali Pacha had condemned her with sixteen others to be tied up in a sack and drown[ed]. He actually met the party on the way to execution, and what with threats and at enormous expense he succeeded in rescuing her. This is the subject of the *Giaour*. [*HVSV*, p. 283.]

Medwin: I hear him now, how he used these words. There was a pathos in them that engraved them indelibly in my mind.

"THE severest fever I ever had was at Patras. I had left Fletcher at Constantinople—[213] convalescent, but unable to move from weakness, and had no attendants but my Albanians, to whom I owe my life.

"They were devotedly attached to me, and watched me day and night. I am more indebted to a good constitution for having got over this attack, than to the drugs of an ignorant Turk, who called himself a physician. He would have been glad to disown the name, and resign his profession too, if he could have escaped from the responsibility of attending me; for my Albanians came the Grand Signor over him, and threatened that if I were not entirely recovered at a certain hour on a certain day, they would take his life. They are not people to make idle threats, and would have carried them into execution had any thing happened to me. You may imagine the fright the poor devil of a doctor was in; and I could not help smiling at the ludicrous way in which his fears shewed themselves. I believe he was more pleased at my recovery than either my faithful nurses, or myself.[214] I had no intention of dying at that time; but if I had died, a similar thing would have been told of me to that related as having happened to Colonel Sherbrooke in America. On the very day my fever was at the highest, a friend of mine declared that he saw me in St. James's Street; and somebody put my name down in the book at the Palace, as having enquired after the King's health!

"Every body would have said that my ghost had appeared."[215]

"But how were they to have reconciled a ghost's writing?" asked I.

"I should most likely have passed the remainder of my life in Turkey, if I had not been called home by my mother's health and my affairs," said he.[216] "I mean to return to Greece, and shall in all probability die there."[217]

Little did I think, at the time he was pronouncing these words, that they were prophetic!

²¹³ *Fletcher*: I was left at Athens in the Convent.

²¹⁴ *Byron, note 11 to Childe Harold, II*: When, in 1810 . . . I was seized with a severe fever in the Morea, these men [his Albanians] saved my life by frightening away my physician, whose throat they threatened to cut if I was not cured within a given time. . . . My poor Arnaouts nursed me with an attention which would have done honour to civilization. [*Poetry*, ii, 175.]

²¹⁵ *Byron to Murray*, October 6, 1820: In the latter end of 1811, I met one evening at the Alfred . . . *Peel*, the Irish Secretary. He told me that, in 1810, he met me, as he thought, in St. James's Street, but we passed without speaking. He mentioned this, and it was denied as impossible, I being then in Turkey. . . . But this is not all: I was *seen* by somebody to *write down my name* amongst the Enquirers after the King's health, then attacked by insanity. Now, at this very period, as nearly as I could make out, I was ill of a *strong fever* at Patras. . . . If I had died there, this would have been a new Ghost Story for you. . . . [*LJ*, v, 87 (M). See also Leigh Hunt on this same story, *HVSV*, p. 335.]

Galt: Barclay of the Stock Exchange in London, might pass for his twin brother. One night last winter this resemblance was noticed in the Opera House, and excited a great sensation, many, who had recollected Lord Byron by sight, believing he had returned home. [*BEM*, xvi, 535.]

²¹⁶ [Earlier editions referred to the *death*, not the *health*, of Mrs. Byron. Although she wrote to Hanson on January 3, 1811, of her ill health and may well have informed Byron, it seems more probable that Medwin misunderstood Byron, who was informed in London of his mother's illness, but before he could depart for Newstead, was told of her death.]

²¹⁷ *Lady Byron*: He had often said before leaving England "I *must* go to the East—to die"—

"I became a member of Drury-lane Committee, at the request of my friend Douglas Kinnaird, who made over to me a share of 500*l.* for the purpose of qualifying me to vote. One need have other qualifications besides money for that office. I found the employment not over pleasant, and not a little dangerous, what with Irish authors and pretty poetesses. Five hundred plays were offered to the Theatre during the year I was Literary Manager. You may conceive that it was no small task to read all this trash, and to satisfy the bards that it was so.[218]

"When I first entered upon theatrical affairs, I had some idea of writing for the house myself, but soon became a convert to Pope's opinion on that subject. Who would condescend to the drudgery of the stage, and enslave himself to the humours, the caprices, the taste or tastelessness, of the age? Besides, one must write for particular actors, have them continually in one's eye, sacrifice character to the personating of it, cringe to some favourite of the public, neither give him too many nor too few lines to spout, think how he would mouth such and such a sentence, look such and such a passion, strut such and such a scene. Who, I say, would submit to all this? Shakspeare had many advantages: he was an actor by profession, and knew all the tricks of the trade. Yet he had but little fame in his day: see what Jonson and his contemporaries said of him. Besides, how few of what are called Shakspeare's plays are exclusively so! and how, at this distance of time, and lost as so many works of that period are, can we separate what really is from what is not his own?

"The players retrenched, transposed, and even altered the text, to suit the audience or please themselves. Who knows how much rust they rubbed off? I am sure there is rust and base metal to spare left in the old plays. When Leigh Hunt comes we shall have battles enough about those old *ruffiani*, the old dramatists, with their tiresome conceits, their jingling rhymes, and endless play upon words. It is but lately that people have been satisfied that Shakspeare was not a god, nor stood alone in the age in which he lived;[219] and yet how few of the plays, even of that boasted time, have survived! and fewer still are now acted. Let us count them. Only one of Massinger's (New Way to pay Old Debts), one of Ford's,* one of Ben Jonson's,*[220] and half-a-dozen of Shakspeare's; and of

* Of which I have forgot the name he mentioned.

these last, 'The Two Gentlemen of Verona' and 'The Tempest' have been turned into operas. You cannot call that having a theatre. Now that Kemble has left the stage, who will endure Coriolanus? Lady Macbeth died with Mrs. Siddons, and Polonius will with Munden.[221] Shakspeare's Comedies are quite out of date; many of them are insufferable to read, much more to see. They are gross food, only fit for an English or German palate; they are indigestible to the French and Italians, the politest people in the world. One can hardly find ten lines together without some gross violation of taste or decency. What do you think of Bottom in the 'Midsummer Night's Dream?' or of Troilus and Cressida *passim.*"

Here I could not help interrupting him by saying, "You have named the two plays that, with all their faults, contain perhaps some of the finest poetry."

"Yes," said he, "in 'Troilus and Cressida:'

> —————'Prophet may you be!
> If I be false, or swerve a hair from truth.
> When Time is old, and hath forgot itself,
> When water-drops have worn the stones of Troy,
> And blind Oblivion swallow'd cities up,
> And mighty states characterless are grated
> To dusty nothing,—yet let memory
> From false to false, among false maids in love,
> Upbraid my falsehood! when they've said,–As false
> As air, as water, wind, or sandy earth,
> As fox to lamb, as wolf to heifer's calf,
> Pard to the hind, or stepdame to her son;
> Yea, let them say, to stick the heart of falsehood—
> As false as Cressid!' "

These lines he pronounced with great emphasis and effect, and continued:

"But what has poetry to do with a play, or in a play? There is not one passage in Alfieri strictly poetical; hardly one in Racine."

Here he handed me a prospectus of a new translation of Shakspeare into French prose, and read part of the first scene in 'The Tempest,' laughing inwardly, as he was used to do; and afterwards produced a passage from Chateaubriand, contending that we have no theatre.

"The French very properly ridicule our bringing in *'enfant au premier acte, barbon au dernier.'* I was always a friend to the unities, and believe that subjects are not wanting which may be treated in strict conformity to their rules. No one can be absurd enough to contend, that the preservation of the unities is a defect,—at least a fault.[222] Look at Alfieri's plays, and tell me what is wanting in them. Does he ever deviate from the rules prescribed by the ancients, from the classical simplicity of the old models? It is very difficult, almost impossible, to write any thing to please a modern audience. I was instrumental in getting up 'Bertram,' and it was said that I wrote part of it myself. That was not the case. I knew Maturin to be a needy man, and interested myself in his success; but its life was very feeble and ricketty.[223] I once thought of getting Joanna Baillie's 'De Montfort' revived; but the winding-up was faulty.[224] She was herself aware of this, and wrote the last act over again; and yet, after all, it failed. She must have been dreadfully annoyed, even more than Lady Dacre was. When it was bringing out, I was applied to to write a prologue; but as the request did not come from Kean, who was to speak it, I declined it.[225] There are fine things in all the Plays on the Passions: an idea in 'De Montfort' struck me particularly; one of the characters said that he knew the footsteps of another.*

"There are four words in Alfieri that speak volumes. They are in 'Don Carlos.' The King and his Minister are secreted during an interview of the Infant with the Queen Consort: the

---

* "*De Montfort.*—'Tis Rezenvelt: I heard his well-known foot! From the first staircase, mounting step by step.
"*Freberg.*—How quick an ear thou hast for distant sound! I heard him not."

Act II. Scene 2.

following dialogue passes, which ends the scene:—'*Vedesti?*
Vedi. Udisti? Udi.' All the dramatic beauty would be lost in
translation—the nominative cases would kill it.²²⁶ Nothing
provokes me so much as the squeamishness that excludes the
exhibition of many such subjects from the stage;—a squeamishness, the produce, as I firmly believe, of a lower tone of the
moral sense, and foreign to the majestic and confident virtue
of the golden age of our country. All is now cant—methodis-
tical cant. Shame flies from the heart, and takes refuge in the
lips; or, our senses and nerves are much more refined than
those of our neighbours.

---

²¹⁸ *Byron in his "Detached Thoughts"*: When I belonged to the
D. L. Committee, and was one of the S. C. of Management, the
number of plays upon the shelves were about *five* hundred. . . . I
do not think that, of those which I saw, there was one which could
be conscientiously tolerated. . . . Then the Scenes I had to go
through! The authours, and the authoresses, the Milliners, the wild
Irishmen . . . who came in upon me! To all of whom it was proper
to give a civil answer, and a hearing, and a reading. [*LJ*, v, 442-
443 (M).]

²¹⁹ *Leigh Hunt*: He affected to doubt whether Shakespeare was
so great a genius as he has been taken for, and whether fashion
had not a great deal to do with it. [*HVSV*, p. 320.]

²²⁰ *William Hazlitt*: Captain Medwin or his Lordship must have
made a mistake in the enumeration of plays of that period still
acted. There is one of Ben Jonson's, "Every Man in his Humour;"
and one of Massinger's, "A New Way to Pay Old Debts;" but there
is none of Ford's . . . acted. [*Collected Works of William Hazlitt*,
ed. A. R. Waller and Arnold Glover (London, 1903), vii, 313.]

²²¹ [On June 26, 1815, Byron imitated the manner of Joseph S.
Munden, the leading comedian of his day, for George Ticknor
(*HVSV*, p. 127). Mrs. Siddons, famous for her Lady Macbeth,
called earlier in the day.]

²²² *Goethe, reported by Eckermann*: Goethe . . . laughed to think
that Lord Byron, who, in practical life, could never adapt himself,
and never even asked about a law, finally subjected himself to the
stupidest of laws—that of the THREE UNITIES. [*Conversations with
Eckermann*, p. 95.]

²²³ *Byron in his "Detached Thoughts"*: Maturin was very kindly recommended to me by Walter Scott, to whom I had recourse. . . . Maturin sent his Bertram. . . . I sent him a favourable answer, and something more substantial. [*LJ*, v, 442 (M).]

²²⁴ [See Edmund Kean's letter to Byron, who had requested Kean to reread *De Monfort*, with an eye to revival (*LJ*, III, 197, note).]

²²⁵ [William Lamb wrote the prologue to *Ina*, by Lady Dacre, then Mrs. Wilmot. Byron saw the play on April 22, 1815.]

²²⁶ [The lines are misquoted from Alfieri's *Filippo*, II, v:

> *Filippo*. Udisti?
>
> *Gomez*.   Udii.
>
> *Filippo*.   Vedesti?
>
> *Gomez*.   Io vidi.

The play is a dramatization of the conflict between Philip II of Spain and his son Don Carlos. Medwin's remark about the "nominative cases" is not clear. Perhaps he means an English translation of the second and fourth speeches would have to express the nominative pronoun: "Did you hear?" "I heard." "Did you see?" "I saw."]

"We should not endure the Œdipus story, nor 'Phædra.' 'Myrra,' the best worked-up, perhaps, of all Alfieri's tragedies, and a favourite in Italy, would not be tolerated. 'The Mysterious Mother' has never been acted,²²⁷ nor Massinger's 'Brother and Sister.'²²⁸ Webster's 'Duchess of Malfy' would be too harrowing: her madness,²²⁹ the dungeon-scene, and her grim talk with her keepers and coffin-bearers, could not be borne: nor Lillo's 'Fatal Curiosity.'²³⁰ The 'Cenci' is equally horrible, though perhaps the best tragedy modern times have produced.²³¹ It is a play,—not a poem, like 'Remorse' and 'Fazio;'²³² and the best proof of its merit is, that people are continually quoting it. But what could be expected from such a beginning?

"The Germans are colder and more phlegmatic than we are, and bear even to see Werner's play, 'The Twenty Eighth of February,' acted.²³³

"To write any thing to please, at the present day, is the despair of authors."

²²⁷ [Horace Walpole's *Mysterious Mother*, described as late as 1911 by *The Encyclopædia Britannica* (11th ed.) as "too horrible for representation on any stage," was not intended for public performance.]

²²⁸ *Harness*: There is no such play—probably he means *'Tis Pity she's a Whore*, by Ford—a masterpiece of its kind, and of which my late noble school-fellow entertained the highest admiration. [*BEM*, xvi, 539.]

Medwin: What play Lord Byron meant is not clear. The Noble Poet was not very well read in the Old Plays—and for my part, I neither knew, know, nor desire to know anything about them.

²²⁹ [It is not the Duchess of Malfi who goes mad but Ferdinand, her brother.]

²³⁰ [Earlier editions referred to Lillo's *Fatal Marriage*. Harness suggested in his review that Byron had probably mentioned Lillo's *Fatal Curiosity*, a hint picked up by Medwin. But Byron may well have referred to Thomas Southerne's *Fatal Marriage*, the main character in which is named Biron.]

²³¹ *Byron to Shelley*, April 26, 1821: I read *Cenci*—but, besides that I think the *subject* essentially *un*dramatic, I am not an admirer of our old dramatists *as models*. I deny that the English have hitherto had a drama at all. Your *Cenci*, however, was a work of power, and poetry. [*LJ*, v, 268 (M).]

²³² [*Fazio* is by Henry Hart Milman.]

²³³ *Medwin*: These words [the preceding six words] were omitted by Mr. Colburn, who in his ignorance did not understand them or had never heard of such a play. [Medwin refers to *Der Vierundzwanzigste Februar*, 1815.] The Scene of this Play is very appropriately laid in a lone house at the top of the Gemmi, one of the most frightful and desolate passes of the Alps, where there is a Lake perpetually frozen, at least I found it so in July. It is a most harrowing Domestic Tragedy. None but German nerves could bear reading such a play, much less the representation on the stage. [Werner's play was first produced in 1810, published 1815.]

It was easy to be perceived that during this tirade against the stage and Shakspeare, he was smarting under the ill reception 'Marino Faliero' had met with, and indignant at the critics, who had denied him the dramatic faculty. This, however, was not the only occasion of his abusing the old dramatists.

Some days after I revived the subject of the drama, and led him into speaking of his own plays.

"I have just got a letter," said he, "from Murray. What do you think he has enclosed me? A long dull extract from that long dull Latin epic of Petrarch's, *Africa*, which he has the modesty to ask me to translate for Ugo Foscolo, who is writing some Memoirs of Petrarch, which he has got Moore, Lady Dacre, &c. to contribute to. What am I to do with the death of Mago? I wish to God, Medwin, you would take it home with you, and translate it; and I will send it to Murray. We will say nothing about its being yours, or mine; and it will be curious to hear Foscolo's opinion upon it. Depend upon it, it will not be an unfavourable one."

In the course of the day I turned it into couplets, (and lame enough they were,) which he forwarded by the next courier to England.

Almost by return of post arrived a furiously complimentary epistle in acknowledgment, which made us laugh very heartily.[234]

"There are three good lines*," said Lord Byron, "in Mago's speech, which may be thus translated:

"Yet, thing of dust!
Man strives to climb the earth in his ambition,
Till death, the monitor that flatters not,
Points to the grave, where all his hopes are laid."[235]

* Ugo Foscolo afterwards took them for his motto.

[234] [Medwin's translation was sent to Murray (*LJ*, vi, 7, note 2), and it seems probable that the translation from Petrarch's *Africa*, Book VI, "The Death of Mago," which appears in Ugo Foscolo's *Essays on Petrarch* (London: John Murray, 1823), pp. 215, 217, was in fact written by Medwin, although the name of Byron appears at the end of it. The lines are not included in either E. H. Coleridge's or P. E. More's edition of Byron's poetical works. See also *LJ*, v, 554: ". . . who ever dreams of his Latin *Africa?*"]

[235] [In Foscolo, p. 217, the lines are translated as follows:

> Yet, thing of dust, and on the verge of night,
> Man dares to climb the stars, and on the height
> Of heaven his owlet vision dares to bend
> From that low earth, where all his hopes descend.

It may be noted that the lines attributed in the *Conversations* to Byron are not in couplets, although Medwin stated that his own version was written in couplets, the form which the translation takes in Foscolo.]

"WHAT do you think of Ada?" said he, looking earnestly at his daughter's miniature, that hung by the side of his writing-table. "They tell me she is like me—but she has her mother's eyes.

"It is very odd that my mother was an only child;—I am an only child; my wife is an only child; and Ada is an only child. It is a singular coincidence; that is the least that can be said of it. I can't help thinking it was destined to be so;[236] and perhaps it is best. I was once anxious for a son; but, after our separation, was glad to have had a daughter; for it would have distressed me too much to have taken him away from Lady Byron, and I could not have trusted her with a son's education. I have no idea of boys being brought up by mothers. I suffered too much from that myself: and then, wandering about the world as I do, I could not take proper care of a child; otherwise I should not have left Allegra, poor little thing!* at Ravenna.[237] She has been a great resource to me, though I am not so fond of her as of Ada; and yet I mean to make their fortunes equal—there will be enough for them both.[238] I have desired in my will that Allegra shall not marry an Englishman.[239] The Irish and Scotch make better husbands than we do. You will think it was an odd fancy, but I was not in the best of humours with my countrymen at that moment— you know the reason. I am told that Ada is a little termagant; I hope not. I shall write to my sister to know if this is the case:[240] perhaps I am wrong in letting Lady Byron have entirely her own way in her education. I hear that my name is not mentioned in her presence; that a green curtain is always kept over my portrait, as over something forbidden;[241] and that she is not to know that she has a father, till she comes of age. Of course she will be taught to hate me; she will be brought up to it.[242] Lady Byron is conscious of all this, and is afraid

* She appears to be the Leila of his Don Juan:
"Poor little thing! She was as fair as docile,
And with that gentle, serious character———"
Don Juan, Canto X. Stanza 52.

that I shall some day carry off her daughter by stealth or force. I might claim her of the Chancellor, without having recourse to either one or the other.[243] But I had rather be unhappy myself, than make her mother so; probably I shall never see her again."

Here he opened his writing-desk, and shewed me some hair, which he told me was his child's.[244]

[236] *Byron in his "Detached Thoughts"*: I have been thinking of an odd circumstance. My daughter, my wife, my half sister, my mother, my sister's mother, my natural daughter, and myself are
$$\underset{1}{\text{daughter}} \quad \underset{2}{\text{wife}} \quad \underset{3}{\text{half sister}}$$
or were all *only* children. . . . Such a complication of *only* children, all tending to *one family*, is singular enough, and looks like fatality almost. [*LJ*, v, 467 (M).]

[237] [Allegra, the natural daughter of Byron and Claire Clairmont, had been placed in a convent at Bagnacavallo, about a dozen miles from Ravenna.]

[238] *Lady Byron*: A Codicil in his Will left her £10,000 (query? *the sum*) and nothing to Ada— But Allegra died after the Will was made—and The Property was left wholly to Mrs. Leigh. It is right that Lady Byron should mention having *in the first week of her marriage* heartily concurred in the propriety of his making an ample provision for his Sister— [See Mrs. Moore's *The Late Lord Byron*, Chapter IV, "Widow, Sister, and Fortune."]

[239] *Byron in his will*: I give and bequeath unto Allegra Biron . . . the sum of five thousand pounds [to be paid] to her on her attaining the age of twenty-one years, or on the day of her marriage, on condition that she does not marry with a native of Great Britain, which shall first happen. [Moore, *Life*, p. 666 (M).]

[240] *Lady Byron*: Mrs. Leigh saw but little of her Niece.

[241] *Lady Byron*: This Portrait in the Albanian Costume, was bought of Philips, the Painter, by Lady Noel (Ly B's Mother) in 1815—when Ld. & Ly B. were in London, *he* being unable to afford the money. Sir Ralph being also under pecuniary embarrassments, Lady Noel parted with some of her diamonds to obtain the £300 (or Guineas) for the purchase.— It was hung over a chimney-piece at Kirkby, & *was* covered with a green curtain: *not* for the reason above supposed.— [Lady Noel's will specified that Ada was not to be shown Byron's portrait until she reached the age of twen-

ty-one. Byron learned of this provision of Lady Noel's will from Hanson and wrote to him of it on March 22, 1822 (*LJ*, vi, 42 and note).]

²⁴² *Lady Byron*: She cried very much on hearing that her father was dead. A short time before some crystals had been given her, sent by her father. Lady Byron had spoken to her of a father who was abroad, with kind feeling simply. She was not old enough to render it necessary to consider in what light the Separation should be put to her.

²⁴³ *Lady Byron*: The Guardianship of the Child was given by the Court to the Mother. A letter to Lady B. from Sir Sam. Romilly states the certainty of its being continued to *her*. [Although Ada was made a ward in Chancery in 1817, Byron retained or thought he retained certain rights in her guardianship and education. See Marchand, p. 685 (note 4) and p. 830.]

²⁴⁴ *Lady Byron*: This Hair had been sent to him by Ly Byron, and also a Miniature of the Child—mentioned p. 101. [Byron thanked his wife for the hair on November 17, 1821 (*LJ*, v, 479).]

During our drive and ride this evening he declined our usual amusement of pistol-firing, without assigning a cause. He hardly spoke a word during the first half-hour, and it was evident that something weighed heavily on his mind. There was a sacredness in his melancholy that I dared not interrupt. At length he said:

"This is Ada's birthday, and might have been the happiest day²⁴⁵ of my life: as it is, ————!" He stopped, seemingly ashamed of having betrayed his feelings. He tried in vain to rally his spirits by turning the conversation; but he created a laugh in which he could not join, and soon relapsed into his former reverie. It lasted till we came within a mile of the Argine gate. There our silence was all at once interrupted by shrieks that seemed to proceed from a cottage by the side of the road. We pulled up our horses, to enquire of a *contadino* standing at the little garden-wicket. He told us that a widow had just lost her only child, and that the sounds proceeded from the wailings of some women over the corpse. Lord Byron was much affected; and his superstition, acted upon by a sadness that seemed to be presentiment, led him to augur some disaster.

"I shall not be happy," said he, "till I hear that my daughter is well. I have a great horror of anniversaries: people only laugh at, who have never kept a register of them. I always write to my sister on Ada's birthday. I did so last year; and, what was very remarkable, my letter reached her on my wedding-day, and her answer reached me at Ravenna on my birthday![246] Several extraordinary things have happened to me on my birth-day; so they did to Napoleon; and a more wonderful circumstance still occurred to Marie Antoinette."

[245] [The date seems to be January 1, 1822, indicated by Medwin's statement, two paragraphs below, that on the next morning Byron received news of Polidori's death.]

[246] *Byron to Murray*, January 2, 1817: On this day *two* years ago I married. . . . It is odd enough that I this day received a letter from you announcing the publication of *Cd. Hd.*, etc., etc., on the day of the date of *The Corsair*; and that I also received one from my Sister, written on the 10th of Decr., my daughter's birthday (and relative chiefly to my daughter), and arriving on the day of the date of my marriage, this present 2d of January, the month of my birth,—and various other Astrologous matters. . . . [*LJ*, IV, 38-39 (M) written from Venice. No letters to Augusta written on December 10 seem to be extant.]

The next morning's courier brought him a letter from England. He gave it me as I entered, and said:

"I was convinced something very unpleasant hung over me last night: I expected to hear that somebody I knew was dead; —so it turns out! Poor Polidori is gone! When he was my physician, he was always talking of Prussic acid,[247] oil of amber, blowing into veins, suffocating by charcoal, and compounding poisons; but for a different purpose to what the Pontic Monarch did, for he has prescribed a dose for himself that would have killed fifty Mithridates',—a dose whose effect, Murray says, was so instantaneous that he went off without a spasm or struggle. It seems that disappointment was the cause of this rash act. He had entertained too sanguine hopes of literary fame, owing to the success of his 'Vampyre,' which, in consequence of its being attributed to me, was got up as a melo-drame at Paris. The foundation of the story *was* mine; but I was forced to disown the publication, lest the world should suppose that I had vanity enough, or was egotist enough, to write in that ridiculous manner about myself.* Notwithstanding which, the French editions still persevere in including it with my works.[248] My real 'Vampyre' I gave at the end of 'Mazeppa,' something in the same way that I told it one night at Diodati, when Monk Lewis, and Shelley and his wife, were present. The latter sketched on that occasion the outline of her Pygmalion story, 'The Modern Prometheus,'[249] the making of a man, (which a lady who had read it afterwards asked Sir Humphrey Davy, to his great astonishment, if he could do); Lewis told a story something like 'Alonzo and Imogene';[250] and Shelley himself (or 'The Snake,'[251] as he used sometimes to call him,) conjured up some frightful woman of an acquaintance of his at home, a kind of Medusa, who was suspected of having eyes in her breasts.[252]

* He alluded to the Preface and the Postscript, containing accounts of his residence at Geneva and in the Isle of Mitylene.

---

[247] [Polidori died on August 24, 1821; E. E. Williams heard of his suicide at Byron's on January 2, 1822, probably the same day that Medwin heard the news. The young physician died after taking prussic acid, although the coroner's report stated that he "died by the visitation of God" (*The Diary of John William Polidori*, ed. William Michael Rossetti, London, 1911, p. 4). His depression was brought about, it seems, by heavy gambling losses, which he could not repay.]

[248] *Medwin*: Singularly enough, Lord Byron's fame in Paris was increased by this spurious publication. It must therefore have had some merit. [Contrast Coulmann's remarks, *HVSV*, p. 339.]

²⁴⁹ *Mary Shelley to Hobhouse*, November 10, 1824: The conversation said to have been held at Diodati is fictitious, since I never saw [Monk] Lewis in my life—and the stories alluded to (with the exception of that of Lewis) were never *related*. . . . The Preface to Frankenstein proves that that story was conceived *before* Lord Byron's and Shelley's tour around the lake [June 22–July 1, 1816], and that Lewis did not arrive at Geneva until some time *after* [in mid-August]. [*Captain Medwin*, pp. 200-201.]

Moore: During a week of rain at this time, having amused themselves with reading German ghost-stories, they agreed, at last, to write something in imitation of them. "You and I," said Lord Byron to Mrs. Shelley, "will publish ours together." He then began his tale of the Vampire; and, having the whole arranged in his head, repeated to them a sketch of the story one evening. . . . The most memorable result, indeed, of their story-telling compact, was Mrs. Shelley's . . . Frankenstein. . . . From his remembrance of this [Byron's] sketch, Polidori afterwards vamped up his strange novel of the Vampire. . . . [Moore, *Life*, p. 319 and note 4; Moore's source is very probably Mary Shelley.]

Medwin: Monk Lewis was not present. It was before his arrival. But this mixing up of the different occasions of the Monk Lewis Narratives is of very little import. It appears that it was on another occasion and before the arrival of Lewis that the Frankenstein Story was sketched out.

²⁵⁰ ["Alonzo the Brave and Fair Imogine" is a ballad by M. G. Lewis. See pp. 190-191 and note 442, below.]

²⁵¹ [On Shelley's nickname, see *LJ*, v, 495-496.]

²⁵² *Byron to Murray*, May 15, 1819: The story of Shelley's agitation is true. . . . Shelley . . . certainly had the fit of phantasy which Polidori describes [in the preface to his *Vampyre*], though *not exactly* as he describes it. [*LJ*, iv, 296-297 (M). Prothero quotes Polidori's account, *LJ*, iv, 296, note 2. Cf. Polidori's *Diary*, p. 128. The episode occurred on June 18, 1816, about two months before Monk Lewis arrived.]

"Perhaps Polidori had strictly no right to appropriate my story to himself; but it was hardly worth it: and when my letter, disclaiming the narrative part, was written,²⁵³ I dismissed the matter from my memory. It was Polidori's own fault that we did not agree. I was sorry when we parted, for

I soon get attached to people; and was more sorry still for the scrape he afterwards got into at Milan. He quarrelled with one of the guards at the Scala, and was ordered to leave the Lombard States twenty-four hours after: which put an end to all his Continental schemes, that I had forwarded by recommending him to Lord ———;[254] and it is difficult for a young physician to get into practice at home, however clever, particularly a foreigner, or one with a foreigner's name. From that time, instead of making out prescriptions, he took to writing romances; a very unprofitable and fatal exchange, as it turned out.

"I told you I was not oppressed in spirits last night without a reason. Who can help being superstitious? Scott believes in second-sight. Rousseau tried whether he was to be d—d or not, by aiming at a tree with a stone; I forget whether he hit or missed. Goethe trusted to the chance of a knife's striking the water, to determine whether he was to prosper in some undertaking.[255] The Italians think the dropping of oil very unlucky. Pietro (Count Gamba) dropped some the night before his exile, and that of his family, from Ravenna.[256] Have you ever had your fortune told? Mrs. Williams told mine. She predicted that twenty-seven and thirty-seven were to be dangerous ages in my life.* One has come true."

"Yes," added I, "and did she not prophecy that you were to die a monk and a miser? I have been told so."

"I don't think these two last very likely; but it was part of her prediction. But there are lucky and unlucky days, as well as years and numbers too. Lord Kinnaird was dining at a party, where Raikes observed that they were thirteen. 'Why don't you make us twelve?' was the reply; and an impudent one it was—but he could say those things.[257] You would not visit on a Friday, would you? You know you are to introduce me to Mrs. Beauclerc. It must not be to-morrow, for it is a Friday."[258]

* He was married in his twenty-seventh, and died in his thirty-seventh year. If true, a good guess.

²⁵³ [A letter to the Editor of *Galignani's Messenger*, April 27, 1819 (*LJ*, ɪᴠ, 286-288).]

²⁵⁴ *Byron to Murray*, November 1, 1816: About a week ago, in consequence of a quarrel at the theatre with an Austrian officer . . . he has contrived to get sent out of the territory. . . . Next day he had an order from the government to be gone in 24 hours. . . . [*LJ*, ɪɪɪ, 379-380 (M). Byron may have recommended him as a physician to Lord Guilford, who for a time did employ Polidori, on whom see Medwin's *Shelley*, pp. 148-152.]

²⁵⁵ [On Goethe's superstitiously throwing his pocketknife into the water, see E. M. Butler, *Byron and Goethe* (London, 1956), p. 112.]

²⁵⁶ *Hobhouse*: Peter count Gamba did no such thing. [*WR*, ɪɪɪ, 28.]

²⁵⁷ *Medwin*: The joke was attributed to Brummell.

²⁵⁸ [On Byron and Mrs. Beauclerk, see Medwin's *Shelley*, p. 368.]

"A fine day," said I, as I entered; "a day worth living for."

"An old hag of a world!" replied he, shaking me by the hand. "You should have been here earlier. Taaffe has been here with a most portentous and obstetrical countenance, and it seems he has been bringing forth an ode—a birth-day *ode*—not on Ada, but on a lady. An *odious* production it must have been! He threatened to inflict, as Shelley calls it; but I fought off. As I told him, Stellas are out of date now: it is a bad compliment to remind women of their age.

"Talking of days, this is the most wretched day of my existence; and I say and do all sorts of foolish things* to drive away the memory of it, and make me forget.

> * "So that it wean me from the weary dream
> Of selfish grief, or gladness!—so it fling
> Forgetfulness around me!"
> > *Childe Harold*, Canto III. Stanza 4.
> "And if I laugh at any mortal thing,
> 'Tis that I may not weep;—and if I weep,
> 'Tis that our nature cannot always bring
> Itself to apathy"——&c.
> > *Don Juan*, Canto IV. Stanza 4.

"I will give you a specimen of some epigrams I am in the habit of sending Hobhouse, to whom I wrote on my first wedding-day,[259] and continue to write still:

> 'This day of ours has surely done
>   Its worst for me and you!
> 'Tis now *five* years since we were *one*,
>   And *four* since we were *two*.'

"And another on his sending me the congratulations of the season, which ended in some foolish way like this:

> 'You may wish me returns of the season:
> Let us, prithee, have none of the day!' "

I think I can give no stronger proof of the sociability of Lord Byron's disposition, than the festivity that presided over his dinners.

Wednesday being one of his fixed days: "You will dine with me," said he, "though it is the 2d of January."[260]

His own table, when alone, was frugal, not to say abstemious*; but on the occasion of these meetings every sort of wine, every luxury of the season, and English delicacy, were displayed. I never knew any man do the honours of his house with greater kindness and hospitality. On this eventful anniversary he was not, however, in his usual spirits, and evidently tried to drown the remembrance of the day by a levity that was forced and unnatural;—for it was clear, in spite of all his efforts, that something oppressed him, and he could not help continually recurring to the subject.

One of the party proposed Lady Byron's health, which he gave with evident pleasure, and we all drank it in bumpers.

---

* His dinner, when alone, cost five Pauls; and thinking he was overcharged, he gave his bills to a lady of my acquaintance to examine†. At a Christmas-day dinner he had ordered a plum-pudding *à l'Anglaise*. Somebody afterwards told him it was not good. "Not good!" said he: "why, it ought to be good; it cost fifteen Pauls."

† He ordered the remnants to be given away, lest his servants (as he said) should envy him every mouthful he ate, and there was always in the Hall a beggar ready to receive them.

The conversation turning on his separation, the probability of their being reconciled was canvassed.

"What!" said he, "after having lost the five best years of our lives?—Never! But," added he, "it was no fault of mine that we quarrelled: I have made advances enough. I had once an idea that people are happiest in the marriage state, after the impetuosity of the passions has subsided,—but that hope is all over with me!"

Writing to a friend the day after our party, I finished my letter with the following remark:

"Notwithstanding the tone of raillery with which he sometimes speaks in 'Don Juan' of his separation from Lady Byron, and his saying, as he did to-day, that the only thing he thanks Lady Byron for is, that he cannot marry, &c., it is evident that it is the thorn in his side—the poison in his cup of life! The veil is easily seen through. He endeavours to mask his griefs, and to fill up the void of his heart, by assuming a gaiety that does not belong to it. All the tender and endearing ties of social and domestic life rudely torn asunder, he has been wandering on from place to place, without finding any to rest in. Switzerland, Venice, Ravenna, and I might soon have added Tuscany, were doomed to be no asylum for him,"[261] &c.

------

[259] *Hobhouse*: Mr. Hobhouse was with lord Byron on his wedding-day: his lordship could not write to him on that day. This fiction is the more unlucky, as the Conversation-writer afterwards mentions, that Mr. Hobhouse was with lord Byron on the day alluded to. [*WR*, iii, 28. A long, confused marginal note written by Medwin makes it clear that he finally realized, after reading Moore's *Life*, that this epigram and the one following it were sent to Moore, to whom, it may be noted, Byron wrote letters on January 2, 1820 and 1821. No letter to Moore written on January 2, 1815, has survived, but Byron did write to him one week after his marriage. I cannot believe that Medwin's versions of the two epigrams are true variants; instead, they suggest what Medwin remembered rather than what Byron said. Medwin got the rhyme words correct. See *LJ*, iv, 394; v, 112.]

[260] *Medwin*: It was the anniversary of his wedding day. [Medwin is correct: January 2, 1822, fell on Wednesday.]

[261] *Trelawny*: No such thing—cant of the author! [The quotation marks closing Medwin's letter, supposedly written on January 3, 1822, should be placed, presumably, at the end of the next to the last sentence of it, not the last, where he is perhaps paraphrasing the letter in the light of later events.]

I observed himself and all his servants in deep mourning. He did not wait for me to enquire the cause.

"I have just heard," said he, "of Lady Noel's death.[262] I am distressed for poor Lady Byron! She must be in great affliction, for she adored her mother! The world will think I am pleased at this event, but they are much mistaken. I never wished for an accession of fortune; I have enough without the Wentworth property. I have written a letter of condolence to Lady Byron,—you may suppose in the kindest terms,—beginning, 'My dear Lady Byron.'[263]

"If we are not reconciled, it is not my fault!"

"I shall be delighted," I said, "to see you restored to her and to your country; which, notwithstanding all you say and write against it, I am sure you like. Do you remember a sentiment in 'The Two Foscari?'—

'He who loves *not* his country, can love nothing.'

"I am becoming more weaned from it every day," said he after a pause, "and have had enough to wean me from it!— No! Lady Byron will not make it up with me now, lest the world should say that her mother only was to blame! Lady Noel certainly identifies herself very strongly in the quarrel, even by the account of her last injunctions; for she directs in her will that my portrait, shut up in a case by her orders, shall not be opened till her grand-daughter be of age, and then not given to her if Lady Byron should be alive.[264]

"I might have claimed all the fortune for my life, if I had chosen to have done so; but have agreed to leave the division

{ 111 }

of it to Lord Dacre and Sir Francis Burdett.[265] The whole management of the affair is confided to them; and I shall not interfere, or make any suggestion or objection, if they award Lady Byron the whole."

I asked him how he became entitled? "The late Lord Wentworth," said he, "bequeathed a life-interest in his Lancashire estates to Lady Byron's mother,[266] and afterwards to her daughter: that is the way I claim."

Some time after, when the equal partition had been settled, he said:

"I have offered Lady Byron the family mansion in addition to the award, but she has declined it: this is not kind."[267]

---

[262] [Byron heard of the death of Lady Noel on February 15, 1822; she had died on January 28.]

[263] [No such letter survives or was written that I know of. However, Byron wrote to Augusta, assuming perhaps that his sentiments would be passed on to Lady Byron, "I regret the pain which the privation must occasion to Sir R. N. and to L^y B. . . . I bear her memory no malice" (*Astarte*, p. 309).]

[264] *Lady Byron*: The passage in the Will is not accurately quoted. It should be referred to,—& certainly would not bear that construction. On Lady Lovelace's marriage (or soon after) the picture was sent to her by Ly Byron. [See above, p. 101 and note 241. Medwin is essentially correct: the portrait was not to be shown to Ada until she became twenty-one and then only with the consent of Lady Byron, if still alive (*LJ*, vi, 42, note).]

[265] *Hobhouse*: Lord Byron could not have claimed all lord Wentworth's fortune for his life, at lady Noel's death. He had before, at his separation from lady Byron, agreed to a division of it. What was referred to sir F. Burdett and lord Dacre, was, *how* the property should be divided. [*WR*, iii, 28-29. Hobhouse is quibbling again. Byron could have controlled the Wentworth property ultimately, but he agreed to arbitration, and Dacre and Burdett decided that the income from the property should be shared. Lady Byron admitted, "it was at his option to make a provision for me out of it or not" (Mrs. Moore, *The Late Lord Byron*, p. 129). See also Marchand, pp. 970-971.]

[266] *Lady Byron*: Another instance of Medwin's blunders—*Leicestershire*. It should be mentioned that just before Lady Noel's death, she desired Lady B— to send her kind forgiveness to Lord Byron. It was transmitted—how received, a letter of his will shew. [See above, p. 112, note 263.]

[267] *Lady Byron*: The whole being in Trust, no such arrange^t was feasible. [As Elwin points out, p. 434, "In those days before the Married Women's Property Acts Annabella's husband would control the estate during her lifetime," *if* Byron had not agreed to arbitration, which he did. For statements of Byron's generosity concerning Kirkby Mallory, see *Correspondence*, II, 213, 215, 221.]

THE conversation turned after dinner on the lyrical poetry of the day, and a question arose as to which was the most perfect ode that had been produced. Shelley contended for Coleridge's on Switzerland, beginning, "Ye clouds,"[268] &c.; others named some of Moore's Irish Melodies, and Campbell's Hohenlinden; and, had Lord Byron not been present, his own Invocation in Manfred, or Ode to Napoleon, or on Prometheus, might have been cited.

"Like Gray," said he, "Campbell smells too much of the oil: he is never satisfied with what he does; his finest things have been spoiled by over-polish—the sharpness of the outline is worn off.[269] Like paintings, poems may be too highly finished. The great art is effect, no matter how produced.

"I will shew you an ode you have never seen, that I consider little inferior to the best which the present prolific age has brought forth." With this he left the table, almost before the cloth was removed, and returned with a magazine, from which he read the following lines on Sir John Moore's burial, which perhaps require no apology for finding a place here:

Not a drum was heard, not a funeral note,
    As his corse to the ramparts we hurried;
Not a soldier discharged his farewell shot
    O'er the grave where our hero we buried.

We buried him darkly at dead of night,
    The sods with our bayonets turning,—
By the struggling moonbeam's misty light,
    And the lantern dimly burning.

No useless coffin confined his breast,
    Nor in sheet nor in shroud we wound him;
But he lay like a warrior taking his rest,
    With his martial cloak around him.

Few and short were the prayers we said,
    And we spoke not a word of sorrow:
But we stedfastly gazed on the face that was dead,
    And we bitterly thought of the morrow.

We thought, as we hollow'd his narrow bed,
    And smooth'd down his lonely pillow,
That the foe and the stranger would tread o'er his head,
    And we far away on the billow!

Lightly they'll talk of the spirit that's gone,
    And o'er his cold ashes upbraid him;
But nothing he'll reck, if they let him sleep on
    In the grave where a Briton has laid him.

But half of our heavy task was done,
    When the clock told the hour for retiring;
And we heard the distant and random gun
    Of the enemy sullenly firing.

Slowly and sadly we laid him down,
    From the field of his fame fresh and gory;
We carved not a line, and we raised not a stone,
    But we left him alone with his glory.

The feeling with which he recited these admirable stanzas, I shall never forget. After he had come to an end, he repeated the third, and said it was perfect, particularly the lines

But he lay like a warrior taking his rest,
    With his martial cloak around him.

"I should have taken," said Shelley, "the whole for a rough sketch of Campbell's."[270]

"No," replied Lord Byron: "Campbell would have claimed it, if it had been his."

I afterwards had reason to think that the ode was Lord
Byron's; that he was piqued at none of his own being mentioned; and, after he had praised the verses so highly, could
not own them.* No other reason can be assigned for his not
acknowledging himself the author,²⁷¹ particularly as he was a
great admirer of General Moore.

* This conjecture is erroneous. It appears that the ode was the production of the late Rev. ———— Wolfe, whose fame rests on it, with
the exception of a very beautiful description of the Dargle. The published posthumous volume displays no remarkable poetical talent.

²⁶⁸ [Coleridge's ode beginning "Ye Clouds! that far above me float
and pause" is on France, not Switzerland.]

²⁶⁹ *Byron in conversation with George Ticknor*, June 25, 1815:
Lord Byron told me that he [Campbell] had injured his poem of
Gertrude, by consulting his critical friends too much, and attempt-
ing to reconcile and follow all their advice. [*HVSV*, p. 127.]

²⁷⁰ [For the history of Charles Wolfe's "The Burial of Sir John
Moore," see Harold A. Small, *The Field of His Fame* (Berkeley
and Los Angeles, 1953), who suggests, p. 5, that Shelley may
have mentioned Campbell as the author because Campbell had in
fact written lines celebrating Sir John Moore.]

²⁷¹ *Mary Shelley to Hobhouse*, November 10, 1824: L. B[yron]
was incapable of praising his own verses—& was certainly satisfied
with the opinion all present had of his talents— Shelley was a warm
admirer of his poetry. [*Captain Medwin*, p. 200.]

Medwin: My opinion for thinking the ode Lord Byron's was cor-
roborated by that of others present. Nor did the pique which I attributed to him accord ill with his character. No man was more
vain—it was a natural vanity—and without vanity—a sense of his
own superiority and a confidence of his own power—no one can
write well. All great poets—Milton was one—have been vain.

Talking after dinner of swimming, he said: "Murray published a letter I wrote to him from Venice, which might have
seemed an idle display of vanity; but the object of my writing
it, was to contradict what Turner had asserted about the im-

possibility of crossing the Hellespont from the Abydos to the Sestos side, in consequence of the tide.

"One is as easy as the other; we did both."[272] Here he turned round to Fletcher, to whom he occasionally referred, and said, "Fletcher, how far was it Mr. Ekenhead and I swam?" Fletcher replied, "Three miles and a half, my Lord." (Of course he did not diminish the distance.) "The real width of the Hellespont," resumed Lord Byron, "is not much above a mile; but the current is prodigiously strong, and we were carried down notwithstanding all our efforts. I don't know how Leander contrived to stem the stream, and steer straight across; but nothing is impossible in love or religion. If I had had a Hero on the other side, perhaps I should have worked harder. We were to have undertaken this feat some time before, but put it off in consequence of the coldness of the water;[273] and it was chilly enough when we performed it. I know I should have made a bad Leander, for it gave me an ague that I did not so easily get rid of. There were some sailors in the fleet who swam further than I did—I do not say than I could have done, for it is the only exercise I pride myself upon, being almost amphibious.

"I remember being at Brighton, many years ago, and having great difficulty in making the land,—the wind blowing off the shore, and the tide setting out. Crowds of people were collected on the beach to see us. Mr. ——— (I think he said Hobhouse) was with me; and," he added, "I had great difficulty in saving him—he nearly drowned me.[274]

"When I was at Venice, there was an Italian who knew no more of swimming than a camel, but he had heard of my prowess in the Dardanelles, and challenged me. Not wishing that any foreigner at least should beat me at my own arms, I consented to engage in the contest. Alexander Scott proposed to be of the party, and we started from Lido. Our land-lubber was very soon in the rear, and Scott saw him make for a gondola. He rested himself first against one, and then against another, and gave in before we got half way to St. Mark's Place. We saw no more of him, but continued our course through the Grand Canal, landing at my palace-stairs. The water of the Lagunes is dull, and not very clear or agreeable to bathe in.[275] I can keep myself up for hours in the sea: I delight in it, and come out with a buoyancy of spirits I never feel on any other occasion.

"If I believed in the transmigration of your Hindoos, I should think I had been a *Merman* in some former state of existence, or was going to be turned into one in the next."

---

[272] *Hobhouse*: Lord Byron did *not* do both, he only swam from the Sestos to the Abydos side. [*WR*, iii, 29.]

Medwin: There were two subjects on which Lord Byron was fond of vapourising. Shooting and Swimming. His Duel with Hobhouse was one instance and his saying that he swam from Sestos to Abydos *and* from the Asiatic to the European side of the Bosphorus another. In fact he did not do both. [For Byron's published reply to William Turner, see *LJ*, v, 246-251.]

[273] *Hobhouse*: Lord Byron and Mr. Ekenhead did undertake this feat some time before—they did not "put it off" in consequence of the coldness of the water—they *gave it up* in consequence of the coldness of the water, when about half over the strait.

If the Conversation-writer had read the note to lord Byron's lines written to commemorate this exploit, he would not have framed this conversation in this way. [*WR*, iii, 29.]

[274] *Hobhouse*: In 1808, lord Byron was swimming with the *Hon. Mr. Lincoln Stanhope*. Both of them were very nearly drowned; but lord Byron did not touch Mr. Stanhope; he very judiciously kept aloof, but cried out to him to keep up his spirits. The by-standers [including Hobhouse] sent in some boatmen with ropes tied round them, who at last dragged lord Byron and his friend from the surf, and saved their lives. [*WR*, iii, 30. Moore, *Life*, p. 106, note 1, states that the place was Brighton and Hobhouse present.]

[275] *Medwin*: It was Insanitary enough. It was very trashy. [For Byron's several accounts of this exploit, see *LJ*, v, 248 (M) and *Correspondence*, ii, 83-85. Angelo Mengaldo was "a noted Italian swimmer who traversed the Danube in Napoleon's campaigns," as Byron explained; Byron did not get out at his palace stairs: he swam the entire length of the Grand Canal "and got out where the Laguna once more opens to Fusina."]

"When I published 'Marino Faliero' I had not the most distant view to the stage.[276] My object in choosing that historical subject was to record one of the most remarkable incidents in the annals of the Venetian Republic, embodying it in what I considered the most interesting form—dialogue, and giving my work the accompaniments of scenery and manners studied on the spot. That Faliero should, for a slight to a woman, become a traitor to his country, and conspire to massacre all his fellow-nobles, and that the young Foscari should have a sickly affection for his native city, were no inventions of mine. I painted the men as I found them, as they were,—not as the critics would have them. I took the stories as they were handed down; and if human nature is not the same in one country as it is in others, am I to blame?—can I help it? But no painting, however highly coloured, can give an idea of the intensity of a Venetian's affection for his native city. Shelley, I remember, draws a very beautiful picture of the tranquil pleasures of Venice in a poem* which he has not published, and in which he does not make me cut a good figure. It describes an evening we passed together.

"There was one mistake I committed: I should have called 'Marino Faliero' and 'The Two Foscari' dramas, historic

* The lines to which Lord Byron referred are these:
> "If I had been an unconnected man,
> I from this moment should have form'd the plan
> Never to leave fair Venice—for to me
> It was delight to ride by the lone sea;
> And then the town is silent—one may write
> Or read in gondolas by day or night,
> Having the little brazen lamp alight,
> Unseen, uninterrupted: books are there,
> Pictures, and casts from all those statues fair
> Which were twin-born with poetry,—and all
> We seek in towns, with little to recall
> Regrets for the green country. I might sit
> In Maddalo's great palace," &c.

Julian and Maddalo.[277]

poems, or any thing, in short, but tragedies or plays. In the first place, I was ill-used in the extreme by the Doge being brought on the stage at all, after my Preface. Then it consists of 3500 lines:* a good acting play should not exceed 1500 or 1800; and, conformably with my plan, the materials could not have been compressed into so confined a space.

"I remember Hogg the Ettrick Shepherd[278] telling me, many years ago, that I should never be able to condense my powers of writing sufficiently for the stage, and that the fault of all my plays would be their being too long for acting. The remark occurred to me when I was about 'Marino Faliero;' but I thought it unnecessary to try and contradict his prediction, as I did not study stage-effect, and meant it solely for the closet. So much was I averse from its being acted, that, the moment I heard of the intention of the Managers, I applied for an injunction; but the Chancellor refused to interfere, or issue an order for suspending the representation.[279] It was a question of property, of great importance in the literary world. He would neither protect me nor Murray. But the manner in which it was got up was shameful!† All the declamatory parts were left, all the dramatic ones struck out; and Cooper,[280] the new actor, was the murderer of the whole. Lioni's soliloquy, which I wrote one moonlight night after coming from the Benzons', ought to have been omitted altogether, or at all events much curtailed. What audience will listen with any patience to a mere tirade of poetry, which stops the march of the action?[281] No wonder, then, that the unhappy Doge should have been damned! But it was no pleasant news to me; and the letter containing it was accompanied by another, to inform me that an old lady, from whom I had great expectations, was likely to live to an hundred. There is an autumnal shoot in some old people, as in trees; and I fancy her consti-

* He gave me the copy, with the number of lines marked with his own pencil. I have left it in England.[282]
† Acted at Drury Lane, April 25, 1821.

tution has got some of the new sap. Well, on these two pleasant pieces of intelligence I wrote the following epigram, or
elegy[283] it may be termed, from the melancholy nature of the
subject:—

> Behold the blessings of a happy lot!
> My play is damn'd, and Lady Noel not!

"I understand that Louis Dix-huit, or *des huitres*,[284] as Moore
spells it, has made a *traduction* of poor 'Faliero;' but I should
hope it will not be attempted on the *Théatre François*. It is
quite enough for a man to be damned once. I was satisfied with
Jeffrey's critique*[285] on the play, for it abounded in extracts.
He was welcome to his own opinion,—which was fairly stated.
His summing up in favour of my friend Sir Walter amused
me: it reminded me of a schoolmaster, who, after flogging a
bad boy, calls out the head of the class, and, patting him on
the head, gives him all the sugar-plums.

> * "However, I forgive him; and I trust
> He will forgive himself:—if not, I must.
> Old enemies who have become new friends,
> Should so continue;—'tis a point of honour."
> *Don Juan*, Canto X. Stanzas 11 and 12.

---

[276] *Byron in the Preface to Marino Faliero*: I have had no view to
the stage. . . . [*Poetry*, IV, 337.]

[277] [Ll. 547-559, with variants.]

[278] [An anonymous writer signing himself "N." and offering no
evidence states in *Notes and Queries*, 5th Series, II (August 22,
1874), 158, "an anecdote has been recorded" that Byron met Hogg
at Rydal. This may well be no more than a vague recollection of
"Noctes Ambrosianae," *Blackwood's*, XVI (November, 1824), 591-
592. Hogg's daughter, Mrs. Garden, editor of *Memorials of James
Hogg* (Paisley, 1885), pp. 103-104, states that Byron and Hogg
never met.]

[279] [Prothero, *LJ*, V, 226-227, note 2, summarizes the details of
the performance of *Marino Faliero* and the injunction, secured and
then suspended.]

²⁸⁰ [Cooper had the title role.]

²⁸¹ [Lioni's soliloquy in IV, i, is 112 lines long.]

²⁸² [Medwin's copy of *Marino Faliero*, inscribed "To Capt. T. Medwin from the Author," was recently purchased by the Seven Gables Bookshop for Mr. Robert H. Taylor of Yonkers, N. Y.]

²⁸³ [Byron sent the epigram, calling it an "Elegy," to Murray on May 25, 1821. He had heard of Lady Noel's recovery as early as April 26 (*LJ*, v, 270), knew that *Marino Faliero* had been "universally condemned" by May 14, 1821 (*LJ*, v, 285).]

²⁸⁴ [Louis d'huîtres is Louis the barrel of oysters. Byron repeatedly referred to him as Louis the Gouty.]

²⁸⁵ [Jeffrey reviewed *Marino Faliero* in the *Edinburgh Review*, xxxv (July, 1821), 271-285.]

"The common trick of Reviewers is, when they want to depreciate a work, to give no quotations from it. This is what 'The Quarterly' shines in;—the way Milman put down Shelley, when he compared him to Pharaoh, and his works to his chariot-wheels,²⁸⁶ by what contortion of images I forget;—but it reminds me of another person's comparing me in a poem to Jesus Christ, and telling me, when I objected to its profanity, that he²⁸⁷ alluded to me in situation, not in person! 'What!' said I in reply, 'would you have me crucified? We are not in Jerusalem, are we?' But this is a long parenthesis. The Reviewers are like a counsellor, after an abusive speech, calling no witnesses to prove his assertions.

"There are people who read nothing but these *trimestrials*, and swear by the *ipse dixit* of these autocrats—these Actæon hunters of literature. They are fond of raising up and throwing down idols. 'The Edinburgh' did so with Walter Scott's poetry, and,—perhaps there is no merit in my plays? It may be so; and Milman may be a great poet, if Heber is right and I am wrong. He has the dramatic faculty, and I have not.²⁸⁸ So they pretended to say of Milton. I am too happy in being coupled in any way with Milton, and shall be glad if they find any points of comparison between him and me.

"But the praise or blame of Reviewers does not last long now-a-days. It is like straw thrown up in the air.*

"I hope, notwithstanding all that has been said, to write eight more plays this year, and to live long enough to rival Lope de Vega, or Calderon. I have two subjects that I think of writing on,—Miss Lee's German tale 'Kruitzner,'[289] and Pausanias.[290]

* He seemed to think somewhat differently afterwards, when, after the review in 'The Quarterly' of his plays, he wrote to me, saying, "I am the most unpopular writer *going!*" a vulgarism of expression one would have scarcely suspected from Byron, but in his correspondence he affected this.

[286] *Harness*: Lord Byron knew from the best authority that it was written by a nephew of Coleridge. [*BEM*, XVI, 539. The review of Shelley's *Revolt of Islam* was written by Sir John Taylor Coleridge. Shelley also believed that the author was Milman. See Shelley's *Letters*, II, 128, note 7, where the passage referred to by Byron is quoted. I find no evidence that Byron was aware of the true authorship of the article. He also assigned Croker's remarks on Keats's *Endymion* (*Quarterly Review*, XIX, 204-208) to Milman.]

[287] *Medwin*: The Author of a Poem of Much promise entitled *Magya* [by Sir John St. Aubyn?], a promise which he did not redeem, and in the Preface to which he attacks Gifford furiously, not only on account of the obscenities in his Journal [*The Quarterly Review*] but with bad taste on the lowness of his extraction. [Gifford's father was a glazier.] *Magya* was a Poem which, if it had been written before *The Corsair*, would have had much popularity; as it was not, it fell almost dead from the Press. [See E. E. Williams, *Journal*, November 16, 1821: "M[edwin] calls, and brought with him St. Aubyn's 'magya' a venetian tale in imitation of the Corsair, of which the preface with the exception of some coarse abuse of Gifford, is the best part."]

[288] [On Heber's comparison of Milman and Byron, which appeared originally in the *Quarterly Review*, and Byron's tribute to Milman's dramatic powers, see *LJ*, v, 54, note 2.]

[289] [Byron's *Werner*, heavily indebted to Harriet Lee's *Kruitzner*, was completed January 20, 1822.]

{ 123 }

[290] *Medwin*: Lord Byron seems to have taken the idea of writing on the subject of Pausanias from the following passage of Goethe: "turning his sad contemplation inwards, he applies to himself the fatal history of the king of Sparta." [Medwin quotes from Goethe's review of *Manfred*, translated by Moore, *Life*, pp. 448-449. See *Manfred*, II, ii, 164-204, and Byron's note. All that may be said with certainty is that Byron knew the story of Pausanias.]

"What do you think of Pausanias? The unities can be strictly preserved, almost without deviating from history. The temple where he took refuge, and from whose sanctuary he was forced without profaning it, will furnish complete unities of time and place.[291]

"No event in ancient times ever struck me as more noble and dramatic than the death of Demosthenes. You remember his last words to Archias?[292]—But subjects are not wanting."

I told Lord Byron, that I had had a letter from Procter*, and that he had been jeered on 'The Duke of Mirandola' not having been included in his (Lord B.'s) enumeration of the dramatic pieces of the day; and that he had added, he had been at Harrow with him.[293]

"Ay," said Lord Byron, "I remember the name: he was in the lower school, in such a class. They stood Farrer, Procter, Jocelyn."[294]

* Barry Cornwall.

[291] [Pausanias the Spartan, who had incited the helots to revolt, took refuge in the sanctuary of Athena on the Spartan Acropolis, was there walled up, and then was dragged out to die only after he had nearly starved to death.]

[292] [The last words of Demosthenes, who had taken refuge in an ancient temple of Poseidon, are recorded by Plutarch. Discovered and threatened by Archias, a former tragic actor now in the pay of Antipater, Demosthenes sucked poison from his pen, allowed it time to take effect, and said, as he moved toward the door of the temple, "Now you can play the part of Creon in the

tragedy as soon as you like and cast forth my body unburied. But I, O gracious Poseidon, quit thy temple while I yet live; Antipater and his Macedonians have done what they could to pollute it."]

²⁹³ [B. W. Procter's *Mirandola* was produced at Covent Garden on January 9, 1821. Byron had seen it advertised and wrote to Murray, January 4, 1821, "If I had been aware that he was in that line, I should have spoken of him in the preface to *M[arino] F[aliero]*." On March 6, 1822, Byron stated (*LJ*, vi, 35) that he had received a letter from Procter, who entered Harrow in February, 1801, several months before Byron.]

²⁹⁴ [Thomas Farrer entered Harrow in April, 1801, as did Byron (*LJ*, i, 73, note 3). In 1813 Byron listed Lord Jocelyn with Powerscourt and Delawarr among his early friends (*LJ*, ii, 259). He was at Harrow with the latter two, may have known Jocelyn there also, although this is uncertain.]

I have no doubt Lord Byron could have gone through all the names, such was his memory. He immediately sat down, and very good-naturedly gave me the following note to send to Barry Cornwall, which shews that the arguments of the Reviewers had not changed his Unitarian opinions, (as he called them):

"Had I been aware of your tragedy when I wrote my note to 'Marino Faliero,' although it is a matter of no consequence to you, I should certainly not have omitted to insert your name with those of the other writers who still do honour to the drama.

"My own notions on the subject altogether are so different from the popular ideas of the day, that we differ essentially, as indeed I do from our whole English *literati*, upon that topic. But I do not contend that I am right—I merely say that such is my opinion; and as it is a solitary one, it can do no great harm. But it does not prevent me from doing justice to the powers of those who adopt a different system."

I introduced the subject of Cain: "When I was a boy," said he, "I studied German, which I have now entirely forgotten. It was very little I ever knew of it. Abel was one of the first books my German master read to me; and whilst he was crying his eyes out over its pages, I thought that any other than Cain had hardly committed a crime in ridding the world of so dull a fellow as Gessner made brother Abel.[295]

"I always thought Cain a fine subject, and when I took it up I determined to treat it strictly after the Mosaic account. I therefore made the snake a snake, and took a Bishop for my interpreter.[296]

"I had once an idea of following the Armenian Scriptures, and making Cain's crime proceed from jealousy,[297] and love of his uterine sister; but, though a more probable cause of dispute, I abandoned it as unorthodox.

"One mistake crept in,—Abel's should have been made the first sacrifice:[298] and it is singular that the first form of religious worship should have induced the first murder.

"Hobhouse has denounced 'Cain' as irreligious, and has penned me a most furious epistle, urging me not to publish it, as I value my reputation or his friendship. He contends that it is a work I should not have ventured to put my name to in the days of Pope, Churchill, and Johnson, (a curious trio!) Hobhouse used to write good verses once himself, but he seems to have forgotten what poetry is in others, when he says my 'Cain' reminds him of the worst bombast of Dryden's. Shelley, who is no bad judge of the compositions of others, however he may fail in procuring success for his own, is most sensitive and indignant at this critique, and says (what is not the case) that 'Cain' is the finest thing I ever wrote, calls it worthy of Milton,[299] and backs it against Hobhouse's poetical Trinity.[300]

---

[295] *Hobhouse in his diary*, September 20, 1820: Amongst other *scherzi* he said that Cain was right to kill Abel, that he might not have the bore of passing 200 years with him. [*HVSV*, p. 316.

In the preface to *Cain*, published December 19, 1821, Byron recalled reading at the age of eight, with "delight," Solomon Gessner's *Death of Abel*.]

[296] *Medwin*: Warburton's *Divine Legation*. See Preface to *Cain*.

[297] [On Cain's motivation, see *LJ*, v, 470, where Byron explains that "envy of Abel" would have made Cain merely "contemptible."]

[298] *Medwin*: No man was so open to criticism as Lord Byron. This observation came from my pointing out the inconsistency of making Cain say, "Life cannot be so slight, as to be quench'd/ Thus quickly" [III, i, 351-352], when he had just seen Abel's burnt flesh offering, perhaps the agonies of death of the lamb or kid on his brother's altar. [The nature of the "mistake" in *Cain* is not clear.]

[299] *Shelley to John Gisborne*, January 26, 1822: In my opinion it contains finer poetry than has appeared in England since the publication of Paradise Regained.—Cain is apocalyptic. . . . [*Letters*, ii, 388 (M).]

[300] *Hobhouse*: Mr. Hobhouse, to whom at that time Lord Byron's poems were generally transmitted previously to their publication, thought it his duty to recommend to Lord Byron not to publish "Cain;" but he did not do it in the terms alluded to by the conversation-writer. Mr. Hobhouse did speak of Lord Byron's reputation, to which he attached the highest importance; but the remark respecting his own friendship, is a pure invention.

Mr. Hobhouse did speak of Pope, and Churchill, and Johnson, but he spoke of them not as poets, but as satirists and critics. He did not join them, or, as the conversation-writer says, make a poetical trinity of them; but he told Lord Byron that he thought he would not venture publishing his "Cain" if Pope were alive,—or Johnson,—or *even* Churchill. The nonsense put into Mr. Hobhouse's letter belongs to the conversation-writer; Lord Byron was extremely incensed at the time, but he afterwards changed his opinion of the poem, and in one of his letters to Mr. Hobhouse, written at the very time to which Mr. Medwin alludes, he said to him, "And it seems that you were not far wrong about 'Cain'."

It is very melancholy that the duty of detecting imposture should render necessary the disclosure of the private correspondence of any man of honour. [Hobhouse's suppressed pamphlet, "Exposure of the Mis-statements Contained in Captain Medwin's Pretended 'Conversations of Lord Byron.' "]

J. W. Croker: The anecdote is so creditable to Mr. Hobhouse, that we are glad to see that he does not at all shake its authenticity; but does his explanation not give the most convincing proof of Mr. Medwin's veracity? How could he have known that Mr. Hobhouse had written at all on the subject—how could he have known so minute a detail as that Mr. Hobhouse had quoted Pope, Churchill, and Johnson? The main facts then are true, and the injurious and ridiculous colouring given to them is quite in character with the disposition of the man who could have amused such an acquaintance as Mr. Medwin, with an account of the private and confidential correspondence of such a friend as Mr. Hobhouse.

In every one of these cases it is undeniable that the facts *must* have been communicated by Lord Byron; what reason can there be to doubt that he supplied the *colouring* also? Mr. Medwin had no interest in travestying them: He evidently does sometimes not even see the malice intended; whilst on the other hand the erroneous matter was all favourable to Lord Byron's own views; . . . thus altered and garnished, they [the facts] became his Lordship's justification. We therefore think we are well founded in our original assertion, that Mr. Hobhouse's Notes tend mainly to support Mr. Medwin's general veracity, and to show that Lord Byron did communicate to him matters which a man of a well regulated mind and a nice sense of honour, never could have promulgated beyond the circle of confidence in which they originally occurred. [Medwin states in his *Shelley*, p. 334, that Byron read Hobhouse's letter to him and Shelley. Byron received it on November 23, 1821, told Hobhouse the next year that it "had made him nearly mad" (Marchand, p. 1031). For Byron's replies to Hobhouse, see *Correspondence*, ii, 204-206, 207-208.]

"The *Snake's* rage has prevented my crest from rising. I shall write Hobhouse a very unimpassioned letter, but a firm one. The publication shall go on, whether Murray refuses to print it or not.

"I have just got a letter, and an admirable one it is, from Sir Walter Scott, to whom I dedicated 'Cain.'[301] The sight of one of his letters always does me good. I hardly know what to make of all the contradictory opinions that have been sent me this week. Moore says, that more people are shocked with the blasphemy of the sentiments, than delighted with the beauty of the lines. Another person thinks the Devil's arguments irresistible, or irrefutable. —— says that the Liberals like it, but that the Ultraists are making a terrible outcry; and that the *he* and *him* not being in capitals, in full dress uniform, shocks the High-church and Court party. Some call me an Atheist, others a Manichean,—a very bad and a hard-sounding name, that shocks the *illiterati* the more because they don't know what it means.[302] I am taxed with having made my drama a peg to hang on it a long, and some say tiresome, dissertation on the principle of Evil; and, what is worse, with having given Lucifer the best of the argument; all of which I am accused of taking from Voltaire.

"I could not make Lucifer expound the Thirty-nine Articles, nor talk as the Divines do:[303] that would never have suited his purpose,—nor, one would think, theirs. They ought to be grateful to him for giving them a subject to write about. What would they do without evil in the Prince of Evil? Othello's occupation would be gone. I have made Lucifer say no more in his defence than was absolutely necessary,—not half so much as Milton makes his Satan do. I was forced to keep up his dramatic character. *Au reste*, I have adhered closely to the Old Testament, and I defy any one to question my moral.

[301] *Medwin*: This Letter appears among Moore's Memoirs [*Life*, p. 547, note 1; dated December 4, 1821]. It is a gem.

[302] *Byron in the original draft of the Preface to Cain*, omitted from early editions: I am prepared to be accused of Manicheism, or some other hard name ending in *ism*, which makes a formidable figure and awful sound in the eyes and ears of those who would be as much puzzled to explain the terms so bandied about, as the liberal and pious indulgers in such epithets. [*Poetry*, v, 209 (M). See also *LJ*, v, 54, note 2, which quotes from the *Quarterly Review* article in which Heber had accused Byron of Manicheism. Byron denied the charge: "I am not a Manichean, nor an *Any*-chean."]

[303] [Cf. Byron's Preface to *Cain*: With regard to the language of Lucifer, it was difficult for me to make him talk like a clergyman. . . .]

"Johnson, who would have been glad of an opportunity of throwing another stone at Milton, redeems him from any censure for putting impiety and even blasphemy into the mouths of his infernal spirits. By what rule, then, am I to have all the blame? What would the Methodists at home say to Goethe's 'Faust'? His devil not only talks very familiarly *of* Heaven, but very familiarly *in* Heaven. What would they think of the colloquies of Mephistopheles and his pupil, or the more daring language of the prologue, which no one will ever venture to translate?[304] And yet this play is not only tolerated and admired, as every thing he wrote must be, but acted, in Germany.[305] And are the Germans a less moral people than we are? I doubt it much. Faust itself is not so fine a subject as Cain. It is a grand mystery. The mark that was put upon Cain is a sublime and shadowy act: Goethe would have made more of it than I have done*."[306]

---

* On Mr. Murray being threatened with a prosecution, Lord Byron begged me to copy the following letter for him:—

"Attacks upon me were to be expected; but I perceive one upon you in the papers which, I confess, I did not expect.

"How and in what manner you can be considered responsible for what I publish, I am at a loss to conceive. If 'Cain' be blasphemous, 'Paradise Lost' is blasphemous; and the words of the Oxford gentleman, 'Evil, be thou my good!' are from that very poem, from the mouth of Satan,—and is there any thing more in that of Lucifer, in the Mystery? 'Cain' is nothing more than a drama, not a piece of argument. If Lucifer and Cain speak as the first rebel and the first murderer may be supposed to speak, nearly all the rest of the personages talk also according to their characters; and the stronger passions have ever been permitted to the drama. I have avoided introducing the Deity, as in Scripture, though Milton does, and not very wisely either; but have adopted his angel as sent to Cain instead, on purpose to avoid shocking any feelings on the subject, by falling short of what all uninspired men must fall short in,—viz. giving an adequate notion of the effect of the presence of Jehovah. The old Mysteries introduced Him liberally enough, and all this I avoided in the new one.

"The attempt to bully you because they think it will not succeed with me, seems as atrocious an attempt as ever disgraced the times. What! when Gibbon's, Hume's, Priestley's, and Drummond's publishers have been allowed to rest in peace for seventy years, are you to be singled out for a work of fiction, not of history or argument?

"There must be something at the bottom of this—some private enemy of your own; it is otherwise incredible. I can only say, '*Me, me, adsum qui feci;'* that any proceedings against you may, I beg, be transferred to me, who am willing and ought to endure them all; that if you have lost money by the publication, I will refund any or all of the copyright: that I desire you will say, that both you and Mr. Gifford remonstrated against the publication, and also Mr. Hobhouse; that I alone occasioned it, and I alone am the person who, either legally or otherwise, should bear the burthen.

"If they prosecute, I will come to England; that is, if by meeting in my own person I can save yours. Let me know. You shan't suffer for me, if I can help it. Make any use of this letter you please."

[304] *Medwin*: He was mistaken. Shelley, Anstey, and others have done so.

[305] [E. M. Butler, *Byron and Goethe*, p. 114, points out that "Byron was wrong in thinking that *Faust* had been performed in Germany"; he also refers to Lord Leveson-Gower's translation of *Faust* (1829), which appeared without the Prologue.]

[306] [At this point Medwin omits "a drinking-song composed one morning—or perhaps evening, after one of our dinners." Medwin had learned from Hobhouse's review that the poem, "Fill the goblet again," had appeared in *Hours of Idleness*.]

DINING with him another day, the subject of private theatricals was introduced. "I am very fond of a private
theatre," said he. "I remember myself and some friends at
Cambridge getting up a play; and that reminds me of a thing
which happened, that was very provoking in itself, but very
humorous in its consequences.

"On the day of representation, one of the performers took
it into his head to make an excuse, and his part was obliged
to be read. Hobhouse came forward to apologize to the audience, and told them that a Mr. Tuke had declined to perform
his part, &c. The gentleman was highly indignant at the '*a*,'
and had a great inclination to pick a quarrel with Scrope Davies, who replied, that he supposed Mr. Tuke wanted to be
called *the* Mr. so and so. He ever after went by the name of
the '*Definite Article*.'[307]

"After this preface, to be less indefinite, suppose we were
to get up a play. My hall, which is the largest in Tuscany,
would make a capital theatre; and we may send to Florence
for an audience, if we cannot fill it here. And as to decorations,
nothing is easier in any part of Italy than to get them: besides
that, Williams will assist us."

It was accordingly agreed that we should commence with
"Othello."[308] Lord Byron was to be Iago. Orders were to be
given for the fitting up of the stage, preparing the dresses,
&c., and rehearsals of a few scenes took place. Perhaps Lord
Byron would have made the finest actor in the world. His
voice had a flexibility, a variety in its tones, a power and
pathos beyond any I ever heard;[309] and his countenance was
capable of expressing the tenderest, as well as the strongest
emotions. I shall never forget his reading Iago's part in the
handkerchief-scene.[310]

[307] *Mary Shelley to Hobhouse*, November 10, 1824: How completely he spoils your story of the Definite Article; I have it as
recorded by one of abler memory where it cuts a much better

figure. [*Captain Medwin*, p. 201. Medwin's version is much superior to that recorded in Edward E. Williams' journal, December 28, 1821 (*HVSV*, p. 264) and much closer to the story which Byron recorded in his "Detached Thoughts" (*LJ*, v, 427). Medwin's spelling, *Tuke*, for Byron's *Tulk*, reflects rather clearly the oral origins of Medwin's version. Moore did not print the anecdote.]

[308] *Edward E. Williams in his journal*, February 18, 1822: Called on Lord B[yron] who talks of getting up *Othello*. [*HVSV*, p. 282.]

[309] *Leigh Hunt*: This is harmless, as an instance of the effect which his Lordship had upon the Captain; but, from all I ever heard of it [Byron's voice], I should form a very different judgment. His voice, as far as I was acquainted with it, though not incapable of loudness, nor unmelodious in its deeper tones, was confined. He made an effort when he threw it out. The sound of it in ordinary, except when he laughed, was pretty and lugubrious. He spoke inwardly, and slurred over his syllables, perhaps in order to hide the *burr*. In short, it was as much the reverse of any thing various and powerful, as his enunciation was of any thing articulate. But I do not know what passion might have made of it. The few times I saw him in a state of violent emotion, it was lower than ever. I can imagine him to have been loud in reciting a declamation, if he chose to be so. He could be loud in singing; and he then threw out at once the best and most powerful tones in his voice; but the effect (as I have already described it) had always an appearance of effort. After all, there may have been greater strength in his voice than it was my chance to witness; but the "flexibility," and the "variety of tones," to say nothing of the pathos, were assuredly in the Captain's imagination. [*HVSV*, pp. 307-308.]

[310] *Trelawny*: He [Byron] recited a great portion of his [Iago's] part with great gusto; it exactly suited him—he looked it too. [*HVSV*, p. 282.]

"Shakspeare was right," said he, after he had finished, "in making Othello's jealousy turn upon that circumstance.* The

* Calderon says, in the *Cisma de l'Inglaterra*, (I have not the original,)

> "She gave me, too, a handkerchief,—a spell—
> A flattering pledge, my hopes to animate—
> An astrologic favour—fatal prize,
> That told too true what tears must weep these eyes!"

handkerchief is the strongest proof of love, not only among the Moors, but all Eastern nations: and yet they say that the plot of 'Marino Faliero' hangs upon too slight a cause."

All at once a difficulty arose about a Desdemona, and the Guiccioli put her Veto on our theatricals.[311] The influence of the Countess over Lord Byron reminded me of a remark of Fletcher's, that Shelley once repeated to me as having overheard: "That it was strange every woman should be able to manage his Lordship, but her Ladyship!"[312]

[311] *Edward E. Williams in his journal*, February 28, 1822: Othello that was talked of laid aside. [Williams, *Journal*, p. 132.]

[312] *Fletcher*: It is very odd, but I never yet knew a lady that could not manage my Lord, *except* my Lady. [Marchand, p. 547, quoting Moore's *Life*.]

Discussing the different actors of the day, he said: "Dowton,[313] who hated Kean, used to say that his Othello reminded him of Obi, or Three-fingered Jack,[314]—not Othello. But, whatever his Othello might have been, Garrick himself never surpassed him in Iago.[315] I am told that Kean is not so great a favourite with the public since his return from America, and that party strengthened against him in his absence. I *guess* he could not have staid long enough to be spoiled; though I *calculate* no actor is improved by their stage. How do you *reckon?*[316]

"Kean began by acting Richard the Third when quite a boy, and gave all the promise of what he afterwards became.[317] His Sir Giles Overreach was a wonderful performance.[318] The actresses were afraid of him; and he was afterwards so much exhausted himself, that he fell into fits. This, I am told, was the case with Miss O'Neill.*

* And he might have added Pasta.

"Kemble did much towards the reform of our stage. Classical costume was almost unknown before he undertook to revise the dresses. Garrick used to act Othello in a red coat and epaulettes, and other characters had prescriptive habits equally ridiculous.[319] I can conceive nothing equal to Kemble's Coriolanus;[320] and he looked the Roman so well, that even 'Cato,' cold and *stiltish* as it is, had a run. That shews what an actor can do for a play! If he had acted 'Marino Faliero,' its fate would have been very different.

---

[313] [For William Dowton and Byron, see *HVSV*, pp. 139-142.]

[314] [Cf. Medwin's *Shelley*, i, 246, where he states that the story of William Tell killing Gessler is "about as true as the exploits of Munchausen, Obi, or three-fingered Jack."]

[315] *Byron to Moore, c.* May 7, 1814: Was not [Kean's] Iago perfection? particularly the last look. I was *close* to him (in the orchestra), and never saw an English countenance half so expressive. [*LJ*, iii, 81 (M).]

[316] [In his use of the italicized words, Byron is ridiculing American English.]

[317] [Kean began his career at the age of fourteen, in York Theatre, appearing as Hamlet, Hastings, and Cato. He played Richard III at Drury Lane on February 12, 1814.]

[318] *Medwin*: I find in looking over the Journal omitted, "By the way, Lord Lonsdaile was the Sir Giles Overreach of his day." What he meant I leave to a future Commentator. I know nothing about his History. [This is probably the first Earl of Lonsdale (1736-1802), a man of immense wealth known as the "bad earl" and described by Junius as "the little contemptible tyrant of the north," whom Byron in *The Blues* confused with Wordsworth's patron, the second earl. For Byron's hysterical reaction to Kean's Sir Giles Overreach, see *LJ*, iv, 340 (M).]

[319] ["Even the witches in *Macbeth*, as produced by Garrick's company, wore powdered wigs, rouge, red stomachers, point lace aprons, and mittens" (Karl J. Holzknecht, *The Backgrounds of Shakespeare's Plays*, New York, 1950, p. 425). John Philip Kemble, as manager of Drury Lane and later of Covent Garden, made

the most important changes in the direction of authentic stage costume, but even he played Lear and Macbeth in "a flowered-satin lounging robe" (*ibid.*, p. 426).]

[320] *Byron to Harness*, December 15, 1811: Last night I saw Kemble in Coriolanus;—he *was glorious* and exerted himself wonderfully. [*LJ*, ii, 90 (M). This was Kemble's greatest role.]

"Kemble pronounced several words affectedly, which should be cautiously avoided on the stage.[321] It is nothing that Campbell writes it *Sepulcrè* in 'Hohenlinden.'[322] The Greek derivation is much against his pronunciation of *ache*."[323]

He now began to mimic Kemble's voice and manner of spouting, and imitated him inimitably[324] in Prospero's lines:

——— 'Yea, the great globe itself,
And all which it inherit, shall dissolve,
And, like the baseless fabric of a vision,
Leave not a *rack* behind!'

"When half seas over, Kemble used to speak in blankverse: and with practice, I don't think it would be difficult. Good prose resolves itself into blank-verse. Why should we not be able to improvise in hexameters, as well as the Italians? Theodore Hook is an improvisatore."[325]

[321] *Medwin*: He alluded to Kemble's pronunciation of the *aches* in the *Tempest*, "We rack thy bones with aches" [i, ii, 370, misquoted], which for the sake of the rhythm he pronounced *atches*. The audience hissed him. [The old disyllabic pronunciation of the noun plural has been used on the stage even in the twentieth century.]

[322] [In the last line of "Hohenlinden," Campbell rhymed *sepulchre* and *chivalry*.]

[323] [English *ache* does not derive from the Greek, although it was once thought to.]

[324] *George Ticknor in his diary*, June 26, 1815: Lord Byron asked me what actors I had heard, and when I told him, imitated

to me the manner of Munden, Braham, Cooke, and Kemble, with exactness, as far as I had heard them. [*HVSV*, p. 127.]

Leigh Hunt: In his wine he would volunteer an imitation of somebody, generally of Incledon. He was not a good mimic in the detail; but he could give a lively broad sketch; and over his cups his imitations were good-natured. . . . [*HVSV*, p. 329; see also Hunt's *Autobiography* (London, 1850), III, 67-68, for Byron imitating Braham.]

[325] *Medwin*: I was present at Port Louis in the Mauritius when Theodore Hook sang an improvised Song—giving a Verse to every one present at the Governor's Table—and not even sparing his Uncle Farquhar, which offended him mortally. He soon after sent him home. His celebrated witticism on landing, on being asked the reason of his return is well known: "It was occasioned by there being something wrong in the *Chest*." [Byron knew Hook at Harrow and had seen a number of his early plays. He was recalled as accountant general of the Mauritius in 1817 because of a deficiency of £12,000 in his accounts—or, as he put it, "on account of a disorder in his chest."]

"The greatest genius in that way that perhaps Italy ever produced," said Shelley, "is Sgricci."

"There is a great deal of knack in these gentry," replied Lord Byron; "their poetry is more mechanical than you suppose. More verses are written yearly in Italy, than millions of money are circulated. It is usual for every Italian gentleman to make sonnets to his mistress's eyebrow before he is married,—or the lady must be very uninspiring indeed.

"But Sgricci! To extemporize a whole tragedy seems a miraculous gift."

"I heard him improvise a five-act play at Lucca," said Shelley, "on the subject of the '*Iphigenia in Tauris*,' and never was more interested. He put one of the finest speeches into the mouth of Iphigenia I ever heard. She compared her brother Orestes to the sole remaining pillar on which a temple hung tottering, in the act of ruin. The idea, it is true, is from Euripides, but he made it his own."

"I have never read his play since I was at school," replied Lord Byron. "I don't know how Sgricci's tragedies may appear in print, but his printed poetry is tame stuff.[326]

"The inspiration of the *improviser* is quite a separate talent: —a consciousness of his own powers, his own elocution—the wondering and applauding audience,—all conspire to give him confidence; but the deity forsakes him when he coldly sits down to think. Sgricci is not only a fine poet, but a fine actor. Mrs. Siddons," continued Lord Byron, "was the *beau idéal* of acting;[327] Miss O'Neill I would not go to see, for fear of weakening the impression made by the queen of tragedians.[328] When I read Lady Macbeth's part, I have Mrs. Siddons before me, and imagination even supplies her voice, whose tones were superhuman, and power over the heart supernatural.

"It is pleasant enough sometimes to take a peep behind, as well as to look before the scenes.

"I remember one leg of an elephant saying to another, 'D—n your eyes, move a little quicker!' and overhearing at the Opera two people in love, who were so *distraits* that they made the responses between the intervals of the recitative, instead of during the recitative itself. One said to the other, 'Do you love me?' then came the flourish of music, and the reply sweeter than the music, 'Can you doubt it?' "

----

[326] *Medwin*: Lord Byron alluded to his vers de societe. Several of Sgricci's Tragedies were taken down in Short hand and published at Paris. [Byron knew Tommaso Sgricci (1788-1836) at Ravenna in 1820 (*LJ*, iv, 413); the Shelleys met him on December 1, 1820, at Pisa, where they heard him in *Iphigenia in Tauris* on December 20, 1820, not Lucca, as Medwin reports. In Lucca on January 12, 1821, Mary alone heard him in *Inez de Castro*. See *The Letters of Mary W. Shelley*, ed. Frederick L. Jones (Norman, Okla., 1944), i, 117, note 4.]

[327] *Medwin*: A misprint of Colburn's. It was in the manuscript *an actress*. [See note 328, below.]

[328] *Byron in the Preface of Marino Faliero:* Miss O'Neill I never saw, having made and kept a determination to see nothing which should divide or disturb my recollections of Siddons. Siddons and Kemble were the *ideal* of tragic action. . . . [*Poetry*, IV, 338, note 1.]

"I have just been reading Lamb's Specimens," said he, "and am surprised to find in the extracts from the old dramatists so many ideas that I thought exclusively my own. Here is a passage, for instance, from 'The Duchess of Malfy,' astonishingly like one in 'Don Juan.'

" '*The leprosy of lust*' I discover, too, is not mine. '*Thou tremblest,*'—' '*Tis with age then,*' which I am accused of borrowing from Otway, was taken from the Old Bailey proceedings. Some judge observed to the witness, 'Thou tremblest;'—' 'Tis with cold then,' was the reply.[329]

[329] *Hobhouse*: Who does not know that this famous speech, which the Conversation-writer made his lord Byron say, was made in the OLD BAILEY—was uttered by "*Bailly*," the Mayor of Paris, on his way to the scaffold? That the real lord Byron should make so ludicrous a blunder is morally impossible. [*WR*, III, 30.]

Medwin: On this blunder of mine, which indeed is sufficiently ludicrous, Mr. Hobhouse, who is *better read in revolutions* than I am, is very facetious. Old Bailli it should be. [Bailly, first mayor of Paris, made the remark when waiting his turn at the Guillotine on November 12, 1793, a cold wet day.] But can stronger evidence of the Authenticity of these Conversations be adduced than this very blunder. For the anecdote is quoted in the Notes of *Marino Faliero* [*Poetry*, IV, 454, note 2, where Byron also defends himself against possible charges of plagiarism from Otway's *Venice Preserved*], and if I had [read them] . . . I should not have made it [the error]. The confusion of "*Vieux Bailli*" and the "Old Bailey" furnishes indisputable proof of the authenticity of the Conversations. [Last sentence from Medwin's *Shelley*, II, 217. Byron wrote in *Marino Fa-*

liero, V, iii, 8, "Thou tremblest, Faliero!" " 'Tis with age, then."]

J. W. Croker: Now this ridiculous blunder seems to us an additional proof of Mr. Medwin's veracity—nay, of his servile attempts at accuracy. No one can doubt that Lord Byron told the story, correctly, of Old Bailly, the celebrated mayor of Paris. . . . Let us pause for a moment on this instance, which, as one of the few that involves no personal discredit to Lord Byron, or pain to others, we may submit to Mr. Hobhouse's own judgment and candour. Does the case in any degree impugn Mr. Medwin's veracity?—Does Mr. Hobhouse doubt that the story is substantially true?—Is he not convinced that Lord Byron quoted the instance of M. Bailly?—Does the ridiculous error of Mr. Medwin in reporting the story alter either its substance or our belief that Lord Byron told it? Certainly not: why, then, we ask Mr. Hobhouse, should other errors, not more important, induce us to disbelieve other parts of Mr. Medwin's relation?

"These Specimens of Lamb's I never saw till to-day.[330] I am taxed with being a plagiarist,[331] when I am least conscious of being one; but I am not very scrupulous, I own, when I have a good idea, how I came into possession of it. How can we tell to what extent Shakspeare is indebted to his contemporaries, whose works are now lost? Besides which, Cibber adapted his plays to the stage.

"The invocation of the witches was, we know, a servile plagiarism from Middleton.[332] Authors were not so squeamish about borrowing from one another in those days. If it be a fault, I do not pretend to be immaculate. I will lend you some volumes of Shipwrecks, from which my storm in 'Don Juan' came."[333]

"Lend me also 'Casti's Novelle,' "[334] said I. "Did you never see in Italian,—

> 'Round her she makes an atmosphere of light;
> The very air seem'd lighter from her eyes'?"

[330] [Lamb's *Specimens of English Dramatic Poets contemporary with Shakespeare* appeared in 1808.]

[331] [Although Byron was repeatedly charged with plagiarism by reviewers who wished to show their learning, Alaric A. Watts between February 24 and May 5, 1821, had published a series of six articles on "Lord Byron's Plagiarisms" in *The Literary Gazette*, whose reviewer of Byron's *Marino Faliero* made the same charge on April 28, 1821.]

[332] [Medwin refers to *Macbeth*, IV, i. On the relation between Middleton's *The Witch* and Shakespeare's play, see Furness's edition of *Macbeth* (third ed., 1903), pp. 361-379. Gifford thought that Shakespeare was the debtor, and Charles Lamb also pointed out similarities between the plays.]

[333] [On Byron's freely and proudly confessed sources for the shipwreck scene of *Don Juan*, II, see Willis W. Pratt, *Byron's Don Juan: Notes on the Variorum Edition* (Austin, 1957), p. 58 and following.]

[334] *Medwin*: "I mean," said I one day, "to translate the *Novelle*." Byron seemed rather alarmed at the idea. "Casti," said he; "why you could not have a notion of such a thing. There are not ten Englishmen who have ever read the *Novelle*. They are a Sealed book to Women. The Italians think nothing of it."—"What do you think of it, Byron?"—"I sha'n't tell you," he replied laughing. In my *Life of Shelley* I have shown [pp. 335-336] what his obligations were to the *Diavolessa*. Without it, perhaps, *Don Juan* would never have been written. He first saw the *Novelle* at Brussels in 1816. *Vide New Monthly Magazine*. [The dialogue above appears, with omissions and unimportant variants, in Medwin's *Shelley Papers*, pp. 71-72, note. Medwin in his *Life of Shelley*, p. 335, refers to an anonymous article of 1816 in *The New Monthly*. It was Pryse Gordon who presented the *Novelle* to Byron in 1816 and, it seems, another copy to Polidori. See Gordon's *Personal Memoirs* (London, 1830), ii, 328, and Polidori's *Diary*, p. 70.]

"The Germans," said he, "and I believe Goethe himself, consider that I have taken great liberties with 'Faust.' All I know of that drama is from a sorry French translation,[335] from an occasional reading or two into English of parts of it by Monk Lewis when at Diodati, and from the Hartz mountain-scene, that Shelley versified the other day.[336] Nothing I envy him so much as to be able to read that astonishing production in the original. As to originality, Goethe has too much sense to pretend that he is not under obligations to authors, ancient and modern;—who is not? You tell me the plot is almost entirely Calderon's.[337] The fête, the scholar, the argument about the *Logos*, the selling himself to the fiend, and afterwards denying his power; his disguise of the plumed cavalier; the enchanted mirror,—are all from Cyprian. That *Magico Prodigioso* must be worth reading, and nobody seems to know any thing about it but you and Shelley. Then the vision is not unlike that of Marlowe's, in his 'Faustus.' The bed-scene is from 'Cymbeline;' the song or serenade, a translation of Ophelia's, in 'Hamlet;' and, more than all, the prologue is from Job, which is the first drama in the world, and perhaps the oldest poem.[338] I had an idea of writing a 'Job,' but I found it too sublime. There is no poetry to be compared with it."

I told him that Japhet's soliloquy in 'Heaven and Earth,' and address to the mountains of Caucasus, strongly resembled Faust's.[339]

"I shall have commentators enough by and by," said he, "to dissect my thoughts, and find owners for them."

"When I first saw the review of my 'Hours of Idleness,'* I was furious; in such a rage as I never have been in since.

* Written in 1808.

---

[335] [Butler, *Byron and Goethe*, p. 114, identifies the "sorry French translation" of *Faust* as that of Madame de Staël in *De l'Allemagne*, which Byron had read in 1813 (*LJ*, ii, 354, note).]

[336] *Byron to Murray*, October 12, 1817: I heard Mr. Lewis translate verbally some scenes of *Goethe's Faust* . . . last summer;—which is all I know of the history of that magical personage. . . .

[*LJ*, IV, 174 (M). Shelley's translations from *Faust*, made in the spring of 1822, were published in part in *The Liberal*.]

[337] *Shelley to John Gisborne*, April 10, 1822: Have you read Calderon's *Magico Prodigioso*? I find a striking similarity between Faust and this drama. . . . *Cypriano* evidently furnished the *germ* of Faust. . . . [*Letters*, II, 407. Shelley translated portions of the Spanish play in March, 1822. Medwin stated in his *Shelley*, p. 382, that "what Byron said" on the subject of the similarities between Goethe and Calderon "was derived from" Shelley. There seems to be no evidence that Byron had read Calderon.]

[338] *Goethe to Eckermann*: I have for the most part not even read all those fine things Lord Byron mentions; still less were they in my thoughts when I was writing *Faust*. But Lord Byron is only great when he is writing poetry; as soon as he reflects, he is a child. . . . My Mephistopheles sings a song from Shakespeare, and why not? Why should I trouble to invent one of my own, when Shakespeare's was so apt and said exactly what I wanted? If therefore the exposition of my *Faust* has some similarity with *Job*, that's quite right too, and I should be praised rather than blamed for it. [Quoted by Butler, pp. 115, 117. It may be noted that Medwin attributes to Byron a much greater familiarity with *Faust* than the other evidence suggests. See Butler, p. 116, for Goethe's actual knowledge (great) of the works referred to.]

[339] *Medwin*: I alluded to when Faust comes out of the Cavern [Faust's opening speech in the "Forest and Cavern" scene].

> Spirit of spirits, all I possess is thine.
> All—all I ask—thou grantest. Nor in vain
> On me thy countenance in fire has beamed.
> To me this glorious universe of things
> Thou gavest as a kingdom, nor with it
> A lifeless admiration, but the power
> And faculty to feel and to enjoy
> Nature and dwell upon her mysteries,
> And look into her deep bosom as we read
> The bosom of a friend.
>
> —*Author's Translation.*

[Japhet's soliloquy opens the third scene of *Heaven and Earth*. See E. H. Coleridge's note (*Poetry*, V, 294) on this passage and *Faust*.]

"I dined that day with Scrope Davies, and drank three bottles of claret to drown it; but it only boiled the more.[340] That critique was a masterpiece of low wit, a tissue of scurrilous abuse. I remember there was a great deal of vulgar trash in it which was meant for humour, 'about people being thankful for what they could get,'—'not looking a gift horse in the mouth,' and such stable expressions.[341] The severity of 'The Quarterly' killed poor Keats, and neglect, Kirke White;[342] but I was made of different stuff, of tougher materials. So far from their bullying me, or deterring me from writing, I was bent on falsifying their raven predictions, and determined to shew them, croak as they would, that it was not the last time they should hear from me. I set to work immediately, and in good earnest, and produced in a year 'The English Bards and Scotch Reviewers.'[343] For the first four days after it was announced, I was very nervous about its fate. Generally speaking, the first fortnight decides the public opinion of a new book. This made a prodigious sensation, more perhaps than any of my works, except 'The Corsair.'

"In less than a year and a half it passed through four editions, and rather large ones. To some of them, contrary to the advice of my friends, I affixed my name. The thing was known to be mine, and I could not have escaped any enemies in not owning it; besides, it was more manly not to deny it. There were many things in that satire which I was afterwards sorry for, and I wished to cancel it. If Galignani chose to reprint it, it was no fault of mine.[344] I did my utmost to suppress the publication, not only in England, but in Ireland.[345] I will tell you my principal reason for doing so: I had good grounds to believe that Jeffrey (though perhaps really responsible for whatever appears in 'The Edinburgh,' as Gifford is for 'The Quarterly,' as its editor) was not the author of that article,—was not guilty of it.[346] He disowned it; and though he would not give up the aggressor, he said he would convince me, if I ever came to Scotland, who the person was. I have every reason to believe it was a certain other lawyer, who hated me for something I once said of Mrs. ———.[347] The technical language about 'minority pleas,' 'plaintiffs,' 'grounds of action,' &c. a jargon only intelligible to a lawyer, leaves no doubt in my mind on the subject.[348] I bear no animosity to him now, though independently of this lampoon, which does him no credit, he gave me cause enough of offence.[349]

[340] *Byron in his journal*, November 22, 1813: I remember the effect of the *first Edinburgh Review* on me. I heard of it six weeks before,—read it the day of its denunciation,—dined and drank three bottles of claret, (with S. B. Davies, I think,) neither ate nor slept the less, but, nevertheless, was not easy till I had vented my wrath and my rhyme, in the same pages, against everything and everybody. [*LJ*, ii, 330 (M).]

[341] *Brougham in The Edinburgh Review*: Let us take what we get and be thankful . . . nor look the gift horse in the mouth. [xi (January, 1808), 289.]

[342] [See Byron's "Who killed John Keats?" in *Poetry*, vii, 76 and note 1. Keats was also attacked in *Blackwood's*, August, 1818. Henry Kirke White, the son of a Nottingham butcher, died in 1806, supposedly as a result of excessive study at Cambridge for holy orders. His *Clifton Grove* (1803) was violently attacked in the *Monthly Review*, February, 1804.]

[343] [Byron's "in a year" is misleading. Although Brougham's review appeared in January, 1808, and *English Bards* in March, 1809, it will be remembered that the poem is a recast and enlarged version of *British Bards*, 380 lines of which had been completed in October, 1807. Thus the review provided only partial provocation for the poem.]

[344] [Galignani reprinted *English Bards* in 1818.]

[345] *Medwin*: On his return to England a fifth Edition was prepared for the press by himself with considerable care but supprest and, except one copy, destroyed on the eve of Publication. [There are two known copies extant.]

[346] *Jeffrey to Byron*, May 12, 1812: It will give me great pleasure to have the honor of being made known to your Lordship—and perhaps I may at some future time disclose some particulars in our

Reviewing history which may convince you that your resentment has hitherto been misdirected. [Marchand, p. 346.]

[347] *Byron to Augusta Leigh,* May 10, 1817: She is surrounded by people who detest me—Brougham the lawyer—who never forgave me for saying that Mrs. G^e Lamb was a damned fool (by the way I did not then know he was in love with her) in 1814, & for a former savage note [to l. 524] in my foolish satire. . . . [*Astarte,* p. 284.]

[348] [All the legal concepts named in the text appear in Brougham's review, although not in a form to suggest that Medwin had it before him when writing.]

[349] *J. W. Croker*: In this statement [*i.e.*, the greater part of the paragraph] Lord Byron's object was to clear himself from the inconsistency of having bespattered and bepraised the Edinburgh reviewers, and of having libelled and then formed an intimacy with the conductor of that publication; and for this trifling purpose he does not hesitate to impart to Mr. Medwin some alleged conduct of Mr. Jeffrey. . . . Whoever wrote the article, the editor [Jeffrey] must have approved it. The whole story is then, we fear not to pronounce, false; but is it the invention of Mr. Medwin? We think not; for it is a mere introduction to a tirade against Mr. Brougham, with whom as an adverse counsel, Lord Byron was displeased. It is highly improbable that he could have known, except from Lord Byron, how much his Lordship resented Mr. Brougham's professional zeal on that occasion; and the terms in which his feelings towards that gentleman are expressed, are such as Mr. Medwin could never have dreamt of.

"The occasion was this:—In my separation-cause, that went before the Chancellor as a matter of form,[350] when the proceedings came on, he took upon himself to apply some expressions, or make some allusions to me, which must have been of a most unwarrantable nature, as my friends consulted whether they should acquaint me with the purport of them.[351] What they precisely were I never knew, or should certainly have made him retract them. I met him afterwards at Coppet, but was not at that time acquainted with this circumstance. He took on himself the advocate also, in writing to Madame de Staël, and advising her not to meddle in the quarrel between Lady Byron and myself. This was not kind; it was a gratuitous and unfeed act of hostility.[352] But there was another reason that influenced me even more than my cooled resentment against Jeffrey, to suppress 'English Bards and Scotch Reviewers.' In the duel-scene I had unconsciously made part of the ridicule fall on Moore. The fact was, that there was no imputation on the courage of either of the principals. One of the balls fell out in the carriage, and was lost; and the seconds, not having a further supply, drew the remaining one.[353]

"Shortly after this publication I went abroad: and Moore was so offended by the mention of the leadless pistols, that he addressed a letter to me in the nature of a challenge, delivering it to the care of Mr. Hanson,[354] but without acquainting him with the contents. This letter was mislaid,—at least never forwarded to me.

[350] *Lady Byron*: What?—not the Separation.

[351] [Byron knew that Brougham had gossiped maliciously about him in 1816. See Hobhouse, *Recollections*, I, 337.]

[352] [For a particularly malicious letter that Brougham wrote from Geneva in 1816, see Mrs. Moore, pp. 126-127.]

[353] [On the Moore-Jeffrey duel, see Marchand, pp. 299-300, notes 7 and 8, and *Letters of Thomas Moore*, pp. 104-105 and notes.]

[354] *Medwin*: Hodgson. Byron mouthed his words so much that the mistake is most easy [to] account for. [Moore sent the challenge, appropriately, in care of James Cawthorn, publisher of *English Bards*, who forwarded it to Hodgson. Hodgson, suspecting a challenge, took care to preserve the seal unbroken, and so it remained as late as October 29, 1811, when Byron offered to open the letter in Moore's presence.]

"But on my return to England in 1812,[355] an enquiry was made by Moore if I had received such a letter? adding, that particular circumstances (meaning his marriage, or perhaps the suppression of the satire) had now altered his situation, and that he wished to recall the letter, and to be known to me through Rogers.[356] I was shy of this mode of arranging matters, one hand presenting a pistol, and another held out to shake; and felt awkward at the loss of a letter of such a nature, and the imputation it might have given rise to. But when, after a considerable search, it was at length found, I returned it to Moore with the seal unbroken; and we have since been the best friends in the world. I correspond with no one so regularly as with Moore.

"It is remarkable that I should at this moment number among my most intimate friends and correspondents those whom I most made the subjects of satire in 'English Bards.' I never retracted my opinions of their works,—I never sought their acquaintance;[357] but there are men who can forgive and forget. The Laureate is not one of that disposition, and exults over the anticipated death-bed repentance of the objects of his hatred. Finding that his denunciations or panegyrics are of little or no avail here, he indulges himself in a pleasant *vision* as to what will be their fate hereafter. The third Heaven is hardly good enough for a king, and Dante's worst birth in the 'Inferno' hardly bad enough for me. My kindness to his brother-in-law might have taught him to be more charitable. I said in a Note to 'The Two Foscari,' in answer to his vain boasting, that I had done more real good in one year than Mr. Southey in the whole course of his shifting and turn-coat existence,[358] on which he seems to reflect with so much complacency. I did not mean to pride myself on the act to which I have just referred, and should not mention it to you, but that his self-sufficiency calls for the explanation. When Coleridge was in great distress, I borrowed 100*l.* to give him."[359]

Some days after this discussion appeared Mr. Southey's reply to the Note in question. I happened to see 'The Literary Gazette' at Mr. Edgeworth's,[360] and mentioned the general purport of the letter to Lord Byron during our evening ride.

[355] [*I.e.*, 1811.]

[356] *Moore in his Life of Byron*: During the interval of a year and a half which elapsed before Lord Byron's return, I had taken upon myself obligations, both as husband and father, which make most men . . . less willing to expose themselves unnecessarily to danger. [Pp. 142-143 (M). Moore then wrote to Byron, "The time which has elapsed . . . has, in many respects, materially altered my situation" and closed by saying, "it would give me sincere pleasure, if, by any satisfactory explanation, he would enable me to seek the honour of being henceforth ranked among his acquaintance." The famous meeting took place at the home of Rogers, November 4, 1811.]

Moore to James Power, October, 1824: If Captain Medwin is as inaccurate about more important things as he is about the circumstances of my first acquaintance with Lord Byron he will have a good deal to answer in various quarters. [*Notes from the Letters of Thomas Moore to His Music Publisher, James Power* (New York, n. d.), p. 115. Medwin's account is substantially correct. See Marchand, pp. 299-301, 303-304, and *Letters of Thomas Moore*, pp. 165-167 and notes.]

[357] *Medwin*: He alludes [among others] to Lord Holland—for whose introduction to him see Dallas [p. 201]. "Lord Holland's age, experience, and other acquired distinctions, certainly, in point of form, demanded that the visit should have been paid at his house. This I am confident Lord Byron at that time would not have done. . . ." [Lord Holland called at Byron's lodgings in St. James's Street.]

[358] *Byron in the Appendix to The Two Foscari*: I, "in my degree," have done more real good in any one given year, since I was twenty, than Mr. Southey in the whole course of his shifting and turncoat existence. [*LJ*, vi, 389.]

[359] *Byron to Murray*, September 11, 1822: I immediately sent him [Coleridge] one hundred pounds. . . . [*LJ*, vi, 113 (M).]

[360] [A brother of Maria Edgeworth. Southey's attack appeared originally in the *Courier*, dated January 5, 1822. Byron saw it a month later.]

His anxiety to get a sight of it was so great, that he wrote me two notes in the course of the evening, entreating me to procure the paper. I at length succeeded, and took it to the Lanfranchi palace at eleven o'clock, (after coming from the opera,) an hour at which I was frequently in the habit of calling on him.

He had left the Guiccioli earlier than usual, and I found him waiting with some impatience. I never shall forget his countenance as he glanced rapidly over the contents. He looked perfectly awful: his colour changed almost prismatically; his lips were as pale as death. He said not a word. He read it a second time, and with more attention than his rage at first permitted, commenting on some of the passages as he went on. When he had finished, he threw down the paper, and asked me if I thought there was any thing of a personal nature in the reply that demanded satisfaction; as, if there was, he would instantly set off for England and call Southey to an account,—muttering something about whips, and branding-irons, and gibbets, and wounding the heart of a woman,—words of Mr. Southey's. I said that, as to personality, his own expressions of "cowardly ferocity," "pitiful renegado," "hireling," were much stronger than any in the letter before me.[361] He paused a moment, and said:

"Perhaps you are right; but I will consider of it. You have not seen *my* 'Vision of Judgment.' I wish I had a copy to shew you; but the only one I have is in London. I had almost decided not to publish it; but it shall now go forth to the world. I will write to Douglas Kinnaird by to-morrow's post, to-night, not to delay its appearance. The question is, whom to get to print it. Murray will have nothing to say to it just now, while the prosecution of 'Cain' hangs over his head. It was offered to Longman; but he declined it on the plea of its injuring the sale of Southey's Hexameters, of which he is the publisher. Hunt shall have it."[362]

Another time he said: "I am glad Mr. Southey owns that

article on 'Foliage,' which excited my choler so much. But who else could have been the author? Who but Southey would have had the baseness, under the pretext of reviewing the work of one man, insidiously to make it a nest-egg for hatching malicious calumnies against others?

"It was bad taste, to say the least of it, in Shelley to write Aθεος after his name at Mont Anvert. I knew little of him at that time, but it happened to meet my eye, and I put my pen through the word, and Μωρος too, that had been added by some one else by way of comment—and a very proper comment too, and the only one that should have been made on it. There it should have stopped. It would have been more creditable to Mr. Southey's heart and feelings if he had been of this opinion; he would then never have made the use of his travels he did, nor have raked out of an album the silly joke of a boy, in order to make it matter of serious accusation against him at home. I might well say he had impudence enough, if he could confess such infamy. I say nothing of the critique itself on 'Foliage;'[363] with the exception of a few sonnets, it was unworthy of Hunt. But what was the object of that article? I repeat, to vilify and scatter his dark and devilish insinuations against me and others. Shame on the man who could wound an already bleeding heart,—be barbarous enough to revive the memory of a fatal event that Shelley was perfectly innocent of,—and found scandal on falsehood! Shelley taxed him with writing that article some years ago;[364] and he had the audacity to admit that he had treasured up some opinions of Shelley's, ten years before, when he was on a visit at Keswick, and had made a note of them at the time.[365] But his bag of venom was not full; it is the nature of the reptile. Why does a viper have a poison-tooth, or the scorpion claws?"[366]

---

[361] [Medwin has quoted correctly from both Southey's letter to the *Courier* (the phrases which Byron muttered) and from Byron's appendix to *The Two Foscari*. See *LJ*, vi, 388-389, 391-392.]

[362] [Byron wrote on February 6, 1822, to Kinnaird, directing him to find a publisher for *The Vision of Judgment* and stating that he would come to England to fight Southey. *The Vision* was first published by John Hunt in *The Liberal*.]

[363] *Southey in the Courier*, December 8, 1824: That his lordship spoke to this effect, and in this temper, I have no doubt. . . . I take these Conversations to be authentic. . . . Now, then, to the point. . . . *The reviewal in question I did not write.* [*LJ*, VI, 395-396. The *Quarterly Review* article on Hunt's *Foliage* was in fact written by the same John Taylor Coleridge who attacked Shelley's *Revolt of Islam* in the *Quarterly* for April, 1819, supposed for a time by Shelley to have been written also by Southey. Byron thus had good reason for supposing the reviewer of *Foliage* to be Southey. J. T. Coleridge had even referred to Shelley's writing of the word *atheos* after his name in an inn register (Newman I. White, *Shelley*, New York, 1940, II, 27), an inscription which Southey copied into a note book and talked about in England. Byron omitted to say that Shelley also wrote the words *democrat* and *great lover of mankind*. See White, *Shelley*, I, 456 and 714, note 48; and for a full account, Garvin de Beer, "An 'Atheist' in the Alps," *Keats-Shelley Memorial Bulletin*, IX (1958), 1-15.]

[364] *Southey in the Courier*, December 8, 1824: It is not true that Shelley ever inquired of me whether I was the author of that paper. . . . But in this part of Lord Byron's statement there may be some mistake, mingled with a great deal of malignant falsehood. Mr. Shelley addressed a letter to me from Pisa [on June 26, 1820], asking if I were the author of a criticism in the Quarterly Review, upon his Revolt of Islam, not exactly, in Lord Byron's phrase, *taxing* me with it. . . . I . . . assured him that I had not written the paper. . . . [*LJ*, VI, 396.]

[365] *Southey in the Courier*, December 8, 1824: What truth is mixed up with the slander of this statement, I shall immediately explain. . . . Mr. Shelley, having, in the letter alluded to [that of June 26, 1820], thought proper to make some remarks upon my opinions, I took occasion, in reply, to comment upon his, and to ask him . . . whether he had found them conducive to his own happiness, and the happiness of those with whom he had been most nearly connected? This produced a second letter [on August 17, 1820] from him, written in a tone, partly of justification, partly of attack. I replied to this also, not by any such absurd admission as Lord Byron has stated, but by recapitulating to him, as a practical

illustration of his principles, the leading circumstances of his own life, from the commencement of his career at University College. The earliest facts I stated upon his own authority, as I had heard them from his own lips [in 1811-1812, at Keswick]; the latter were of public notoriety. [*LJ*, vi, 397.]

[366] *Medwin*: It seems to be a mystery what Byron's cause of animosity against Southey could have been except from jealousy—in that he took up Shelley's wrongs against the Quarterly. There must have been some deeper cause than appears on the surface, and the fault must have been with Southey himself. . . . There was a stinging and acrid venom in the Assailants. [Medwin's note is of interest because it reveals that neither Byron nor Shelley ever told him that Southey was spreading stories in England about a "League of Incest" and "promiscuous intercourse" in 1816 involving Byron, Claire, Shelley, and Mary.]

Some days after these remarks, on calling on him one morning, he produced 'The Deformed Transformed.' Handing it to Shelley, as he was in the habit of doing his daily compositions, he said:

"Shelley, I have been writing a *Faustish* kind of drama: tell me what you think of it."

After reading it attentively, Shelley returned it.

"Well," said Lord Byron, "how do you like it?"

"Least," replied he, "of any thing I ever saw of yours. It is a bad imitation of 'Faust;' and besides, there are two entire lines of Southey's in it."

Lord Byron changed colour immediately, and asked hastily what lines? Shelley repeated,

> 'And water shall see thee,
> And fear thee, and flee thee.'

"They are in 'The Curse of Kehama.' "[367]

His Lordship, without making a single observation, instantly threw the poem into the fire.[368] He seemed to feel no chagrin at seeing it consume—at least his countenance betrayed none, and his conversation became more gay and lively than usual. Whether it was hatred of Southey, or respect for Shelley's opinions, which made him commit an act that I considered a sort of suicide, was always doubtful to me. I was never more surprised than to see, two years afterwards, 'The Deformed Transformed' announced, (supposing it to have perished at Pisa); but it seems that he must have had another copy of the manuscript, or had re-written it perhaps, without changing a word, except omitting the 'Kehama' lines. His memory was remarkably retentive of his own writings. I believe he could have quoted almost every line he ever wrote.

One day a correspondent of Lord Byron's sent him from Paris the following lines[369]—a sort of epitaph for Southey— which he gave me leave to copy.

> Beneath these poppies buried deep,
>   The bones of Bob the Bard lie hid;
> Peace to his manes! may he sleep
>   As soundly as his readers did!
>
> Through every sort of verse meandering,
>   Bob went without a hitch or fall,
> Through Epic, Sapphic, Alexandrine,
>   To verse that was no verse at all;
>
> Till Fiction having done enough
>   To make a bard at least absurd,
> And give his readers *quantum suff.*,
>   He took to praising George the Third:
>
> And now in virtue of his crown,
>   Dooms us, poor Whigs, at once to slaughter;
> Like Donellan of bad renown,
>   Poisoning us all with laurel water.
>
> And yet at times some awkward qualms he
>   Felt about leaving honour's track;
> And though he has got a butt of Malmsey,
>   It may not save him from a sack.

Death, weary of so dull a writer,
    Put to his works a *finis* thus.
O! may the earth on him lie lighter
    Than did his quartos upon us!

" 'Heaven and Earth' was commenced," said he, "at Ravenna, on the 9th October last. It occupied about fourteen days. Douglas Kinnaird tells me that he can get no bookseller to publish it. It was offered to Murray; but he is the most timid of God's booksellers, and starts at the title. He has taken a dislike to that three-syllabled word *Mystery*, and says, I know not why, that it is another 'Cain.' I suppose he does not like my making one of Cain's daughters talk the same language as her father's father, and has a prejudice against the family.

---

[367] [Cf. Eve's speech in Byron's *Cain*, III, i, 419-443, with the following lines from Southey's *Curse of Kehama*, Canto II:

    And Water shall hear me,
        And know thee and fly thee;
    And the Winds shall not touch thee
        When they pass by thee . . .
    And thou shalt seek Death
        To release thee in vain.

The Deformed Transformed is not indebted to *The Curse of Kehama*.]

[368] *Trelawny to Murray*, January 15, 1833: This is a plumper—I was in the room—*half a sheet* of M.S. of The Deformed Transformed was given Shelley to read—which had been written in the night—& that half which was distroyed [*sic*]—other parts which Shelley had seen before he admired—& he said the lyrical incantation beginning "from the red earth like Adam" &c &c [I, i, 385] incomperable [*sic*]. [Unpublished; in the collection of Sir John Murray.]

[369] *Medwin*: The lines are by Moore. All the Editions of this Work were Marred with Errata of the Press. There are two in the first two [*sic*] lines—*did* for *hid* and *peace to his manes and may he sleep* for *peace to his manes, may he sleep*. Mr. Colburn thought *manes* had only one syllable. The printing of books in England is

particularly disagreeable. In Germany no man can be a publisher without passing a strict classical examination. It would be well if such a law existed with us.

I could not make her so unnatural as to speak ill of her grandfather. I was forced to make her aristocratical, proud of her descent from the eldest born. Murray says, that whoever prints it will have it pirated, as 'Cain' has been,—that a Court of justice will not sanction it as literary property.[370] On what plea? There is nothing objectionable in it, that I am aware of. You have read it; what do you think? If 'Cain' be immoral (which I deny), will not the Chancellor's refusal to protect, and the cheapness of a piratical edition, give it a wider circulation among the lower classes? Will they not buy and read it for the very reason that it is considered improper, and try to discover an evil tendency where it was least meant? May not impiety be extracted by garbling the Bible? I defy the common people to understand such mysteries as the loves of the Angels,—at least they are mysteries to me. Moore, too, is writing on the same text.[371] Any thing that he writes must succeed."

I told him that the laughter of the fiends in the Cave of Caucasus reminded me of the snoring of the Furies in the 'Eumenides' of Æschylus.[372]

"I have never read any of his plays since I left Harrow," said Lord Byron. "Shelley, when I was in Switzerland, translated the 'Prometheus' to me[373] before I wrote my ode; but I never open a Greek book. Shelley tells me that the choruses in 'Heaven and Earth' are deficient. He thinks that lyrical poetry should be metrically regular. Surely this is not the case with the Greek choruses that he makes such a fuss about.[374] However, Hunt will be glad of it for his new periodical work. I talked of writing a second part to it; but it was only as Coleridge promised a second part to 'Christabel.' I will tell you how I had an idea of finishing it:

"Let me see—where did I leave off? Oh, with Azazael [sic] and Samiasa refusing to obey the summons of Michael [sic], and throwing off their allegiance to Heaven. They rise into the air with the two sisters, and leave this globe to a fate which, according to Cuvier, it has often undergone, and will undergo again. The appearance of the land strangled by the ocean will serve by way of scenery and decorations. The affectionate tenderness of Adah [sic] for those from whom she is parted, and for ever, and her fears contrasting with the loftier spirit of Aholibamah triumphing in the hopes of a new and greater destiny, will make the dialogue. They in the mean time continue their aërial voyage, every where denied admittance in those floating islands on the sea of space, and driven back by guardian-spirits of the different planets, till they are at length forced to alight on the only peak of the earth uncovered by water. Here a parting takes place between the lovers, which I shall make affecting enough. The fallen Angels are suddenly called, and condemned,—their destination and punishment unknown. The sisters still cling to the rock, the waters mounting higher and higher. Now enter Ark. The scene draws up, and discovers Japhet endeavouring to persuade the Patriarch, with very strong arguments of love and pity, to receive the sisters, or at least Adah, on board. Adah joins in his entreaties, and endeavours to cling to the sides of the vessel. The proud and haughty Aholibamah scorns to pray either to God or man, and anticipates the grave by plunging into the waters. Noah is still inexorable. The surviving daughter of Cain is momentarily in danger of perishing before the eyes of the Arkites. Japhet is in despair. The last wave sweeps her from the rock, and her lifeless corpse floats past in all its beauty, whilst a sea-bird screams over it, and seems to be the spirit of her angel lord. I once thought of conveying the lovers to the moon, or one of the planets; but it is not easy for the imagination to make any unknown world more beautiful than this; besides, I did not think they would approve of the moon as a residence.

I remember what Fontenelle said of its having no atmosphere, and the dark spots being caverns where the inhabitants reside. There was another objection: all the human interest would have been destroyed, which I have even endeavoured to give my Angels. It was a very Irish kind of compliment Jeffrey paid to Moore's 'Lalla Rookh,' when he said the loves were those of Angels; meaning that they were like nothing on earth. What will he say of 'The Loves of the Angels?'—that they are like (for he has nothing left) nothing in Heaven?"

"I wrote 'The Prophecy of Dante' at the suggestion of the Countess. I was at that time paying my court to the Guiccioli, and addressed the dedicatory sonnet to her. She had heard of my having written something about Tasso, and thought Dante's exile and death would furnish as fine a subject. I can never write but on the spot. Before I began 'The Lament,' I went to Ferrara, to visit the Dungeon. Hoppner was with me, and part of it, the greater part, was composed (as 'The Prisoner of Chillon') in the prison.[375] The place of Dante's fifteen years' exile, where he so pathetically prayed for his country, and deprecated the thought of being buried out of it; and the sight of his tomb, which I passed in my almost daily rides,—inspired me. Besides, there was somewhat of resemblance* in our destinies—he had a wife, and I have the same feelings about leaving my bones in a strange land.

> * "The day may come she would be proud to have
> The dust she doom'd to strangers, and transfer
> Of him whom she denied a home—the grave."
> *Prophecy of Dante.*
>
> "Where now my boys are, and that fatal she"
> *Ibid.*
> "They made an exile, not a slave of me." *Ibid.*

[370] *Byron to Moore,* February 28, 1822: I hear that *Cain* has been pirated, and that the Chancellor has refused to give Murray any redress. [*LJ*, vi, 27 (M).]

[371] [Moore's *Loves of the Angels* was published in December, 1822.]

[372] [On the laughter of the fiends, see *Heaven and Earth*, I, iii, 57 and note 1 (*Poetry*, v, 296).]

[373] [The *Prometheus* of Aeschylus is listed among Shelley's reading for 1816.]

[374] *Medwin*: Byron was wrong. The Greek Choruses are in regular metre, the strophe and antistrophe corresponding.

[375] *Medwin*: This seems to be a fiction or a mystification. [Medwin's note refers, presumably, to Byron's statement that the greater part of *The Lament of Tasso* was composed in the prison. Byron told Millingen that it was composed in two nights (*HVSV*, p. 467). The manuscript is dated April 20, 1817; Byron's original plan was to leave Venice on April 17. I find no evidence that Byron knew Hoppner at this time; he stated on March 25 that he did not have "the slightest acquaintance" with him (*LJ*, IV, 83-84).]

⌣

"I had, however, a much more extensive view in writing that poem than to describe either his banishment or his grave. Poets are sometimes shrewd in their conjectures. You quoted to me the other day a line in 'Childe Harold,' in which I made a prediction about the Greeks*: in this instance I was not so fortunate as to be prophetic. This poem was intended for the Italians and the Guiccioli, and therefore I wished to have it translated. I had objected to the *Versi sciolti* having been used in my Fourth Canto of 'Childe Harold;' but this was the very metre they adopted in defiance of my remonstrance, and in the very teeth of it;[376] and yet I believe the Italians liked the work. It was looked at in a political light, and they indulged in my dream of liberty, and the resurrection of Italy. Alas! it was only a dream!

"*Terza Rima* does not seem to suit the genius of English poetry—it is certainly uncalculated for a work of any length in our language, however, it may do for a short ode. The public at least thought my attempt a failure, and the public is in the main right. I never persecute the public. I always bow

* "Will Gaul or Muscovite redress ye? No!"
   Childe Harold, Canto II. Stanza 75.

{ *159* }

to its verdict, which is generally just. But if I had wanted a sufficient reason for my giving up the Prophecy—the Prophecy failed me.

"It was the turn political affairs took that made me relinquish the work.[377] At one time the flame was expected to break out over all Italy, but it only ended in smoke, and my poem went out with it. I don't wonder at the enthusiasm of the Italians about Dante. He is the poet of liberty. Persecution, exile, the dread of a foreign grave, could not shake his principles. There is no Italian gentleman, scarcely any well-educated girl, that has not all the finer passages of Dante at the fingers' ends,—particularly the Ravennese. The Guiccioli, for instance, could almost repeat any part of the 'Divine Comedy;' and, I dare say, is well read in the 'Vita Nuova,' that prayer-book of love.

[376] *Byron in the Preface to* The Prophecy of Dante: I have had the fortune to see the fourth canto of *Childe Harold* translated into Italian *versi sciolti*,—that is, a poem written in the *Spenserean stanza* into *blank verse*, without regard to the natural divisions of the stanza or the sense. If the present poem . . . should chance to undergo the same fate, I would request the Italian reader to remember that . . . I have failed in imitating that which all study and few understand. . . . [*Poetry*, iv, 244.]

[377] *Byron to Richard B. Hoppner*, May 31, 1821: What you say of the *Dante* is the first I have heard of it. . . . Continue it!—Alas! what could Dante himself *now* prophesy about Italy? [*LJ*, v, 302 (M). The Italian revolutionary movement had collapsed in 1821.]

"Shelley always says that reading Dante is unfavourable to writing, from its superiority to all possible compositions.[378] Whether he be the first or not, he is certainly the most untranslatable of all poets. You may give the meaning; but the charm, the simplicity—the classical simplicity,—is lost. You might as well clothe a statue, as attempt to translate Dante. He is better, as an Italian said, '*nudo che vestito.*'

"There's Taaffe is not satisfied with what Cary has done, but he most be *traducing* him too.[379] What think you of that fine line in the 'Inferno' being rendered, as Taaffe has done it?

'I Mantuan, capering, squalid, squalling.'

There's alliteration and inversion enough, surely! I have advised him to frontispiece his book with his own head, *Capo di Traditore*, 'the head of a *traitor;*' then will come the title-page comment—Hell!"

I asked Lord Byron the meaning of a passage in 'The Prophecy of Dante.' He laughed and said:

"I suppose I had some meaning when I wrote it: I believe I understood it then."*

> * "If *you* insist on grammar, though
> I never think about it in a heat—"
>
> *Don Juan*, Canto VII. Stanza 42.
>
> "I don't pretend that I quite understand
> My own meaning when I would be very fine."
>
> *Don Juan*, Canto IV. Stanza 5.

---

[378] *Medwin*: In a memr. Book from which I compiled my Life of Shelley . . . I find a Dialogue between Shelley and Lord Byron which may here find a place.

Byron. "You say that reading Dante has a hindering effect on your poetical powers—that it draws away your Oestrum. You call it a great poem—a great poem indeed. That should have a uniformity of design, a combination of parts all lending to a great whole, all contributing to the development. The action should go on increasing in beauty and power. Has the *Divine Comedy* any of these characters? Who can read with patience 14,000 lines made up of prayers, dialogues, and questions without sticking in the [thousand turns and winding of the inextricable labyrinths of his three-times-nine circles?] But what is the *Divine Comedy*? It is a scientific treatise of some theological student, one moment treating of angels and the next of demons, far the most interesting personages in his Drama—shewing that he had a better concept of Hell than Heaven. It is true, it might have pleased his contemporaries and been sung about the streets, as were the poems of Homer; but at the present day, either human nature is much changed or the poem is so obscure, tiresome, and insupportable that no one can read it for half an hour without yawning and going to sleep over it like Malagigi; and the hundred times I have made the attempt to read it, I have lost." [Most of this appears in Medwin's *Life of Shelley*, pp. 376-377, in a slightly more polished form and with some of the sentences in a different order. Byron's first sentence is new, as is Medwin's introductory sentence. The words within brackets have been taken from the printed text to piece out Medwin's holograph note, which omitted them.]

[379] [Taaffe planned an eight-volume commentary on Dante, with Byron's help secured Murray as publisher for the first volume, the only one to appear, and it did not contain Taaffe's translation.]

"That," said I, "is what the disciples of Swedenborg say.[380] There are many people who do not understand passages in your writings, among our own countrymen: I wonder how foreigners contrive to translate them."

"And yet," said he, "they have been translated into all the civilized, and many uncivilized tongues. Several of them have appeared in Danish, Polish, and even Russian dresses.[381] These last, being translations of translations from the French, must be very diluted. The greatest compliment ever paid me has been shewn in Germany, where a translation of the Fourth Canto of 'Childe Harold' has been made the subject of a University prize.[382] But as to obscurity, is not Milton obscure? How do you explain

—— 'Smoothing the raven down
Of darkness till it smiled!'

Is it not a simile taken from the electricity of a cat's back? I'll leave you to be my commentator, and hope you will make better work with me than Taaffe is doing with Dante, who perhaps could not himself explain half that volumes are written about, if his ghost were to rise again from the dead. I am sure I wonder he and Shakspeare have not been raised by their commentators long ago!"

[380] *Medwin*: A great Swedenborgist of my acquaintance, of whom I asked the meaning of a passage in his works, said, "I un-

derstood it the last time I read it and perhaps will another time, but now I cannot explain it." This made Lord Byron laugh.

[381] [*Manfred* was translated into Danish by P. F. Wulff in 1820; *The Siege of Corinth* and *The Corsair* were translated into Polish by Bruno hr Kicinski in the same year; and in 1821 appeared a Russian translation of selected poems, edited by M. Kachenovsky.]

[382] *Byron to Murray*, May 26, 1822: At Leipsic, this year, the highest prize was proposed for a translation of two Cantos of *Childe Harold*. [*LJ*, VI, 74 (M).]

"PEOPLE are always advising me," said he, "to write an epic. They tell me that I shall leave no great poem behind me;—that is, I suppose they mean by great, a heavy poem, or a weighty poem; I believe they are synonymous. They say that 'Childe Harold' is unequal; that the last two Cantos are far superior to the two first. I know it is a thing without form or substance,—a *voyage pittoresque*. But who reads Milton? My opinion as to the inequality of my poems is this,—that one is not better or worse than another. And as to epics, have you not got enough of Southey's? There's 'Joan d'Arc,' 'The Curse of Kehama,' and God knows how many more curses, down to 'The Last (of the Goths!') If you must have an epic, there's 'Don Juan' for you.[383] I call that an epic: it is an epic as much in the spirit of our day as the Iliad was in Homer's. Love, religion, and politics form the argument, and are as much the cause of quarrels now as they were then. There is no want of Parises and Menelauses, and of *Crim.-cons.* into the bargain. In the very first Canto you have a Helen. Then, I shall make my hero a modern Achilles for fighting,—a man who can snuff a candle three successive times with a pistol-ball: and, depend upon it, my moral will be a good one; not even a Dr. Johnson would be able to find a flaw in it!

"Some one has possessed the Guiccioli with a notion that my Don Juan and the Don Giovanni of the Opera are the same person; and to please her I have discontinued his history and adventures;[384] but if I should resume them, I will tell you how I mean him to go on. I left him in the seraglio. There I shall make one of the favourites, a Sultana, (no less a personage,) fall in love with him, and carry him off from Constantinople. Such elopements are not uncommon, nor unnatural either, though it would shock the ladies to say they are ever to blame. Well, they make good their escape to Russia; where, if Juan's passion cools, and I don't know what to do with the lady, I shall make her die of the plague. There are accounts enough of the plague to be met with, from Boccaccio to De Foe;—but I have seen it myself, and that is worth all their descriptions. As our hero can't do without a mistress, he shall next become man-mistress to Catherine the Great. Queens have had strange fancies for more ignoble people before and since. I shall, therefore, make him cut out the ancestor of the young Russian,[385] and shall send him, when he is *hors de combat*, to England as her ambassador. In his suite he shall have a girl whom he shall have rescued during one of his northern campaigns, who shall be in love with him, and he not with her.

"You see I am true to Nature in making the advances come from the females. I shall next draw a town and country life at home,[386] which will give me room for life, manners, scenery, &c. I will make him neither a dandy in town, nor a fox-hunter in the country. He shall get into all sorts of scrapes, and at length end his career in France. Poor Juan shall be guillotined in the French Revolution![387] What do you think of my plot? It shall have twenty-four books too, the legitimate number. Episodes it has, and will have, out of number; and my spirits, good or bad, must serve for the machinery. If that be not an epic, if it be not strictly according to Aristotle, I don't know what an epic poem means."

---

[383] *Byron to Murray*, April 6, 1819: So you and Mr. Foscolo, etc., want me to undertake what you call a "great work?" an Epic poem, I suppose, or some such pyramid. . . . Is *Childe Harold* nothing? You have so many "*divine*" poems, is it nothing to have written a *Human* one? without any of your worn-out machinery. . . . Since you want *length*, you shall have enough of *Juan*, for I'll make 50 cantos. [*LJ*, IV, 283-284 (M).]

Trelawny: I asked Byron to write a novel. He said, "so I would if Scott had not—besides, a man cannot write a novel till he is forty."

[384] *Byron to Murray*, July 6, 1821: At the particular request of the Contessa G. I have promised *not* to continue *Don Juan*. You will therefore look upon these 3 cantos as the last of that poem. She had read the two first in the French translation, and never ceased

beseeching me to write no more of it. The reason of this is not at first obvious to a superficial observer of FOREIGN manners; but it arises from the wish of all women to exalt the *sentiment* of the passions, and to keep up the illusion which is their empire. Now *Don Juan* strips off this illusion, and laughs at that and most other things. [*LJ*, v, 320-321 (M).]

[385] *Medwin*: Prince Suworoff, then at Pisa. [This seems to be a grandson of the great General Suvorov, Prince Italiski.]

[386] *Medwin*: Byron says that the adventures in *Don Juan* are partly indebted to his friends. Martin Hawke used to tell a story which occurred to himself in the City, from which I suspect the scene between Juan and Inez in the 1st canto to have been taken.

[387] *Byron to Murray*, February 16, 1821: I meant . . . to make him finish as *Anacharsis Cloots* in the French revolution. [*LJ*, v, 242. Clootz was guillotined.]

———————

"Murray," said he, "pretends to have lost money by my writings, and pleads poverty: but if he is poor, which is somewhat problematical to me, pray who is to blame?[388] The fault is in his having purchased, at the instance of his great friends, during the last year, so many expensive Voyages and Travels*, which all his influence with 'The Quarterly' cannot persuade people to buy, cannot puff into popularity. The Cookery-book (which he has got a law-suit about) has been for a long time his sheet-anchor; but they say he will have to re-fund—the worst of *funds*.[389] Mr. Murray is tender of my fame! How kind in him! He is afraid of my writing too fast. Why? because he has a tenderer regard for his own pocket, and does not like the look of any new acquaintance, in the shape of a book of mine, till he has seen his old friends in a variety of new faces; *id est*, disposed of a vast many editions of the former works. I don't know what would become of me without Douglas Kinnaird, who has always been my best and kindest friend. It is not easy to deal with Mr. Murray.[390]

* "Death to his publisher—to him 'tis sport."
Don Juan, Canto V. Stanza 52.

[388] *Trelawny*: Murray wrote requesting Lord B. to give him something in his Corsair stile to recover his popularity—then on the wane with the Ladys, besides Gentlemen did not relish or think his mystery &c. comparable to his reputation. Lord B. replied to Murray, "how should *you* know how Gentlemen *think*."

[389] *Byron in his lines "To Mr. Murray"*:

> Along thy sprucest bookshelves shine
> The works thou deemest most divine—
> The Art of Cookery, and mine,
>   My Murray.

[*Poetry*, vii, 57 (M), first published 1830. E. H. Coleridge notes that Murray, after publishing Mrs. Rundell's *Domestic Cookery* for many years, purchased the copyright in 1822 for £2,000.]

[390] *Murray*: Mr. Murray . . . paid, at various times, for the copyright of his Lordship's Poems, sums amounting to upwards of 15,000*l.* [*GM*, cxxxvi, 440.]

J. W. Croker: This list of prices [paid to Byron and published by Murray in the *Gentleman's Magazine*] affords an instance of liberality in Mr. Murray as a tradesman which some readers may think carried too far. . . . There are, we are told, wretches so incapable of understanding such feelings as Mr. Murray here showed, as to suppose that his generosity was a mere calculation of the advantage of getting Lord Byron into his debt—we leave, for the present, such persons to the torment of their own base thoughts; while we contemplate the transaction with peculiar satisfaction, as calculated to excite, as Lord Byron himself expresses it, a higher opinion, not only of the individual, but of human nature. How Lord Byron, or any man who knew these facts, could have uttered, or permitted to be uttered, any imputation against Mr. Murray's pecuniary conduct towards his lordship, is truly astonishing. . . .

Medwin: As to whether £15,000 was an exorbitant price for the works of the most popular writer of the Age (Walter Scott has been said to have received £100,000), The Trade will be the best judge. . . . But it is a Subject Lord Byron would never have mentioned had not Mr. Murray as he said pretended to have lost money by being his publisher. [*Captain Medwin*, p. 187.]

Whether Murray was justly or unjustly attacked by Lord Byron is nothing to me. The bibliopole I had never seen, and had not the slightest cause of difference with him, and it is monstrous to suppose that I could be malignant enough to invent these things against him. I had been passing many years in another hemisphere and knew very little of literature, and less of the literary men of the day.

"Murray offered me, of his own accord, 1000*l.* a Canto for 'Don Juan,' and afterwards reduced it to 500*l.* on the plea of piracy; and complained of my dividing one Canto into two, because I happened to say something at the end of the Third about having done so.[391] It is true enough that 'Don Juan' has been pirated; but whom has he to thank but himself?[392] In the first place, he put too high a price on the copies of the two first Cantos that came out, only printing a quarto edition, at, I think, a guinea and a half. There was a great demand for it, and this induced the knavish booksellers to *buccaneer*. If he had put John Murray on the title-page, like a man, instead of smuggling the brat into the world, and getting Davison, who is a printer and not a publisher, to father it, who would have ventured to question his paternal rights?[393] or who would have attempted to deprive him of them?

"The thing was plainly this: he disowned and refused to acknowledge the bantling; the natural consequence was, that others should come forward to adopt it. Mr. John Murray is the most nervous of God's booksellers. When 'Don Juan' first came out, he was so frightened that he made a precipitate retreat into the country, shut himself up, and would not open his letters.[394] The fact is, he prints for too many Bishops. He is always boring me with piratical edition after edition, to prove the amount of his own losses, and furnish proof of the extent of his own folly. Here is one at two-and-sixpence that came only yesterday. I do not pity him. Because I gave him one of my poems, he wanted to make me believe that I had made him a present of two others, and hinted at some lines in 'English Bards' that were certainly to the point.[395] But I have altered my mind considerably upon that subject:[396] as I once hinted to him, I see no reason why a man should not profit by the sweat of his brain, as well as that of his brow, &c.;

besides, I was poor at that time, and have no idea of aggrandizing booksellers. I was in Switzerland when he made this modest request,—and he always entertained a spite against Shelley for making the agreement, and fixing the price, which I believe was not dear. For the Third Canto of 'Childe Harold,' 'Manfred,' and 'The Prisoner of Chillon,' &c. I got 2400*l*.[397] Depend on it, he did not lose money—he was not ruined by that speculation.

---

[391] [Byron bargained hard with Murray for cantos III, IV, and V, who first offered £1,000 for them but finally paid £1,525, the same price paid for cantos I and II. In the first transaction Murray got 438 stanzas, along with the 160 lines of the "Ode on Venice," and in the second he got 387 stanzas. Byron's price had thus gone up. For Byron's reference to the pirated edition of the first two cantos, in the course of bargaining with Murray, see *LJ*, v, 348.]

[392] *Medwin*: All this *at least* is true.

[393] [Thomas Davison printed the original quarto edition of the first two cantos in 1819 and an octavo edition later in the same year. Pirated editions sold for four shillings and were so advertised on the title page.]

[394] *Byron to Hobhouse*, August 4 and August 20, 1819: Juan is before the public; . . . Murray . . . seems in a state of perturbation; and he had by his own account taken refuge at Wimbledon from the torrent. . . .

I hear nothing of Don Juan but in two letters from Murray; the first very tremulous. . . . [*Correspondence*, ii, 120, 122.]

[395] *J. W. Croker*: Alas! there seems from other passages . . . but too much reason to fear that, in moments of vexation, and in the hurry of impassioned conversation, Lord Byron so far forgot himself and truth as to utter what Mr. Medwin has attributed to him. . . . This imputation, that Mr. Murray attempted to take advantage of Lord Byron's generosity, by converting his lordship's gift of one poem into a right to obtain others *gratis*, is founded on a fact which is true, but which Mr. Medwin could, we think, have learned only from Lord Byron. Lord Byron, it seems, made Mr. Murray a present of two poems, called "The Siege of Corinth" and "Parisina." The donation of these two poems having been made about [*i.e.*, at] the same time, may account for Mr. Medwin's stating the fact only as to *one*; but this inaccuracy, whether his lord-

ship's or Mr. Medwin's, is of no importance. . . . Before Lord Byron's friends can charge Mr. Medwin with having invented this most flagitious insinuation, they must show who it was, except Lord Byron, who could have told Mr. Medwin the only fact in the case which has the least foundation of truth. And is it quite out of the scope of human frailty that Lord Byron,—who could hardly contemplate his [later] acceptance of the money with any great satisfaction,—should have soothed his morbid spirit by endeavouring to turn on Mr. Murray the blame which he felt that the story, if truly told, must have excited against him? [Byron at one point made an outright gift to Murray of *The Siege of Corinth* and *Parisina*, for which Murray had offered £1,000, and later proposed that the money be divided among Godwin, Coleridge, and Maturin. Murray declined to so distribute it, and Byron finally accepted it himself. See *LJ*, III, 251, note 1. Murray may have "hinted at" lines 913-914 of *English Bards*: "Let others spin their meagre lines for hire;/ Enough for Genius, if itself inspire!"]

[396] *Trelawny*: And on every subject too contained in this Book & all others written about him—he pratled on according to the "vain" he was in—or as he said—according to the state of his digestion—or when he saw inquisitive people—in shocking language dragling cower—to get scent of his opinion & draw him out— he then broke out & it would have puzled the devil to follow him in all his shifts & turns—or draw any honest conclusions—he did not possess "invariable principles."

[397] [Byron may have told Medwin that because he had given Murray two poems (*The Siege of Corinth* and *Parisina*, for which he eventually accepted a thousand guineas), the publisher wanted him to make a "present" of another—*Childe Harold*, III, the manuscript of which was carried to England by Shelley, who "insisted that Byron's price was 2,000 guineas instead of the 1,200 guineas Murray had supposed" (White, *Shelley*, I, 465). Shelley thought that Murray bore him "some illwill, as the cause of the unexpected difference in his disbursements of £800" (*Letters*, I, 514).]

"Murray has long prevented 'The Quarterly' from abusing me.[398] Some of its bullies have had their fingers itching to be at me; but they would get the worst of it in a set-to." (Here he put himself in a boxing attitude.) "I perceive, however, that we shall have some sparring ere long. I don't wish to quarrel with Murray, but it seems inevitable. I had no reason to be pleased with him the other day. Galignani wrote to me, offering to purchase the copyright of my works, in order to obtain an exclusive privilege of printing them in France. I might have made my own terms, and put the money in my own pocket; instead of which, I enclosed Galignani's letter to Murray, in order that he might conclude the matter as he pleased. He did so, very advantageously for his own interest;[399] but never had the complaisance, the common politeness, to thank me, or acknowledge my letter.[400] My differences with Murray are not over. When he purchased 'Cain,' 'The Two Foscari,' and 'Sardanapalus,' he sent me a deed, which you may remember witnessing. Well, after its return to England, it was discovered that it contained a clause which had been introduced without my knowledge,—a clause by which I bound myself to offer Mr. Murray all my future compositions;—but I shall take no notice of it."[401]

---

[398] *Murray*: With regard to the 'Quarterly Review,' his Lordship *well knew* that it was established and constantly conducted on principles which absolutely excluded Mr. Murray from all such interference and influence as is implied in the 'Conversations.' [*GM*, CXXXVI, 439. Murray had launched the *Quarterly* in 1809; in 1824 he exercised sufficient influence over it to suppress Croker's too favorable review of Medwin's *Conversations*.]

[399] *Murray*: Mr. Murray derived no advantage from the proposed agreement, which was by no means of the importance here ascribed to it, and therefore was never attempted to be carried into effect. . . . [*GM*, CXXXVI, 439.]

Moore in his journal, December 20 and 21, 1821: Murray wishes me to found a bargain with Galignani, for the right of publishing [*Cain, The Two Foscari*, and *Sardanapalus*] here.

Galignani called and agreed to give a hundred pounds.

[400] *Byron to Murray*, January 19, 1821: You never answered a word about *Galignani*: if you mean to use the two *documents, do*; if *not, burn* them. I do not choose to leave them in any one's possession: suppose some one found them without the letters, what would they *think*? why, that *I* had been doing the *opposite* of what I have

done, to wit, referred the whole thing to you—an act of civility at least, which required saying, "I have received your letter." [*LJ*, v, 224 (M). Medwin also quotes from Byron's letters several other examples of his quarrels with Murray; see *LJ*, iv, 157, 327, 337-338.]

[401] *Murray*: He [Murray] has only to observe upon the subject, that, on referring to the Deed in question, no such clause is to be found; that this instrument was signed in London . . . ; and that the signature of Capt. Medwin is not affixed. [*GM*, cxxxvi, 442.]

J. W. Croker: This charge, thus summarily overthrown, is that upon which Mr. Medwin's veracity might be most reasonably questioned, because he alludes to his own share in a transaction which never took place; and it might be argued that one falsehood being thus proved home on him, his authority in any other point is destroyed. We cannot quite concur in this reasoning; because, in all the former cases, Lord Byron himself must have communicated the facts to Mr. Medwin: and we cannot but think that, in this individual instance, it is highly improbable that the latter should have invented a gratuitous falsehood, and accompanied it with a statement of certain facts which must have led to its immediate detection. . . . We dare say the fact is, that Mr. Medwin did witness some deed or other, for Lord Byron; but that all the superstructure built on this fact was Lord Byron's own. It is not our business (God forbid it were!) to endeavour to trace by what influence of passion or what perversity of intellect Lord Byron should have chosen to invent such a farrago of calumny. Whether he meant to deceive his auditor,—or whether sore, as Mr. Medwin represents him to be, with Mr. Murray's reluctance to publish his irreligious works, his resentment overpowered his reason and his veracity—we cannot venture to decide: all that we can say is, that, after great hesitation and with great reluctance, we find ourselves forced to the conclusion that Mr. Medwin's reports are substantially correct, and we must leave to abler pens and more discriminating understandings the task of clearing Lord Byron's memory from the stain which they at present seem to affix to it.

Medwin: I perceive by reference to my notes that on the 28th Nov[r] 1821 about the time *Cain, The Two Foscari*, and *Sardanapalus* were in the press [all three published December 19, 1821] I witnessed a Deed which I understood to be the Copyright of these Dramas. Lord Byron observed that all the witnesses to it had written books. I remember replying that the wonder nowadays was to meet with a person who had not. . . . I must therefore have confused some other copyright about which Lord Byron was speaking with this—but there is one fact about which I am not mistaken, and which perhaps is the only one of importance in this question: Lord Byron speaking of some Copyright certainly did make use of words to this import. [*Captain Medwin*, p. 188.]

The Editor of the Conversations [Colburn?] to the Editor of the Morning Chronicle: Now, it is to be observed, that it does not appear very conclusive that this is the identical deed referred to by Mr. Medwin; it might have been a deed relative to some former purchase which the party had taken this opportunity of sending for Lord Byron's signature, for it is well known, that although that respecting the *Two Foscari* was signed in London, yet others were sent to Italy to be executed by Lord Byron himself. If Capt. Medwin had desired to practice any deception (which is quite improbable), is it likely he would have committed himself in so unguarded a manner? Certainly not. And I have no doubt, if Mr. Murray had chosen to refer to other deeds, he would have found one witnessed by Mr. Medwin, and containing a clause of the nature alluded to. [*Captain Medwin*, p. 189. Murray had, in fact, not consulted the deed, for it no longer existed; he had consulted his memory. It may be that Medwin witnessed the document assigning Byron's memoirs to Murray; it was signed in November, 1821, the month referred to by Medwin. See *Captain Medwin*, pp. 189-190. Or, Medwin may have witnessed a deed authorizing Murray to dispose of French rights to the three plays concerned.]

Some time afterwards he said: "Murray and I have made up our quarrel;[402] at least, it is not my fault if it should be renewed. The parsons have been at him about 'Cain.' An Oxonian has addressed a bullying letter to him, asking him how so moral a bookseller can stain his press with so profane a book? He is threatened with a prosecution by the *Anti-constitutional* Society.[403] I don't believe they will venture to attack him: if they do, I shall go home and make my own defence."

Lord Byron wrote the same day the letter contained in the Notes on 'Cain.'[404] Some months afterwards he said in a letter:

"Murray and I have dissolved all connection.[405] He had the choice of giving up me or the 'Navy List.' There was no hesitation which way he should decide: the Admiralty carried the day.[406] Now for 'The Quarterly:' their batteries will be opened; but I can fire broadsides too. They have been letting off lots of squibs and crackers against me, but they only make a noise and * * *"[407]

———⌣———

[402] *Byron to Moore*, March 6, 1822: The enclosed letter from Murray hath melted me. . . . You may, therefore, send him the packet of *Werner*. . . . [*LJ*, vi, 34.]

[403] *Byron to Murray*, August 16, 1821: An't you afraid of the Constitutional Assassination of Bridge Street? [*LJ*, v, 344. The Constitutional Association actually brought suit against John Hunt, for publishing Byron's *Vision of Judgment*. The "bullying letter" addressed to Murray as a result of his publishing *Cain* was *A Remonstrance to Mr. John Murray, respecting a Recent Publication* (1822) by "Oxoniensis." Byron's letter to Murray, February 8, 1822, referring to the attack, was versified in "Noctes Ambrosianae," *Blackwood's*, March, 1822.]

[404] [Medwin must be referring to the work of some editor: Byron did not write any notes for the play.]

[405] *Byron to Murray*, February 8, 1822: You will now perceive that it was well for you, that I have decided upon changing my publisher. . . . [*LJ*, vi, 17.]

[406] *Murray*: The passage about the Admiralty is unfounded in fact, and no otherwise deserving of notice than to mark its absurdity. . . . [*GM*, cxxxvi, 439. On the "Navy List," see Byron's "To Mr. Murray," written in 1818 but first published in 1830 (*Poetry*, vii, 56-58). Murray advertised himself as "Bookseller to the Admiralty and the Board of Longitude."]

[407] *Medwin*: Mr. Murray defended himself by what he thought the Evidence of Letters from this attack. At the time this Conversation was held I never had seen Murray, and it is monstrous to suppose that I should have maligned him without cause. He says nothing ever occurred to subvert the friendly sentiments Lord Byron entertained for him. Read the correspondence. It was one squabble throughout. On my quitting Pisa, he gave me a Memorandum on an open sheet of paper, mixed up with other Memoranda (Correspondence) to be read to Mr. Murray or his principal Clerk, and which, not finding the Bibliopolist at home, who was as difficult of access as a Prime Minister, I did so read in Albemarle Street to his said Clerk, couched in these words. Lord Byron wonders he has

not heard from Mr. Murray on the receipt of his new Cantos of Don Juan and desires him to be less negligent in future—!!

I now take my leave of Mr. Murray, and embrace this opportunity of declaring once for all that I do not consider myself responsible in any way for the materials or liable in the most distant degree to be called upon to advocate the authenticity of any one of the facts or anecdotes contained in my Publication. These must rest with Lord Byron, stand or fall upon the authority of Lord Byron, for to me . . . most of the topics of his Conversations were new, almost all the characters among his contemporaries, who were the subject of them, as well as their works, unknown, the name of Mr. Murray no otherwise known to me than through the medium of the Title pages of Lord Byron's Publications. [Last paragraph from Medwin's letter to the Editor of *Galignani's Weekly Register*, presumably unpublished.]

In a letter dated from Genoa the 5th of May, 1823, in answer to one of mine in which I told him that I had executed his Murray commission, he says:

" 'Werner' was the last book Murray published for me, and three months after came out the Quarterly's article on my plays, when 'Marino Faliero' was noticed for the first time," &c.[408]

"I need not say that I shall be delighted by your inscribing your 'Wanderer' to me;[409] but I would recommend you to think twice before you inscribe a work to *me*, as you must be aware that at present I am the most unpopular writer going*, and the odium on the dedicatee may recur on the dedicator. If you do not think this a valid objection, of course there can be none on my part," &c.[410]

* "But Juan was my Moscow, and Faliero
My Leipsic, and my Mont St. Jean seems Cain."
Don Juan, Canto X. Stanza 56.

[408] [*Werner*, the last volume which Murray published for Byron, appeared on November 23, 1822; *Marino Faliero* on April 21,

1821. It received its long delayed review in the *Quarterly* of July, 1822.]

409 [Medwin's poem, *Ahasuerus, The Wanderer,* bore on its dedication page, "To The Right Hon. Lord Byron, This Poem Is Inscribed By His Friend. Paris, March 1, 1823."]

410 *Medwin:* The et caetera, which I did not give from fear of being taxed with vanity, was as follows: "You shewed me, I remember, a passage at Pisa, I suppose intended for the Poem, and which I thought well of. I pede faults, which rendered fully means—look to your feet—or you may be undone by the reviewers." I was at no loss to understand the reference and his views from the circumstance of his having criticized one or two of the lines as lame *of a foot,* with a foot too short. [Prothero does not print this letter, although it would seem to be significant that it bears the same date as Byron's letter introducing Medwin to Hobhouse. Presumably Byron would not have sent the letter of introduction to Medwin without a covering letter. If genuine, it demonstrates that Medwin wrote his dedication page before he received permission from Byron. With the first sentence of the last paragraph of the text of the letter, compare page 123, Medwin's original note.]

O^N my speaking to him with great praise one day of Coleridge's 'Ancient Mariner,' Lord Byron said: "I have been
much taken to task for calling 'Christabel' a wild and singularly original and beautiful poem; and the Reviewers very
sagely come to a conclusion therefrom, that I am no judge
of the compositions of others. 'Christabel' was the origin of
all Scott's metrical tales, and that is no small merit. It was
written in 1795, and had a pretty general circulation in the
literary world, though it was not published till 1816, and then
probably in consequence of my advice. One day, when I was
with Walter Scott (now many years ago), he repeated the
whole of 'Christabel,'[411] and I then agreed with him in thinking this poem what I afterwards called it. Sir Walter Scott
recites admirably. I was rather disappointed when I saw it in
print; but still there are finer things in it than in any tale of
its length; the proof of which is, that people retain them
without effort.

"What do you think of the picture of an English October
day?

'There is not wind enough to twirl
The one red leaf, the last of its clan,
That dances as long as dance it can,
Hanging so light, and hanging so high,
On the topmost twig that looks up at the sky.'[412]

"Some eight or ten lines of 'Christabel'* found themselves
in 'The Siege of Corinth,' I hardly know how;[413] but I adopted
another passage, of greater beauty, as a motto to a little work
I need not name†, and paraphrased without scruple the same
idea in 'Childe Harold.'[414] I thought it good because I felt it

* "Was it the wind through some hollow stone,
    Sent that soft and tender moan?
    He lifted his head—" &c.
                                    Siege of Corinth.

† The stanzas beginning "Fare thee well!"

deeply—the best test of poetry. His psychological poem was always a great favourite of mine, and but for me would not have appeared. What perfect harmony of versification!"

And he began spouting 'Kubla Khan:'

'It was an Abyssinian maid,
And on her dulcimer she play'd,
Singing of Mount Abora'—

"Madame de Staël was fond of reciting poetry that had hardly any thing but its music to recommend it."

"And pray," asked I, "what has 'Kubla Khan?'"

"I can't tell you," said he; "but it delights me."

And he went on till he had finished the Vision.

"I was very much amused with Coleridge's 'Memoirs.' There is a great deal of *bonhommie* in that book, and he does not spare himself. Nothing, to me at least, is so entertaining as a work of this kind—as private biography: Hamilton's 'Memoirs,'[415] for instance, that were the origin of the style of Voltaire. Madame de Staël used to say, that 'De Grammont' was a book containing, with less matter, more interest than any she knew. Alfieri's 'Life' is delightful. You will see my Confessions in good time, and you will wonder at two things—that I should have had so much to confess, and that I should have confessed so much. Coleridge, too, seems sensible enough of his own errors. His sonnet to the Moon is an admirable burlesque on the *Lakists*, and his own style.[416] Some of his stories are told with a vast deal of humour, and display a fund of good temper that all his disappointments could not sour. Many parts of his 'Memoirs' are quite unintelligible, and were, I apprehend, meant for Kant; on the proper pronunciation of whose name I heard a long argument the other evening.

"Coleridge is like Sosia in 'Amphytrion;'—he does not know whether he is himself or not.[417] If he had never gone to Germany, nor spoilt his fine genius by the transcendental philosophy and German metaphysics, nor taken to write lay sermons, he would have made the greatest poet of the day. What poets had we in 1795? Hayley had got a monopoly, such as it was.[418]

Coleridge might have been any thing: as it is, he is a thing 'that dreams are made of.' "

411 *Byron in a note to The Siege of Corinth*: I heard that the wild and singularly original and beautiful poem [*Christabel*] recited [by Scott, in June, 1815 (*Poetry*, III, 471). See also *LJ*, III, 228, note.]

Byron to Moore, December 24, 1816: I hear that the *Edinburgh Review* has cut up Coleridge's *Christabel*, and declared against me for praising it. [*LJ*, IV, 31, on which page in a footnote Prothero quotes the attack on Byron in the *Edinburgh Review*. The first part of *Christabel* was written in 1797, the second in 1800.]

412 [Coleridge, *Christabel*, ll. 48-52, describes a chilly night, not an October day.]

413 *Medwin*: Lord Byron says that it was recited to him (by Walter Scott) after the lines were written. See Notes to *The Siege of Corinth* [*Poetry*, III, 471-472].

414 [Byron refers to *Childe Harold*, III, xciv.]

415 [Anthony Hamilton, *Mémoires de la Vie du Comte de Gramont*, 1713, an English translation of which was edited by Sir Walter Scott in 1811.]

416 [Coleridge's "Sonnet: To the Autumnal Moon" (1796) could not have been intended as a parody of the "Lakists" because of its early date; however, it does exhibit a remarkable number of characteristically romantic elements.]

417 [Sosia, Amphytrion's slave in the comedies of Plautus and Dryden, begins to doubt his identity when he encounters Mercury disguised as himself, guarding his master's door while Jupiter enjoyed Amphytrion's wife within.]

418 [The fame of William Hayley (1745-1820) was so great that upon the death of Thomas Warton in 1790 he was offered the laureateship. Byron satirized him in *English Bards*.]

Being one day at Moloni's the bookseller's at Pisa, a report was in circulation that a subject belonging to the Lucchese States had been taken up for sacrilege, and sentenced to be burnt alive. A priest who entered the library at that moment confirmed the news, and expressed himself thus:—"*Scelerato!*" said he, "he took the consecrated wafers off the altar, and threw them contemptuously about the church! What punishment can be great enough for such a monstrous crime? Burning is too easy a death! I shall go to Lucca,—I would almost go to Spain,—to see the wretch expire at the stake!" Such were the humane and Christian sentiments of a minister of the Gospel! I quitted him with disgust, and immediately hastened to Lord Byron's.

"Is it possible?" said he, after he had heard my story. "Can we believe that we live in the nineteenth century? However, I can believe any thing of the Duchess of Lucca. She is an Infanta of Spain, a bigot in religion, and of course advocates the laws of the Inquisition. But it is scarcely credible that she will venture to put them into effect here. We must endeavour to prevent this *auto da fé*. Lord Guilford is arrived: —we will get him to use his influence. Surely the Grand Duke of Tuscany will interfere, for he has himself never signed a death-warrant since he came upon the throne."[419]

Shelley entered at this moment horror-struck: he had just heard that the criminal was to suffer the next day. He proposed that we should mount and arm ourselves as well as we could, set off immediately for Lucca, and endeavour to rescue the prisoner when brought out for execution, making at full speed for the Tuscan frontiers, where he would be safe. Mad and hopeless as the scheme was, Lord Byron consented, carried away by his feelings, to join in it, if other means should fail. We agreed to meet again in the evening, and in the mean time to get a petition signed by all the English residents at Pisa, to be presented to the Grand Duke.

"I will myself," said he, "write immediately to Lord Guilford."

He did so, and received an answer[420] a few hours after, telling him that the same report had reached Lord Guilford; but that he had learned, on investigation, that it was unfounded.

It appeared that the Duchess had issued a proclamation which made the peasant amenable, when apprehended, to the ancient laws of Spain; but that he had escaped to Florence and given himself up to the police, who had stipulated not to make him over to the authorities at Lucca, but on condition of his being tried by the Tuscan laws.

[419] [On the conclusion of this affair, see C. L. Cline, *Byron, Shelley, and their Pisan Circle* (Cambridge, Mass., 1952), p. 65. The Duchy of Lucca was governed by Maria Luisa, queen of Etruria, and her son Charles Louis.]

[420] *Medwin*: I was mistaken in saying in the *Conversations*, that Shelley [Byron?] had applied to Lord Guildford [*sic*]. . . . The Duchess had issued a proclamation, that the offender, if arrested, should be subject to the Spanish laws; but he had escaped to Florence, and delivered himself up to the police, who had not made him over to the Lucchese authorities, but on condition that he should be tried by the statutes of Tuscany. [*Shelley*, p. 367. Shelley, upon hearing that the culprit had been sentenced to the galleys, directed Byron's courier not to deliver Byron's letter to Guilford. Byron, it seems, had at first expected Shelley to write to Guilford, but then had decided to write himself.]

Speaking of Coppet and Madame de Staël, he said: "I knew Madame de Staël in England. When she came over she created a great sensation, and was much courted in the literary as well as the political world. On the supposition of her being a Liberal, she was invited to a party, where were present Whitbread, Sheridan, and several of the Opposition leaders.[421]

[421] [Byron records in "Some Recollections of my acquaintance with Madame de Staël" (*Murray's Magazine*, January, 1887) that he and de Staël dined together with Sheridan, Whitbread, Grattan, and Lansdowne, all of them Whig leaders.]

"To the great horror of the former, she soon sported her *Ultraisms*. No one possessed so little tact as Madame de Staël, —which is astonishing in one who had seen so much of the world and of society. She used to assemble at her routs politicians of both sides of the House, and was fond of setting two party-men by the ears in argument. I once witnessed a curious scene of this kind. She was battling it very warmly, as she used to do, with Canning, and all at once turned round to (I think he said) Lord Grey, who was at his elbow, for his opinion. It was on some point upon which he could not but most cordially disagree. She did not understand London society, and was always sighing for her *coterie* at Paris. The dandies took an invincible dislike to the De Staëls, mother and daughter. Brummell was her aversion;—she, his.[422] There was a double marriage talked of in town that season:—Auguste (the present Baron) was to have married Miss Milbanke;[423] I, the present Duchess of Broglie.[424] I could not have been worse *embroiled*.

"Madame de Staël had great talent in conversation, and an overpowering flow of words. It was once said of a large party that were all trying to shine, 'There is not one who can go home and think.' This was not the case with her. She was often troublesome, some thought rude, in her questions; but she never offended me, because I knew that her inquisitiveness did not proceed from idle curiosity, but from a wish to sound people's characters. She was a continual interrogatory to me, in order to fathom mine, which requires a long plumbline.[425] She once asked me if my real character was well drawn in a favourite novel of the day ('Glenarvon').[426] She was only singular in putting the question in the dry way she did. There are many who pin their faith on that insincere production.[427]

---

422 *Byron in his "Detached Thoughts"*: The Dandies . . . persecuted and mystified Mᵉ. de Stael . . . damnably. They persuaded Mᵉ. de Stael that Alvanley had a hundred thousand a year, etc.,

etc., till she praised him to his *face* for his *beauty*! and made a set at him for Albertine (*Libertine*, as Brummell baptized her, though the poor Girl was and is as correct as maid or wife can be, and very amiable withal), and a hundred fooleries besides. [*LJ*, v, 423 (M).]

Medwin: Lord Byron frequently spoke and with almost envy of Brummell and prided himself much on his intimacy with him, or rather on Brummell's condescension in patronizing him.

I could have supplied many anecdotes to his [Brummell's] biographer. Like Theodore Hook, the Town was constantly running with Brummell's last joke: His asking someone with whom he was walking and who capped the Regent, "Who's your fat friend?"— and saying, "George, ring the bell," which he did, to order him out of Carlton House. The Prince's saying to the Duke of York, "Your Mr. Brummells are well known." But he paid dearly for one of his whistles. He had expectations from an aunt with whom he made a visit. The old lady had no silver forks, and Brummell, taking up a steel one at the Table, said before a large party, "What's this? Is it to make hay with?" Another of his jokes was on being asked by a Beggar for a half penny. "My friend, I have heard of such a coin, but never touched one." There was a time when if Byron had not been Childe Buren, he would have wished to be Brummell.

[423] *Lady Byron*: They had never conversed together.

[424] *Mary Shelley in Lardner's Cabinet Cyclopaedia*: Lord Byron was among her [Madame de Staël's] favourites. . . . There was a notion at one time that he would marry her daughter. [Albertine, later Duchess of Broglie. Quoted by Elizabeth Nitchie, "Byron, Madame de Staël, and Albertine," *Keats-Shelley Journal*, vii (1958), 8.]

[425] *Trelawny*: She asked Byron why he sat with his eyes half closed. He looked affected. He said, "because you are placed opposite to me."

[426] *Byron to Murray*, July 22, 1816: Of *Glenarvon*, Madame de Stael told me (ten days ago, at Copet) marvellous and grievous things. . . . [*LJ*, iii, 338-339 (M).]

[427] *Medwin*: To wit, Goethe, who considers an anecdote therein about an assassination to apply to Byron himself. [See Goethe's review of *Manfred*, which he read in the light or under the shade of *Glenarvon*.]

"No woman had so much *bonne foi* as Madame de Staël: hers was a real kindness of heart. She took the greatest possible interest in my quarrel with Lady Byron, or rather Lady Byron's with me, and had some influence over my wife,[428]—as much as any person but her mother, which is not saying much. I believe Madame de Staël did her utmost to bring about a reconciliation between us.[429] She was the best creature in the world.

"Women never see consequences—never look at things straight forward, or as they ought. Like figurantes at the Opera, they make a hundred *pirouettes*, and return to where they set out. With Madame de Staël this was sometimes the case. She was very indefinite and vague in her manner of expression. In endeavouring to be new she became often obscure, and sometimes unintelligible. What did she mean by saying that 'Napoleon was a system, and not a man?'

"I cannot believe that Napoleon was acquainted with all the petty persecutions that she used to be so garrulous about, or that he deemed her of sufficient importance to be dangerous: besides, she admired him so much, that he might have gained her over by a word.[430] But, like me, he had perhaps too great a contempt for women; he treated them as puppets, and thought he could make them dance at any time by pulling the wires. That story of '*Gardez vos enfans*' did not tell much in her favour, and proves what I say. I shall be curious to see Las Cases' book, to hear what Napoleon's real conduct to her was."[431]

I told him I could never reconcile the contradictory opinions he had expressed of Napoleon in his poems.

"How could it be otherwise?" said he. "Some of them were called translations,[432] and I spoke in the character of a Frenchman and a soldier. But Napoleon was his own antithesis (if I may say so). He was a glorious tyrant, after all. Look at his public works: compare his face, even on his coins, with those of the other sovereigns of Europe. I blame the manner of his death: he shewed that he possessed much of the Italian character in consenting to live.[433] There he lost himself in his dramatic character, in my estimation. He was master of his own destiny; of *that*, at least, his enemies could not deprive him. He should have gone off the stage like a hero: it was expected of him.

"Madame de Staël, as an historian, should have named him in her 'Allemagne;' she was wrong in suppressing his name, and he had a right to be offended.[434] Not that I mean to justify his persecutions. These, I cannot help thinking, must have arisen indirectly from some private enemy. But we shall see.

"She was always aiming to be brilliant—to produce a sensation, no matter how, when, or where. She wanted to make all her ideas, like figures in the modern French school of painting, prominent and shewy,—standing out of the canvass, each in a light of its own. She was vain; but who had an excuse for vanity if she had not? I can easily conceive her not wishing to change her name, or acknowledge that of Rocca.[435] I liked Rocca; he was a gentleman and a clever man; no one said better things, or with a better grace. The remark about the Meillerie road that I quoted in the Notes of 'Childe Harold,' '*La route vaut mieux que les souvenirs*,'[436] was the observation of a thorough Frenchman."

---

[428] *Lady Byron*: Lady Byron had but a slight acquaintance with M[e]. de Stael. But M[e]. de Stael addressed a letter to Lady Byron,—the only one,—in favor of a reconciliation—The reply was to the effect that such a step as the Sep[n]. could not have been adopted on grounds capable of being changed.

[429] *Moore*: He must endeavour, she told him, to bring about a reconciliation with his wife, and submit to contend no longer with the opinion of the world. [Moore, *Life*, p. 321.]

[430] [Although Madame de Staël carried on a kind of running duel with Napoleon for many years and in 1803 was ordered by him not to reside within forty leagues of Paris, there was a story current that she favored his return in 1815.]

⁴³¹ [The Marquis Las Cases, who accompanied Napoleon to St. Helena and there took notes on his conversation, published his *Mémorial de Ste Hélène* in 1823.]

⁴³² ["From the French" and "Ode from the French."]

⁴³³ *Byron to Lady Byron*, in February, 1815: Bonaparte's conduct since his fall is to be traced entirely to the Italian character— for a Frenchman or Englishman would have shot himself. An Italian will persevere—waiting for any chance or change. [*HVSV*, p. 625, note 50.]

⁴³⁴ *Harness*: Madame de Stael!—an historian!—Allemagne! Has he ever seen the work? What can the man mean! [*BEM*, xvi, 539.]

Medwin: Hobhouse [*i.e.*, Harness] is very facetious about Lord Byron's calling Madame de Stael an Historian. What is her *Allemagne* but a History of the Literature and progress of that Country. [*De l'Allemagne*, suppressed by Napoleon in 1810 as "not French" and published in 1813 in London, is concerned only with the previous half century of German literature, philosophy, art, etc., which are described as being stifled or destroyed by Napoleonic ambition. Napoleon banished the author from France.]

⁴³⁵ *Medwin*: Madame de Stael was married [secretly] to Rocca but did not like to exchange her name for his.

⁴³⁶ [The last line of Byron's note to *Childe Harold*, III, xcix.]

"HERE is a letter I have had to-day," said he. "The writer is a stranger to me, and pleads great distress. He says he has been an officer in the East India service, and makes out a long list of grievances, against the Company and a Mr. Standish. He charges the Government with sending him home without a trial, and breaking him without a Court-martial; and complains that a travelling gentleman, after having engaged him as an interpreter to accompany him to Persia, and put him to great expense in preparations for the journey, has all at once changed his mind, and refused to remunerate him for his lost time, or pay him any of the annual stipend he had fixed to give him. His name seems to be ———. You have been at Bombay,—do you know him?"

"No," answered I; "but I know his story. He was thought to have been hardly used. As to the other part of his complaint, I know nothing."

"He asks me for 50*l*. I shall send it him by to-morrow's post: there is no courier to-day."[437]

---

[437] [Medwin referred to this episode later in his "Hazlitt in Switzerland," *Fraser's Magazine*, XIX (March, 1839), 278.]

"Who would not wish to have been born two or three centuries later?" said he, putting into my hand an Italian letter. "Here is a *savant* of Bologna, who pretends to have discovered the manner of directing balloons by means of a rudder, and tells me that he is ready to explain the nature of his invention to our Government. I suppose we shall soon travel by air-vessels; make air instead of sea-voyages; and at length find our way to the moon, in spite of the want of atmosphere."*

"*Cœlum ipsum petimus stultitia*," said I.

* "Steam-engines will convey him to the moon."
    Don Juan, Canto X. Stanza 2.

"There is not so much folly as you may suppose, and a vast deal of poetry, in the idea," replied Lord Byron. "Where shall we set bounds to the power of steam?[438] Who shall say, 'Thus far shalt thou go, and no farther?' We are at present in the infancy of science. Do you imagine that, in former stages of this planet, wiser creatures than ourselves did not exist? All our boasted inventions are but the shadows of what has been,—the dim images of the past—the dream of other states of existence. Might not the fable of Prometheus, and his stealing the fire, and of Briareus and his earth-born brothers, be but traditions of steam and its machinery? Who knows whether, when a comet shall approach this globe to destroy it, as it often has been and will be destroyed,[439] men will not tear rocks from their foundations by means of steam, and hurl mountains, as the giants are said to have done, against the flaming mass?—and then we shall have traditions of Titans again, and of wars with Heaven."

"A mighty ingenious theory," said I laughing,—and was near adding, in the words of 'Julian and Maddalo':

> "The sense that he was greater than his kind
> Had made, methinks, his eagle spirit blind
> With gazing on its own exceeding light."

Talking of romances, he said: " 'The Monk' is perhaps one of the best in any language, not excepting the German. It only wanted one thing, as I told Lewis, to have rendered it perfect. He should have made the dæmon really in love with Ambrosio: this would have given it a human interest. 'The Monk' was written when Lewis was only twenty, and he seems to have exhausted all his genius on it. Perhaps at that age he was in earnest in his belief of magic wonders. That is the secret of Walter Scott's inspiration: he retains and encourages all the superstitions of his youth. Lewis caught *his* passion for the marvellous, and it amounted to a mania with him, in Germany; but the groundwork of 'The Monk' is neither original nor German; it is derived from the tale of 'Santon Barsisa.' The episode of 'The Bleeding Nun,' which was turned into a melo-drama, is from the German.[440]

"There were two stories which he almost believed by telling. One happened to himself whilst he was residing at Manheim. Every night, at the same hour, he heard or thought he heard in his room, when he was lying in bed, a crackling noise like that produced by parchment, or thick paper. This circumstance caused enquiry, when it was told him that the sounds were attributable to the following cause:—The house in which he lived had belonged to a widow, who had an only son. In order to prevent his marrying a poor but amiable girl, to whom he was attached, he was sent to sea. Years passed, and the mother heard no tidings of him, nor the ship in which he had sailed. It was supposed that the vessel had been wrecked, and that all on board had perished. The reproaches of the girl, the upbraidings of her own conscience, and the loss of her child, crazed the old lady's mind, and her only pursuit became to turn over the Gazettes for news. Hope at length left her: she did not live long,—and continued her old occupation after death.[441]

---

[438] *Edward E. Williams in his diary*, January 6, 1822: He [Byron] has received letters from a mechanic at Bologna signed by a number of Professors of the University there, calling upon him to lend his name and pecuniary assistance to the furthering of the projection of a machine, with which a man, by the aid of wings is to elevate himself to any height—in short to fly—the whole is to be worked by *steam* and the weight of the engine is not considered any impediment. [*HVSV*, p. 265.]

[439] [On this element in Byron's thought, indebted in part to Georges Cuvier, see my *Byron: The Record of a Quest* (Austin, 1949), pp. 198-217.]

[440] [In the "Advertisement" of *The Monk*, Lewis confessed his debt to Addison's "Santon Barsisa" (*The Guardian*, No. 148) and to the German tradition of the Bleeding Nun.]

[441] [A variant of Medwin's story of the rustling newspapers appears in Trelawny's *Records*, ii, 89, where it is also placed in the

mouth of Byron, who may well have recited it of course before both Medwin and Trelawny. There, Lewis's place of residence is properly said to be Weimar, not Mannheim.]

"The other story that I alluded to before, was the original of his 'Alonzo and Imogene,' which has had such a host of imitators. Two Florentine lovers, who had been attached to each other almost from childhood, made a vow of eternal fidelity. Mina was the name of the lady—her husband's I forget, but it is not material. They parted. He had been for some time absent with his regiment, when, as his disconsolate lady was sitting alone in her chamber, she distinctly heard the well-known sound of his footsteps, and starting up beheld, not her husband, but his spectre, with a deep ghastly wound across his forehead, entering. She swooned with horror: when she recovered, the ghost told her that in future his visits should be announced by a passing-bell, and these words, distinctly whispered, 'Mina, I am here!' Their interviews now became frequent, till the woman fancied herself as much in love with the ghost as she had been with the man. But it was soon to prove otherwise. One fatal night she went to a ball:—what business had she there? She danced too; and, what was worse, her partner was a young Florentine, so much the counterpart of her lover, that she became estranged from his ghost. Whilst the young gallant conducted her in the waltz, and her ear drank in the music of his voice and words, a passing-bell tolled! She had been accustomed to the sound till it hardly excited her attention, and now lost in the attractions of her fascinating partner, she heard but regarded it not. A second peal!—she listened not to its warnings. A third time the bell, with its deep and iron tongue, startled the assembled company, and silenced the music! Mina then turned her eyes from her partner, and saw reflected in the mirror, a form, a shadow, a spectre: it was her husband! He was standing between her and the young Florentine, and whispered in a solemn and melancholy tone the accustomed accents, 'Mina, I am here!'—She instantly fell dead.[442]

"Lewis was not a very successful writer. His 'Monk' was abused furiously by Mathias, in his 'Pursuits of Literature,' and he was forced to suppress it.[443] 'Abellino' he merely translated.[444] 'Pizarro' was a sore subject with him, and no wonder that he winced at the name. Sheridan, who was not very scrupulous about applying to himself *literary* property at least, manufactured his play without so much as an acknowledgment, pecuniary or otherwise, from Lewis's ideas;[445] and bad as 'Pizarro' is, I know (from having been on the Drury-Lane Committee, and knowing, consequently, the comparative profits of plays,) that it brought in more money than any other play has ever done, or perhaps ever will do.

---

[442] *Medwin*: See Shelley's Journal, where this story is told in different words. [See *Mary Shelley's Journal*, pp. 57-58, for the story of Minna, as the name was spelled in Shelley's *Essays* (1840), where Mary published it with a few alterations and omissions. Medwin had access to Mary's unpublished journal, with Shelley's entry for August 18, 1816. The clear proof is to be found in the numerous similarities of phrasing, although these do not exclude the possibility that Byron may also have told the story to Medwin, who then refreshed his memory of it by going to Mary's journal or a transcript of it.

The significant similarities between the story of Mina and Lewis's poem "Alonzo the Brave and Fair Imogine" (*The Monk*, ed. Louis F. Peck, New York, 1952, pp. 306-308) are the inclusion in both of an inconstant lady, untrue to her man, who is killed in battle and returns as a ghost, at the sight of which she dies. There are, however, important differences.]

[443] [Thomas James Mathias attacked Lewis's *Monk* for its obscenity in *Pursuits of Literature*, Dialogue iv, both preface and poem. See 16th ed., 1812, pp. 212-216, 305, and elsewhere. An injunction to prohibit sale of the novel was obtained, and Lewis published an expurgated edition in 1798.]

[444] [Lewis's *Rugantino, or the Bravo of Venice. A Grand Romantic Melodrama* (acted 1805) is a dramatization of Lewis's ro-

mance, *The Bravo of Venice* (1805), itself translated from the German of Heinrich Zschokke's *Aböllino der grosse Bandit*.]

[445] [Sheridan's *Pizarro*, produced at Drury Lane on May 24, 1799, was founded on Kotzebue's *Spaniards in Peru*; Lewis's *Rolla*, published in 1799 but never acted and superseded by Sheridan's *Pizarro*, is a translation of Kotzebue's play.]

"But to return to Lewis. He was even worse treated about 'The Castle Spectre,' which had also an immense run, a prodigious success. Sheridan never gave him any of its profits either. One day Lewis being in company with him, said,— 'Sheridan, I will make you a large bet.' Sheridan, who was always ready to make a wager, (however he might find it inconvenient to pay it if lost,) asked eagerly what bet? 'All the profits of my Castle Spectre,' replied Lewis. 'I will tell you what,' said Sheridan, (who never found his match at repartee,) 'I will make you a very small one,—what it is worth.' "[446]

I asked him if he had known Sheridan? "Yes," said he. "Sheridan was an extraordinary compound of contradictions, and Moore will be much puzzled in reconciling them for the Life he is writing. The upper part of Sheridan's face was that of a god—a forehead most expansive, an eye of peculiar brilliancy and fire; but below he shewed the satyr.

"Lewis was a pleasant companion, and would always have remained a boy in spirits and manners—(unlike me!) He was fond of the society of younger men than himself. I myself never knew a man, except Shelley, who was companionable till thirty. I remember Mrs. Hope once asking who was Lewis's male-love this season![447] He possessed a very lively imagination, and a great turn for narrative, and had a world of ghost-stories, which he had better have confined himself to telling. His poetry is now almost forgotten: it will be the same with that of all but two or three poets of the day.

"Lewis had been, or thought he had been, unkind to a brother whom he lost young;[448] and when any thing disagreeable was about to happen to him the vision of his brother appeared: he came as a sort of monitor.

"Lewis was with me for a considerable period at Geneva; and we went to Coppet several times together; but Lewis was there oftener than I.

"Madame de Staël and he used to have violent arguments about the Slave Trade,[449]—which he advocated strongly, for most of his property was in negroes and plantations. Not being satisfied with three thousand a-year, he wanted to make it five; and would go to the West Indies;[450] but he died on the passage of sea-sickness, and obstinacy in taking an emetic."[451]

[446] *Byron in his "Detached Thoughts"*: Sheridan was one day offered a bet by M. G. Lewis. "I will bet you, Mr. Sheridan, a very large sum: I will bet you what you *owe me* as Manager, for my 'Castle Spectre.' " "I never make *large bets*," said Sheridan: "but I will lay you a *very small* one; I will bet you *what it is* WORTH!" [*LJ*, v, 417. Byron told this same story to Hobhouse, who recorded it in his diary for December 22, 1815, in words similar to those used by Medwin. See *Recollections*, I, 326.]

[447] [For a discussion of the problem of Lewis's homosexuality, impossible to prove or disprove conclusively, see Louis F. Peck, *A Life of Matthew G. Lewis* (Cambridge, Mass., 1961), pp. 65-67. Mrs. Hope may be the hostess referred to in Byron's "Detached Thoughts," No. 50.]

[448] [Lewis's younger brother, Barrington, died early, in 1800, from a spinal injury.]

[449] *Byron to Samuel Rogers*, April 4, 1817: Last autumn . . . I set him [Lewis] by the ears with Madame de Stael about the slave-trade. [*LJ*, IV, 97. But Lewis was a very enlightened slave owner; see Peck, pp. 151, 160.]

[450] *Lady Byron*: Lewis's object in going to the W. Indies was to benefit his Slaves, by whom he was beloved.

[451] [Lewis died of yellow fever, but he hastened his end by taking an emetic a few days before his death. See Peck, p. 173.]

I SAID to him, "You are accused of owing a great deal to Wordsworth. Certainly there are some stanzas in the Third Canto of 'Childe Harold' that smell strongly of the Lakes: for instance—

> 'I live not in myself, but I become
> Portion of that around me;—and to me
> High mountains are a feeling!' "

"Very possibly," replied he. "Shelley, when I was in Switzerland, used to dose me with Wordsworth physic even to nausea; and I do remember then reading some things of his with pleasure. He had once a feeling of Nature, which he carried almost to a deification of it:—that's why Shelley liked his poetry.

"It is satisfactory to reflect, that where a man becomes a hireling and loses his mental independence, he loses also the faculty of writing well. The lyrical ballads, jacobinical and puling with affectation of simplicity as they were, had undoubtedly a certain merit*: and Wordsworth, though occasionally a writer for the nursery masters and misses,

> 'Who took their little porringer,
> And ate their porridge there,'[452]

now and then expressed ideas worth imitating; but, like brother Southey, he had his price; and since he is turned tax-gatherer, is only fit to rhyme about asses and waggoners. Shelley repeated to me the other day a stanza from 'Peter Bell' that I thought inimitably good.[453] It is the rumination of Peter's ass,

* "Or Wordsworth unexcised, unhired, who *then*
Season'd his pedlar poems with democracy."
Don Juan, Canto III. Stanza 93.

who gets into a brook, and sees reflected there a family circle, or tea-party. But you shall have it in his own words:

> 'Is it a party in a parlour,
> Cramm'd just as you on earth are cramm'd?
> Some sipping punch, some sipping tea,
> And every one, as you may see,
> All silent and all d——d!'[454]

There was a time when he would have written better; but perhaps Peter thinks feelingly.

"The republican trio, when they began to publish in common, were to have had a community of all things, like the ancient Britons; to have lived in a state of nature, like savages, and peopled some 'island of the blest' with children in common, like ——. A very pretty Arcadian notion![455] It amuses me much to compare the Botany Bay Eclogues, the Panegyric of Martin the Regicide, and 'Wat Tyler,' with the Laureate Odes, and Peter's Eulogium on the Field of Waterloo.[456] There is something more than rhyme in that noted stanza containing

> 'Carnage is God's daughter!'*——[457]

* Wordsworth's Thanksgiving Ode.

---

[452] [Misquoted from "We Are Seven," ll. 47-48.]
Mary Shelley to Hobhouse, November 10, 1824: You justly remark that Lord Byron could not have made an inaccurate quotation —his memory was admirable. . . . [*Captain Medwin*, p. 201.]

[453] *Medwin*: See Shelley's own *Peter Bell* and the admirable stanzas with which Lord Byron was well acquainted, tho' he does not mention it. [Shelley's poem, written in October, 1819, was not published until 1839.]

[454] [A variant of the stanza which serves as a motto for Shelley's *Peter Bell the Third*.]

[455] *Southey to the Editor of the Courier*: I shall only observe . . . that the slander is as worthy of his lordship as the scheme itself would have been. . . . Mr. Wordsworth and I were strangers to each other, even by name, at the time when he represents us as engaged in a Satanic confederacy, and we never published anything in common. [*LJ*, vi, 399. Southey, of course, did not contribute to *Lyrical Ballads*, as may be implied, nor was Wordsworth involved in the Pantisocratic scheme. Southey and Coleridge, however, did collaborate on the *Fall of Robespierre*, 1794, the year which also produced Southey's *Botany Bay Eclogues* and his *Wat Tyler*, piratically published in 1817, to the author's embarrassment.]

[456] [For Byron on Southey's "Elegy on Martin the regicide," see *LJ*, vi, 389, a note in the Appendix to *The Two Foscari*, and *Poetry*, iv, 482, the Preface to *The Vision of Judgment*. The poem referred to is a juvenile work, "Inscription for the Apartment in Chepstow Castle, where Henry Martin, the Regicide, was imprisoned thirty years." "Peter's Eulogium on the Field of Waterloo" probably refers to Southey's *The Poet's Pilgrimage to Waterloo*, 1816; the "Laureate Odes" to Southey's *Odes to . . . the Prince Regent*, 1814. Southey was made poet laureate in 1813.]

[457] [Quoted in *Don Juan*, VIII, ix, with a note, from Wordsworth's "Thanksgiving Ode on the Battle of Waterloo," the first version. Wordsworth later deleted the quoted line. Cf. Shelley's *Peter Bell the Third*, VI, xxxvi.]

I offended the *par nobile* mortally—past all hope of forgiveness—many years ago. I met, at the Cumberland Lakes, Hogg the Ettrick Shepherd, who had just been writing 'The Poetic Mirror,'[458] a work that contains imitations of all the living poets' styles, after the manner of the 'Rejected Addresses.' The burlesque is well done, particularly that of me, but not equal to Horace Smith's. I was pleased with Hogg; and he wrote me a very witty letter,[459] to which I sent him, I suspect, a very dull reply. Certain it is that I did not spare the Lakists in it; and he told me he could not resist the temptation, and had shewn it to the fraternity. It was too tempting; and as I could never keep a secret of my own, as you know, much less that of other people, I could not blame him. I remember saying, among other things, that the Lake poets were such fools as not to fish in their own waters; but this was the least offensive part of the epistle."[460]

---

[458] [It is highly unlikely that Byron ever met Hogg personally and quite certain that they did not meet in 1815 or 1816, when Hogg was writing *The Poetic Mirror*. Mrs. M. Garden, Hogg's daughter, denied that any such meeting ever took place. See her *Memorials of James Hogg, the Ettrick Shepherd*, pp. 188, 196-197. An anonymous writer, signing himself "N." and offering no evidence, states an "anecdote has been recorded" that Byron and Hogg met at Rydal and got drunk together there at an inn (*Notes and Queries*, 5th Series, II, 158).]

[459] *Byron to Murray*, August 3, 1814: I have a most amusing epistle from the Ettrick Bard—Hogg. . . . [*LJ*, III, 115 (M). Hogg's letters to Byron are witty, as Medwin reports. Byron's letters to Hogg were stolen, it seems, by a visitor.]

[460] *Southey to the Editor of the Courier*: No such epistle was ever shown to Mr. Wordsworth or to me; but I remember . . . to have heard that Lord Byron had spoken of us in a letter to Hogg, with some contempt, as fellows who could neither vie with him for skill in angling nor for prowess in swimming. [*LJ*, VI, 398.]

"Bowles is one of the same little order of spirits, who has been fussily fishing on for fame, and is equally waspish and jealous. What could Coleridge mean by praising his poetry as he does?[461]

"It was a mistake of mine, about his making the woods of Madeira tremble,[462] &c.; but it seems that I might have told him that there were no *woods* to make tremble with kisses, which would have been quite as great a blunder.

"I met Bowles once at Rogers's, and thought him a pleasant, gentlemanly man—a good fellow, for a parson. When men meet together after dinner, the conversation takes a certain turn. I remember he entertained us with some good stories.

The reverend gentleman pretended, however, to be much shocked at Pope's letters to Martha Blount.

"I set him and his invariable principles at rest. He did attempt an answer, which was no reply; at least, nobody read it. I believe he applied to me some lines in Shakspeare.*[463] A man is very unlucky who has a name that can be punned upon; and his own did not escape.[464]

"I have been reading 'Johnson's Lives,' a book I am very fond of. I look upon him as the profoundest of critics, and had occasion to study him when I was writing to Bowles.[465]

"Of all the disgraces that attach to England in the eye of foreigners, who admire Pope more than any of our poets, (though it is the fashion to under-rate him among ourselves,) the greatest perhaps is, that there should be no place assigned to him in Poets' Corner. I have often thought of erecting a monument to him at my own expense in Westminster Abbey, and hope to do so yet. But he was a Catholic, and, what was worse, puzzled Tillotson[466] and the Divines. That accounts for his not having any national monument. Milton, too, had very nearly been without a stone; and the mention of his name on the tomb of another was at one time considered a profanation to a church. The French, I am told, lock up Voltaire's tomb. Will there never be an end to this bigotry? Will men never learn that every great poet is necessarily a religious man?—so at least Coleridge says."

"Yes," replied Shelley; "and he might maintain the converse,—that every truly religious man is a poet; meaning by poetry the power of communicating intense and impassioned impressions respecting man and Nature."

* "I do remember thee, my Lord Biron," &c.

---

[461] *Medwin*: Byron is very unjust to Bowles. Look at the poetry that preceded him. His sonnets are perfect—and if he had written nothing but *Coombe Ellen*, he might claim to be classed among the

first descriptive poets of any age. [Coleridge had praised Bowles in *Biographia Literaria.*]

[462] *Byron in a marginal note*, 1816, to *English Bards*: Misquoted [in *English Bards*] and misunderstood by me; but not intentionally. It was not the "woods," but the people in them who trembled—why, Heaven only knows—unless they were overheard making this prodigious smack. [*Poetry*, I, 325, note 1. On the controversy between Byron and Bowles, see *LJ*, v, 522-592.]

Bowles to Murray, April 4, 1813: He [Byron] owes, as he will acknowledge, some amends to me for quoting me as the author of some nonsense which, he now knows, I never wrote, at least with the interpretation put to it. We had an explanation on this subject [at the home of Rogers], and he acknowledg'd how wrong he had been very ingenuously. [*A Wiltshire Parson and His Friends: The Correspondence of William Lisle Bowles*, ed. Garland Greever (Boston, 1926), pp. 143-144.]

[463] [Once Byron had become famous, it was inevitable that the line, here misquoted, on Biron or Berowne from *Love's Labour's Lost* (V, ii, 850) should be "applied" to him; but Bowles pointed out in *A Final Appeal to the Literary Public Relative to Pope, To which are added Some Remarks on Lord Byron's Conversations* (London, 1825), p. 147, that he had used lines from Pope: "Should some more sober critic come abroad,/ If wrong, I smile; if right, I kiss the rod." See J. J. Van Rennes, *Bowles, Byron and the Pope-Controversy* (Amsterdam, 1927), p. 93. (*Biron*, the spelling of the folios, rhymes with *moon*.)]

[464] [Byron's "Letter on Bowles's Strictures," published in March, 1821, used as its motto a line from an old song, "I'll play at *Bowls* with the Sun and Moon."]

[465] [Byron's "Letter" quoted from Johnson's *Lives of the Poets*, "the finest critical work extant" (*LJ*, v, 556, 560).]

[466] *Hobhouse*: D[ied] 1694 when Pope was 6.

—————

When I entered the room, Lord Byron was devouring, as he called it, a new novel of Sir Walter Scott's.[467]

"How difficult it is," said he, "to say any thing new!" Who was that voluptuary of antiquity, who offered a reward for a new pleasure? Perhaps all nature and art could not supply a new idea.

"This page, for instance, is a brilliant one; it is full of wit. But let us see how much of it is original. This passage, for instance, comes from Shakspeare; this *bon mot* from one of Sheridan's Comedies; this observation from another writer (naming the author); and yet the ideas are new-moulded,—and perhaps Scott was not aware of their being plagiarisms. It is a bad thing to have too good a memory."

"I should not like to have you for a critic," I observed.

" 'Set a thief to catch a thief,' " was the reply.[468]

"I never travel without Scott's Novels," said he: "they are a library in themselves—a perfect literary treasure. I could read them once a-year with new pleasure."[469]

I asked him if he was certain about the Novels being Sir Walter Scott's?

"Scott as much as owned himself the author of 'Waverley' to me in Murray's shop," replied he. "I was talking to him about that novel, and lamented that its author had not carried back the story nearer to the time of the Revolution. Scott, entirely off his guard, said, 'Ay, I might have done so, but'—— There he stopped. It was in vain to attempt to correct himself: he looked confused, and relieved his embarrassment by a precipitate retreat.[470]

"On another occasion I was to dine at Murray's; and being in his parlour in the morning, he told me I should meet the author of 'Waverley' at dinner. He had received several excuses, and the party was a small one; and, knowing all the people present, I was satisfied that the writer of that novel must have been, and could have been, no other than Walter Scott.

"He spoiled the fame of his poetry by his superior prose. He has such extent and versatility of powers in writing, that, should his Novels ever tire the public, which is not likely, he will apply himself to something else, and succeed as well.

[467] [On January 27, 1822, Byron was still eagerly awaiting the arrival of Scott's *The Pirate*.]

⁴⁶⁸ *Lady Byron*: Lord Byron was candid in owning what he had borrowed. He shewed in the letters of J. [? Ortrer *or* Ortis, *i.e.*, Ugo Foscolo's *Letters of Jacopo Ortis* (1798)] the original idea of "Burns the slow lamp" a line in The Corsair.

⁴⁶⁹ *Byron to Scott*, January 12, 1822: I never move without them [Scott's novels]; and when I removed from Ravenna to Pisa the other day, and sent on my library before, they were the only books that I kept by me, although I already have them by heart. [*LJ*, vi, 5.]

⁴⁷⁰ *Scott in the General Preface to Waverley*, 1829: I have no recollection whatever of this scene taking place . . . ; and from the manner in which he [Byron] uniformly expressed himself, I knew his opinion was entirely formed, and that any disclamations of mine would only have savoured of affectation. I do not mean to insinuate that the incident did not happen, but only that it could hardly have occurred exactly under the circumstances narrated without my recollecting something positive on the subject. [*Waverley Novels*, ed. Andrew Lang (London, 1892), I, xxx.]

Pryse Lockhart Gordon to Scott, September 2, 1829: I perceive in the preface to the new and beautiful Edition of your works, that you mention your doubts of Mr. Medwin's veracity in his *pretended* Conversations with Lord Byron relative to the Author of the Waverley Novels. I recollect when his lordship passed an evening with me here [Brussels], on his way to Switzerland, and when we were talking about *the Author*, I asked the poet if he had any doubt of this, and whether he had been on the subject with you. "No, Sir," he replied (with a change of countenance which made me regret that I had put the question). "It would have been great impertinence in me to question Mr. Scott on a point of such delicacy—and besides, being a proof of ignorance, for who that has read those delightful works and has besides the advantage of knowing Mr. Scott, could for a moment doubt that *he* was the Author? A contemporary of Shakespeare might as well have asked, who wrote *Hamlet*? [*HVSV*, pp. 180-181.]

Dr. J. R. Fenwick to Lady Byron, May 29, 1815: The broken sentence which fell from W. Scott in conversation with Lord B[yron] leaves no longer any doubt of his being the Author of Waverley. [Elwin, *Lord Byron's Wife*, p. 305. Fenwick is commenting on remarks in a letter from Lady Byron, who had met Scott at some time after April 7, 1815. See also *LJ*, v, 17-18.]

"His mottoes from old plays prove that *he*, at all events, possesses the dramatic faculty, which is denied *me*. And yet I am told that his 'Halidon Hill' did not justify expectation. I have never met with it, but have seen extracts from it."[471]

"Do you think," asked I, "that Sir Walter Scott's Novels owe any part of their reputation to the concealment of the author's name?"

"No," said he: "such works do not gain or lose by it. I am at a loss to know his reason for keeping up the *incognito*,— but that the reigning family could not have been very well pleased with 'Waverley.' There is a degree of *charlatanism* in *some* authors keeping up *the Unknown*. Junius owed much of his fame to that trick; and now that it is known to be the work of Sir Philip Francis, who reads it? A political writer, and one who descends to personalities such as disgrace Junius, should be immaculate as a public, as well as a private character; and Sir Philip Francis was neither. He had his price, and was gagged by being sent to India. He there seduced another man's wife. It would have been a new case for a Judge[472] to sit in judgment on himself, in a *Crim.-con.* It seems that his conjugal felicity was not great, for, when his wife died, he came into the room where they were sitting up with the corpse, and said, 'Solder her up, solder her up!' He saw his daughter crying, and scolded her, saying, 'An old hag—she ought to have died thirty years ago!' He married, shortly after, a young woman. He hated Hastings to a violent degree; all he hoped and prayed for was to outlive him.—[473] But many of the newspapers of the day are written as well as Junius. Mathias's book, 'The Pursuits of Literature,' now almost a deadletter, had once a great fame.[474]

"When Walter Scott began to write poetry, which was not at a very early age, Monk Lewis corrected his verse: he understood little then of the mechanical part of the art. The Fire King in 'The Minstrelsy of the Scottish Border,' was almost all Lewis's.[475] One of the ballads in that work, and, except some of Leyden's, perhaps one of the best, was made from a story picked up in a stagecoach; — I mean that of 'Will Jones.'

> 'They boil'd Will Jones within the pot,
> And not much fat had Will.'[476]

"I hope Walter Scott did not write the review on 'Christabel;' for he certainly, in common with many of us, is indebted to Coleridge. But for him, perhaps 'The Lay of the Last Minstrel' would never have been thought of.[477] The line

> 'Jesu Maria shield thee well!'

is word for word from 'Christabel.'[478]

---

[471] [Byron received Sir Walter Scott's gift of *Halidon Hill, a Dramatic Sketch from Scottish History* (1822), of inferior merit, about November 23, 1822, after his conversation with Medwin.]

[472] *Hobhouse*: He was not a Judge.

[473] *Byron to Rogers*, March 3, 1818: They say Francis is Junius; I think it looks like it. I remember meeting him at Earl Grey's at dinner. Has not he lately married a young woman? and was not he Madame Talleyrand's *Cavalier servente* in India years ago? [*LJ*, IV, 210 (M). Prothero explains, "Sir Philip Francis (1740-1818) was sentenced, in March, 1779, to pay a fine of 50,000 rupees to the husband of Madame Grand, who left India under his protection, and subsequently became the mistress, and, in 1801, the wife of Talleyrand. Sir Philip married, in 1814," a second wife. His first wife died in 1806. His long struggle for power with Warren Hastings led to a duel in India.]

[474] [The 16th ed. of 1812 seems to be the last.]

[475] *Scott to Archibald Constable*, October 22, 1824: He says very truly that I received much instruction from poor Mat Lewis but it related almost entirely to the rhymes in which he was justly *superior* and to the structure of versification for which the poor Monk had a most excellent ear. He wrote no part of "The Fire King" which I finished in one evening after dinner with Heber & Leyden sitting beside me nor do I think he ever helped me to a line save one in which I had made a false quantity sounding Jŭlÿ—Jūlў. [*Letters of Scott*, ed. H. J. C. Grierson and others (London, 1935),

VIII, 408-409. "The Fire-King," written in 1799, was published in *Tales of Wonder*, written and collected by M. G. Lewis, 1801.]

[476] [Lewis heard the grisly story of Bill Jones from Scott, as he explained in the preface to *Romantic Tales* (London, 1808), where we read (IV, 99),

> So he caused the cook make water hot,
> And the corpse, both flesh and bones,
> (To see what fat Bill Jones had got,)
> The Captain boiled in the negro-pot;
> But there wasn't *much* fat in Jones.

The tyrannous captain had killed Bill Jones, whose spirit then returned in sailorly guise to haunt the captain and drive him to suicide.]

[477] *Scott to Mrs. Hughes*, November 11, 1824: You would see in Byron's conversations that I was led to imitate the stile of Coleridge's Christabelle in the Lay of the last Minstrel—it is very true. . . . Byron seems to have thought I had a hand in some ill-natured review of Coleridges wild & wondrous tale which was entirely a mistake. He might have remembered by the way that it was I who first introduced his Lordship to the fragment with a view to interest him in Coleridge's fate and in the play he was then bringing forward. [*Letters of Scott*, VIII, 421.]

[478] [*Christabel*, l. 54, as well as l. 582, is "Jesu, Maria, shield her well!"]

⏜

"Of all the writers of the day, Walter Scott is the least jealous:[479] he is too confident of his own fame to dread the rivalry of others. He does not think of good writing, as the Tuscans do of fever—that there is only a certain quantity of it in the world."*

"What did you mean," said a gentleman[480] who was with

* Travellers in Italy should be cautious of taking *bouquets* of flowers from the *Contadini* children, as they are in the habit of placing them on the breasts of persons having malignant fevers, and think that, by communicating the disorder to another, it will be diminished in the person affected.

Lord Byron, "by calling Rogers a *Nestor* and an *Argonaut*? I suppose you meant to say that his poetry was old and worn out."

"You are very hard upon the *dead** poet,—upon the late lamented Mr. Samuel Rogers, (as he has been called,)—and upon me too, to suspect me of speaking ironically upon so serious a subject."

"It was a very doubtful expression, however, that 'Nestor of little poets,' " rejoined the other. "Compliments ought never to have a double sense—a cross meaning. And you seem to be fond of this mode of writing, for you call Lady Morgan's 'Italy' a fearless and excellent work.[481] What two odd words to be coupled together!"

"Take it as you like," replied Lord Byron, "I say, 'The Pleasures of Memory' *will* live."[482]

---

* He used to tell a story of Rogers and Ward visiting the Catacombs at Paris together. As Rogers, who was last, was making his exit, Ward said to him, "Why, you are not coming out, are you? Surely you are not tired of your *countrymen*! You don't mean to forsake them, do you?" The Poet did not forget the joke and revenged it by the Epigram contained in Page 210.[483]

---

[479] *Byron to Scott*, January 12, 1822: You disclaim "jealousies;" but I would ask, as Boswell did of Johnson, "of *whom could* you be *jealous*?"—of none of the living certainly. . . . [*LJ*, vi, 4.]

[480] [Medwin, *Shelley*, ii, 189, identifies the other conversationalist as Shelley.]

[481] [From a note in the appendix to *The Two Foscari*.]

[482] *Trelawny*: I was with Shelley—& Byron bepraised Rogers to annoy S— for in reality they both thought alike—about the late lamented Mr. Samuel R.

[483] [A similar story of Rogers and John William Ward in the catacombs is told in R. Ellis Roberts, *Samuel Rogers and His Circle* (New York, 1910), p. 65. Rogers appears in Byron's "Letter on Bowles's Strictures" (*LJ*, v, 537) as "the last Argonaut of classic English poetry, and the Nestor of our inferior race of living poets."]

"The Pleasures of *Mummery!** Pray now, (speak candidly,) have you read since you were a schoolboy, or can you, with all your memory, repeat five lines of that boasted 'Essay on Memory' that you have been bepraising so furiously all your life? Instruct me where to find the golden fleece. Be my Jason for once."

"I remember being delighted with 'The Pleasures of Memory' when I was at Harrow; and that is saying a great deal, for I seldom read a book when I was there, and continue to like what I did then.

" 'Jacqueline,' too, is a much finer poem than 'Lara.'[484] Your allowing precedence to the latter amused me. But they soon got a divorce."[485]

"There again: your taste is too fastidious. Rogers was very much offended at its being said that his 'Pleasures,' &c. were to be found shining in green and gold morocco-bindings in most parlour-windows, and on the book-shelves of all young ladies."

"But, don't we all write to please them? I am sure I was more pleased with the fame my 'Corsair'[486] had, than with that of any other of my books. Why? for the very reason because it did shine, and in *boudoirs*. Who does not write to please the women? And Rogers has succeeded: what more can he want or wish?

"There was a Mrs. ——— once fell in love with Shelley for his verses;[487] and a Miss Stafford was so taken with the 'Sofa' (a very different one from Cowper's) that she went to France and married Crebillon.[488]

"These are some of the sweets of authorship. But my day is over. *Vixi*, &c. I used formerly (that *olim*[489] is a bad and a sad word!) to get letters by almost every post, the delicate beauty of whose penmanship suggested the fair, taper fingers that indited them. But my 'Corsair' days are over. Heigh ho!"

* The reader is requested to bear in mind that it is not with the author that this dialogue is held.—ED.

"But what has all this to do with Rogers, or 'The Pleasures of Memory?' Is there one line of that poem that has not been altered and realtered, till it would be difficult to detect in the patchwork any thing like the texture of the original stuff?"

[484] *Lady Byron*: Lady Byron heard the same opinion given in private & with evident sincerity. He always made too high an estimate of the *relative* merits of other Poets.

[485] *Byron to Moore*, August 12, 1814: Murray talks of divorcing Larry and Jacky. . . . [*LJ*, iii, 125. The two poems were originally published together in a single volume.]

Medwin: It was an unnatural and unintelligible conjunction that gave rise to many jokes. [See *LJ*, iii, 136-137.]

[486] *Trelawny*: Seven thousand [copies] sold the day of publication & composed in 15 days. [Ten thousand copies of *The Corsair* were sold on the day of publication; the poem was written in ten days.]

[487] *Medwin*: See Shelley's *Life*. [This note, written at the bottom of the page and unattached to any statement in the text, presumably refers to the mysterious married woman who "once fell in love with Shelley for his verses," described in Medwin's *Life of Shelley*, pp. 204-207. White (*Shelley*, i, 437) believes that it was Shelley, not Medwin, who invented her.]

[488] *Byron in "A Second Letter to Murray on Bowles's Strictures"*: Crebillon . . . writes a licentious novel, and a young English girl of some fortune and family (a Miss Strafford) [*sic*] runs away, and crosses the sea to marry him. . . . [*LJ*, v, 574 (M), first published 1835.]

[489] *Medwin*: "Nuper" he should have said—if he had quoted correctly—"Nuper idoneus."

"Well, if there is not a line or a word that has not been canvassed, and made the subject of separate epistolary discussion, what does that prove but the general merit of the whole piece? And the correspondence will be valuable by and bye, and save the commentators a vast deal of labour, and waste of ingenuity. People do wisest who take care of their fame when they have got it. That's the rock I have split on. It has been said that he has been puffed into notice by his dinners and

Lady Holland. Though he gives very good ones, and female Mæcenases are no bad things now-a-days, it is by no means true. Rogers has been a spoilt child; no wonder that he is a little vain and jealous. And yet he deals praise very liberally sometimes; for he wrote to a little friend of mine,[490] on the occasion of his late publication, that 'he was born with a rose-bud in his mouth, and a nightingale singing in his ear,'—two very prettily turned Orientalisms. Before my wife and the world quarrelled with me, and brought me into disrepute with the public, Rogers had composed some very pretty commendatory verses on me; but they were kept corked up for many long years, under hope that I might reform and get into favour with the world again, and that the said lines (for he is rather costive, and does not like to throw away his effusions) might find a place in 'Human Life.'[491] But after a great deal of oscillation, and many a sigh at their hard destiny—their still-born fate,—they were hermetically sealed, and adieu to my immortality![492]

"Rogers has an unfortunately sensitive temper. We nearly quarrelled at Florence. I asked the officer of the *Dogana* (who had trouble enough with all my live and dead stock), in consequence of his civilities, to dine with me at Schneider's;[493] but Rogers happened to be in one of his ill humours, and abused the Italians.

"He is coming to visit[494] me on his return from Rome, and will be annoyed when he finds I have any English comforts about me. He told a person the other day that one of my new tragedies was intended for the stage, when he knew neither of them was. I suppose he wanted to get another of them damned. Samuel, Samuel! But," added he, after a pause, "these things are, as Lord Kenyon said of Erskine,[495] 'mere spots in the sun.' He has good qualities to counterbalance these littlenesses in his character.

[490] *Medwin*: Moore.

[491] [See *Poetry*, iv, 539 note.]

[492] *Lady Byron*: There are some beautiful lines on Lord Byron in Rogers' "Italy" a noble way of making Ld Byron's Satire harmless. [The lines, published after Byron's death, are quoted in *LJ*, ii, 70, note.]

[493] [On Byron and Rogers at Florence, where they stayed at a "little inn *vis-à-vis* Sneyder's," see Marchand, p. 941.]

[494] *Medwin*: It was during this visit that the Scene occurred which I detailed at some length in the *Angler in Wales* [i, 24-26], in which Tiger and the Monkey play a part, and where he allowed the Dog to bait the Banker bard. The verses contained in Shelley's *Life* [ii, 191-194, "Question and Answer," on Rogers] were probably written about this time. One of the most savage of satires in our language, he had thought to place under the couch where he pressed his caller to sit, enjoying the idea that he was seated in unconscious serenity over this literary Rocket, that would one day explode. [Cf. Trelawny's *Records*, p. 31, and Medwin's *Shelley*, ii, 190.]

Note the Bard at Bay. I have mentioned that Byron had a Cerberus in the shape of an English Bull dog, Tiger by name. The animal was an intelligent one, & tho' as little inclined to make new acquaintances as his master, soon learned to distinguish his master's habitués & allowed them the Entree, contenting himself with growling at one & wagging his tail at another, a compliment however seldom paid to any but Shelley. Byron was much attracted to this fine creature and frequently had him loosed when playing at Billiards, his favourite game. On the occasion of the meeting of Childe Harold and the Bard of Memory, his gruff friend Tiger was called on to play a distinguished part. Rogers, as soon as he dismounted at the Tre Donzelle, in one of his sentimental notes announced the interesting event of his arrival & immediate visit. Knowing that Rogers was momentarily to appear, Byron gave orders to Tita to introduce the Monkey & Bull dog. I think I see Byron in his jacket stumping round the Billiard room with the heavy sound that once heard could not be mistaken, & after making some successful strike, bursting into one of his usual jibes or flashes of merriment, which success always inspired, or dividing his caresses between Jocko and Tiger. There existed no slight jealousy between the favourites, which showed itself on the part of the latter by a short, loud, angry bark at his rival, whilst the ape sat grinning and chattering defiance (perched out of reach,) to the no small amusement of his master. The coming of the expected guest was now announced by a bark of deeper intonation, which Byron made no effort to repress, but turned to the game, to which he affected with one of his cynic grins to pay more than common attention. In the meantime Tiger rushed furiously at the Stranger, who backed into a corner of the room, shivering and breathless with Terror. Byron, without casting a look at the poor bard at bay, contented himself with drawling out at intervals, Ti-i-ger, Ti-i-ger, but in such an accent as rather to encourage than check the baiter, who continued a furious concert of menaces at the Death in Life or Departed Mr. Rogers. Byron at length pretended to discover the cause of the affray; to kick Tiger aside and press his *dear friend* in his arms was only the affair of an instant. It was a fine piece of acting— the mock fervour of his profession of regard, his upbraidings and threats to Tiger—nothing in stage language could surpass the situation. [See *The Angler in Wales*, I, 24-26, where this account appears, with minor differences. Medwin makes no claim of being present. Rogers arrived at Pisa about April 20, 1822, after Medwin had left. I see no reason to assume another, earlier visit from Rogers to Byron. Trelawny says in his *Records*, I, 53-54, that it was he who saved Rogers from the dog, there called Moretto, and that Byron's malice resulted from a London letter accusing Rogers of gossiping about Byron.]

[495] [Byron knew Erskine personally, but not Kenyon, who died in 1802.]

"Rogers is the only man I know who can write epigrams, and sharp bone-cutters too, in two lines; for instance, that on an M. P. who had reviewed his book,[496] and said he wrote very well for a banker:—

'They say he has no heart, and I deny it:
He has a heart,—and gets his speeches by it.' "[497]

[496] [Ward had condemned Rogers's *Columbus* in the *Quarterly Review*. See *LJ*, ii, 69, note.]

[497] *Medwin*: Do not suppose that these Conversations reveal all that passed between us. Some were not very proper for ears polite. [Medwin then supplies a couplet which he says that Byron quoted and which he identifies as from the first (unexpurgated) edition of Martin A. Shee's *Rhymes on Art*: "Noseless himself, he brings home noseless blocks,/ To show what time has done and what— the [pox]." The lines refer to Lord Elgin and the Elgin Marbles.]

"I HAVE been told," said he one Sunday evening during our ride, "that you have got a parson here of the name of Nott. —Nott?[498] I think I should know that name: was he not one of the tutors of a late Princess? If I am not mistaken, 'thereby hangs a tale,' that perhaps would have been forgotten, but for his over-officious zeal,—or a worse motive. The would-be Bishop having himself cracked windows, should not throw stones. I respect the pulpit as much as any man, but would not have it made a forum for politics or personality. The Puritans gave us quite enough of them.—But to come to the point. A person who was at his house to-day, where he has a chapel, tells me that this dignitary of the Church has in a very undignified way been preaching against my 'Cain.'[499] He contends, it seems, that the snake which tempted Eve was not a snake, but the Devil in disguise; and that Bishop Warburton's 'Legation of Moses' is no authority. It may be so, and a poor unlearned man like me may be mistaken: but as there are not three of his congregation who have seen 'Cain,' and not one but will be satisfied that the learned Doctor's object is to preach against and vilify me, under the pretext of clearing up these disputed points, surely his arguments are much misplaced. It is strange that people will not let me alone. I am sure I lead a very quiet, moral life here."

A fortnight after he said: "I hear that your Doctor, in company with some Russians, the other day, called Shelley a *scelerato*, and has been preaching two sermons, two following Sundays, against Atheism. It is pretty clear for whom he means them; and Mrs. Shelley being there, it was still more indecent. The Doctor is playing with penknives when he handles poets."[500]

The next morning he gave us a song upon the Doctor, to the tune of "The Vicar and Moses."[501]

⁴⁹⁸ *Medwin*: This divine was, I believe, a Prebend of Winchester, and . . . obtained . . . the appointment of sub-preceptor to the Princess Charlotte, which situation, from his over-anxiety to become . . . a bishop, and some coquetting with his royal pupil, whom he persuaded to recommend him by a codicil to her will, for a father-in-Godship, in case of accidents, lost him his office. So at least runs the story. . . . He had also been, if he had now ceased to be, "a gay deceiver," and had obtained for himself, by his backing out of more than one matrimonial engagement, the *soubriquet* of Slip-knot (Nott). [*Shelley*, p. 361.]

⁴⁹⁹ *Byron to Moore*, February 20, 1822: The parsons are preaching at it [*Cain*], from Kentish Town and Oxford to Pisa. . . . [*LJ*, vi, 24 (M).]

⁵⁰⁰ *Mary Shelley to Maria Gisborne*, January 18, 1822: Vacca reported that this Doctʳ Nott said in Society that Shelley was a scelerato. We told Taaffe and the little gossip reported it to all the world. Doctʳ Nott heard of it, and sent a message by Medwin to deny it. . . . [F. L. Jones, "Mary Shelley to Maria Gisborne: New Letters, 1818-1822," *Studies in Philology*, LII (January, 1955), 70-71. Mary went to hear Nott preach several times.]

Mary Shelley to Hobhouse, November 10, 1824: Medwin could also have mentioned that as soon as Dr. Nott heard that he was accused of the impropriety of preaching against Shelley, he paid us a visit to exculpate himself from the charge. [*Captain Medwin*, p. 201.]

⁵⁰¹ *Medwin*: "Most unfortunate," Byron used to say, "was the man who had a name that could be punned upon"; and . . . said that the preacher read some of the commandments affirmatively and not negatively, as "Thou shalt, Nott! (not) bear false witness against thy neighbour, &c." The circumstance to which I allude, and that excited Lord Byron's bile, is this: He opened a chapel in his own apartment [in the same building in which Shelley lived], and preached a trilogy of sermons against Atheism, Mrs. Shelley forming one of the congregation, and his eyes being directed on her with a significant expression. . . . These discourses came to Byron's ears, and though Shelley laughed at the malice of the Doctor, the noble bard was indignant at the prostitution of his pulpit, and still more so when he heard that the divine had at Mrs. Beauclerc's called Shelley a "*Scelerato*." . . . The day after, Byron wrote

a little biting satire, a song to the tune of *The Vicar and Moses*, which . . . was supplied to Colburn for the *Conversations*, but thought by him *trop fort*. [*Shelley*, pp. 361-362.]

"I have often wished," said I to Lord Byron one day, "to know how you passed your time after your return from Greece in 1812."[502]

"There is little to be said about it," replied he. "Perhaps it would have been better had I never returned! I had become so much attached to the Morea, its climate, and the life I led there, that nothing but my mother's death*[503] and my affairs would have brought me home. However, after an absence of three years,[504] behold! I was again in London. My Second Canto of 'Childe Harold' was then just published;[505] and the impersonation of myself, which, in spite of all I could say, the world would discover in that poem, made every one curious to know me, and to discover the identity. I received every where a marked attention, was courted in all societies, made much of by Lady Jersey, had the *entré* at Devonshire-house, was in favour with Brummell, (and that was alone enough to make a man of fashion at that time;) in fact, I was a lion[506]—a ball-room bard—a *hot-pressed* darling! 'The Corsair' put my reputation *au comble*, and had a wonderful success, as you may suppose, by one edition being sold in a day.

"Polidori, who was rather vain, once asked me what there was he could not do as well as I? I think I named four things: —that I could swim four miles—write a book, of which four thousand copies should be sold in a day†—drink four bottles of wine—and I forget what the other was,[507] but it was not worth mentioning. However, as I told you before, my 'Corsair' was sufficient to captivate all the ladies.

* In August 1811.
† The fact is that nearly 10,000 copies of several of Lord Byron's productions have been sold on the first day of publication.

[502] *Medwin*: I asked him about 1812 because he often spoke of it, as the epoch of his glory—his Waterloo Era. [Byron returned from Greece in 1811.]

[503] *Medwin*: Misprint—*health*. She died a fortnight after his return after two years absence. [In the text, Medwin has deleted *death* and the sign of the possessive in *mother's*, so that the phrase stands, "my mother and my affairs." It seems barely possible that Byron may have told Medwin that one of the causes for his return was concern for his mother's health, although his letters from abroad to her do not reveal any such concern. She wrote to Hanson, January 3, 1811, "I am neither well nor happy, and *never expect* to be so in this world" (Marchand, p. 272). But see *LJ*, I, 321: ". . . I heard *one* day of her illness, the *next* of her death," which, however, may well refer to the specific illness that led to her death and does not, presumably, eliminate the possibility that Byron knew that she was not in good health.]

[504] *Medwin: Seasons*. Misprint.

[505] *Hobhouse*: The framer of the Conversations does not seem to have recollected that the first and second canto of "Childe Harold" were published together, and never appeared separately. [*WR*, III, 31.]

[506] *Byron in his diary*, January 19, 1821: I had been the lion of 1812. . . . [*LJ*, V, 178.]

Medwin: Speaking of English beauties, he said in his day that there were two [?]—the first, Lady Charlemont—cold as a statue —and Lady Adelaide Forbes. And I suspect it was to the latter that he made an offer, being refused. I saw her set a little in Paris. This was in 1822 or 3. [See *LJ*, II, 230-231, 333, 358; V, 549.]

[507] *Trelawny*: & dup[e] four women.

Moore: "After all," said the physician, "what is there you can do that I cannot?"—"Why, since you force me to say," answered the other, "I think there are three things I can do which you cannot." Polidori defied him to name them. "I can," said Lord Byron, "swim across that river—I can snuff out that candle with a pistol-shot at the distance of twenty paces—and I have written a poem of which 14,000 copies were sold in one day." [Moore, *Life*, p. 319 (M).]

"About this period I became what the French call *un homme à bonnes fortunes*, and was engaged in a *liaison*,—and, I might add, a serious one.

"The lady had scarcely any personal attractions to recommend her. Her figure, though genteel,[508] was too thin to be good,[509] and wanted that roundness which elegance and grace would vainly supply. She was, however, young, and of the first connexions. *Au reste*, she possessed an infinite vivacity, and an imagination heated by novel-reading, which made her fancy herself a heroine of romance, and led her into all sorts of eccentricities. She was married, but it was a match of *convenance*, and no couple could be more fashionably indifferent to, or independent of one another, than she and her husband.[510] It was at this time that we happened to be thrown much together. She had never been in love—at least where the affections are concerned,—and was made without a heart,[511] as many of the sex are; but her head more than supplied the deficiency.

"I was soon congratulated by my friends on the conquest I had made, and did my utmost to shew that I was not insensible to the partiality I could not help perceiving. I made every effort to be in love, expressed as much ardour as I could muster, and kept feeding the flame with a constant supply of *billets-doux* and amatory verses. In short, I was in decent time duly and regularly installed into what the Italians call *service*, and soon became, in every sense of the word, a *patito*.

"It required no Œdipus to see where all this would end. I am easily governed by women, and she gained an ascendancy over me that I could not easily shake off. I submitted to this thraldom long, for I hate *scenes*, and am of an indolent disposition; but I was forced to snap the knot rather rudely at last.[512] Like all lovers, we had several quarrels before we came to a final rupture. One was made up in a very odd way, and without any verbal explanation. She will remember it. Even during our intimacy I was not at all constant to this fair one, and she suspected as much. In order to detect my intrigues she watched me, and earthed a lady into my lodgings,—and came herself, terrier-like, in the disguise of a carman.[513] My valet, who did not see through the masquerade, let her in; when, to the despair of Fletcher, she put off the man, and put on the woman. Imagine the scene: it was worthy of Faublas!

"Her after-conduct was unaccountable madness—a combination of spite and jealousy. It was perfectly agreed and understood that we were to meet as strangers. We were at a ball. She came up and asked me if she might waltz. I thought it perfectly indifferent whether she waltzed or not, or with whom, and told her so, in different terms, but with much coolness. After she had finished, a scene occurred, which was in the mouth of every one.[514]

* * * * *

* * * * * * *

* * * * * * *

* * * * * * *

[508] *Harness*: A word that has long been exploded by all but the apprentices of Cheapside and the milliners of Cranbourne-alley. . . . [*BEM*, xvi, 540.]

[509] *Lady Caroline Lamb to Medwin*, November, 1824: You justly observe, I had few personal attractions. [*LJ*, ii, 452.]

[510] *Lady Caroline Lamb to Medwin*, November, 1824: *I had married for love*. . . . He never could say . . . that I had not loved my husband. In his letters to me he is perpetually telling me I love him the best of the two. . . . [*LJ*, ii, 451.]

[511] *Lady Caroline Lamb to Medwin*, November, 1824: Byron never could say I had no heart. [*LJ*, ii, 451.]

[512] *Lady Caroline Lamb to Medwin*, November, 1824: The last time we parted for ever, as he pressed his lips on mine (it was in the Albany) he said "poor Caro, if every one hates me, you, I see, will never change—No, not with ill usage!" & I said, "yes, I *am* changed, & shall come near you no more."—For then he showed me letters, & told me things I cannot repeat, & all my attachment went. This was our last parting scene—well I remember it. [*LJ*, ii, 453.]

[513] *Lady Caroline Lamb to Medwin*, November, 1824: It *is* true I went to see him as a Carman, after that! [*LJ*, ii, 453; cf. *HVSV*, pp. 58-59.]

[514] *Lady Caroline Lamb to Medwin*, November, 1824: The scene at Lady Heathcote's is nearly true—he had made me swear I was

never to Waltz. Lady Heathcote said, Come, Lady Caroline, you must begin, & I bitterly answered—oh yes! I am in a merry humour. I did so—but whispered to Lord Byron "I conclude I may walze *now*" and he answered sarcastically, "with every body in turn —you always did it better than any one. I shall have a pleasure in seeing you."—I did so you may judge with what feelings. After this, feeling ill, I went into a small inner room where supper was prepared; Lord Byron & Lady Rancliffe entered after; seeing me, he said, "I have been admiring your dexterity." I clasped a knife, not intending anything. "Do, my dear," he said. "But if you mean to act a Roman's part, mind which way you strike with your knife— be it at your own heart, not mine—you have struck there already." "Byron," I said, and ran away with the knife. I never stabbed myself. It is false. Lady Rancliffe & Tankerville screamed and said I would; people pulled to get it from me; I was terrified; my hand got cut, & the blood came over my gown. I know not what happened after—but this is the very truth. [*LJ*, ɪɪ, 452-453. For Byron's account, written the day after the event, see his *Correspondence*, ɪ, 163-164; for other accounts, see *HVSV*, pp. 69-70, 617, note 57.]

"Soon after this she promised young Grattan her favours if he would call me out.[515] Yet can any one believe that she should be so infatuated after all this, as to call at my apartments? (certainly with no view of shooting herself.) I was from home; but finding 'Vathek' on the table, she wrote in the first page, 'Remember me!'

"Yes! I had cause to remember her; and, in the irritability of the moment, wrote under the two words these two stanzas:—

> Remember thee, remember thee!
>   Till Lethe quench life's burning stream,
> Remorse and shame shall cling to thee,
>   And haunt thee like a feverish dream!
>
> Remember thee! Ay, doubt it not;
>   Thy husband too shall think of thee;
> By neither shalt thou be forgot,
>   Thou *false* to him, thou *fiend* to me![516]

[515] [Preceding nine words supplied from Medwin's letter to Edward Bulwer, September 10, 1825, *Captain Medwin*, p. 184.]

[516] [The two words in italics are supplied from E. H. Coleridge's edition of Byron's *Poetry*. This entire section on Lady Caroline appears only in the first edition of the *Conversations*; Medwin did not intend to replace it.]

"I am accused of ingratitude to a certain personage.[517] It is pretended that, after his civilities, I should not have spoken of him disrespectfully.[518] Those epigrams were written long before my introduction to him;[519] which was, after all, entirely accidental, and unsought-for on my part. I met him one evening at Colonel Johnston's.[520] As the party was a small one, he could not help observing me; and as I made a considerable noise at that time, and was one of the lions of the day, he sent General —— to desire I would be presented to him. I would willingly have declined the honour, but could not with decency. His request was in the nature of a command. He was very polite, for he is the politest man in Europe, and paid me some compliments that meant nothing.[521] This was all the civility he ever shewed me, and it does not burthen my conscience much.

[517] *Galt*: His Lordship never was accused of ingratitude to the Prince. He was *blamed* for writing in contempt of the consideration due to the personal feelings of the Prince, as he would have been had he taken the same liberty with the domestic circumstances of any other gentleman. . . . [*BEM*, xvi, 533.]

[518] *R. C. Dallas*: Certain it is, he gave up all ideas of appearing at Court, and fell into the habit of speaking disrespectfully of the Prince. [*HVSV*, pp. 56-57.]

[519] *Medwin*: The Epigrams referred to were to Lady Jersey, to King Charles, and to the Princess Charlotte. [Of "Condolatory Address," "Windsor Poetics," and "Lines to a Lady Weeping," the third only, published March 7, 1812, was written before Byron's introduction to the Prince Regent.]

[520] [The name of Byron's host (or hostess) is given by Murray as *Johnson* (*HVSV*, p. 55), by Galt as *Johnstone* (*BEM*, xvi, 534).]

[521] *Galt*: With regard to the compliments in question, assuredly on the second day after the interview, at Miss Johnstone's ball, he was proud, and pleased with them. [*BEM*, xvi, 533-534. For Byron's accounts of his interview, see *LJ*, ii, 125-129, 134-135; for other accounts, see *HVSV*, pp. 55-57.]

"I will shew you my Irish '*Avatara*.' Moore tells me that it has saved him from writing on the same subject:[521ª] he would have done it much better. I told Moore to get it circulated in Paris: he has sent me a few printed copies; here is one for you.[522] I have said that the Irish Emancipation, when granted, will not conciliate the Catholics, but will be considered as a measure of expediency, and the resort of fear. But you will have the sentiment in the words of the original."

"What a noble fellow," said Lord Byron, after I had finished reading, "was Lord Edward Fitzgerald!—and what a romantic and singular history was his! If it were not too near our times, it would make the finest subject in the world for an historical novel."

"What was there so singular in his life and adventures?" I asked.

"Lord Edward Fitzgerald," said he, "was a soldier from a boy. He served in America, and was left for dead in one of the pitched battles, (I forget which,) and returned in the list of killed. Having been found in the field after the removal of the wounded, he was recovered by the kindness and compassion of a native, and restored to his family as one from the grave. On coming back to England, he employed himself entirely in the duties of his corps and the study of military tactics, and got a regiment. The French Revolution now broke out, and with it a flame of liberty burnt in the breast of the young Irishman. He paid this year a visit to Paris, where he formed an intimacy with Tom Paine, and came over with him to England.

"There matters rested, till, dining one day at his regimental mess, he ordered the band to play 'Ça ira,' the great revolutionary air. A few days afterwards he received a letter from headquarters, to say that the King dispensed with his services.[523]

[521a] [See *Letters of Moore*, ed. Dowden, II, 786; *LJ*, v, 369.]

[522] *Moore in his diary*, January 8, 1822: Have got Lord Byron's Irish verses printed on a single sheet by Galignani. [*Journal*, III, 315.]

Medwin: I have omitted the *Irish Avatara*, as it is now contained in his works. When Moore sent 4 copies of the Satire, Byron stuck them like the layers of an onion in the mirror over his chimney piece—in order to excite our curiosity, which he would not gratify by shewing the Stanzas. He afterwards one evening, then in good humour, made an exception in my favour, and gave me one of the Copies, saying, "Here is one for you," etc. [*The Irish Avatar* was first published in England in the first edition of Medwin's *Conversations*, with a number of the stanzas deleted, which were restored in the "New Edition" of 1824, but printed with asterisks at six points to indicate omissions. These Medwin has supplied in his annotated copy, revealing one variant from E. H. Coleridge's version of stanza 21, last line: Instead of "Like their blood which has flowed, and which yet has to flow," Medwin has, "Like the blood he has shed & may yet have to flow." Byron directed Moore to have twenty copies privately printed, send him six (*LJ*, v, 369).]

[523] *Medwin*: This anecdote coincides with one of Charles [11th] Duke of Norfolk, who gave, at the mess of his command, "The Sovereignty of the People" and was, like Lord Edward Fitzgerald, dismissed from his command.

Some years after, one of his sons, Mr. Stephenson, who had been sent on some foreign Mission, came back with a piece of riband on his Button hole—which much offended his father, who said, "What do you wear that order for?" The son's reply was alluding to the dismissal order for his regiment. "What sort of order did you once get?" [The occasion was a London dinner in 1789; the toast proposed was, "Our sovereign's health—the majesty of the people." George III deprived him of some of his public offices. On his death in 1815, he left no legitimate sons.]

"He now paid a second visit to America, where he lived for two years among the native Indians; and once again crossing the Atlantic, settled on his family estate in Ireland, where he fulfilled all the duties of a country gentleman and magistrate. Here it was that he became acquainted with the O'Connors, and in conjunction with them zealously exerted himself for the emancipation of their country. On their imprisonment he was proscribed, and secreted himself for six weeks in what are called the liberties of Dublin; but was at length betrayed by a woman.

"Major Sirr and a party of the military entered his bedroom, which he always kept unlocked. At the voices he started up in bed and seized his pistols, when Major Sirr fired and wounded him. Taken to prison, he soon after died of his wound, before he could be brought to trial. Such was the fate of one who had all the qualifications of a hero and a patriot! Had he lived, perhaps Ireland had not now been a land of Helots."[524]

[524] *Medwin*: Lord Byron derived this Sketch of Lord Ed. Fitzgerald from Mrs. Beauclerk, his half-sister, in a Conversation with her. She was the depository of his Papers relative to the Revolution, which she gave Moore for the Life of the Irish Patriot and rebel. [The spirit of the account is authentic and, although there are numerous errors of detail, the main outlines of Fitzgerald's life are given correctly, with one exception. His second visit to America took place before, not after, his intimacy with Paine in Paris and his dismissal from the British army. Byron wrote on March 10, 1814, "If I had been a man, I would have made an English Lord Edward Fitzgerald" (*LJ*, II, 396). It should be added that Medwin was an old friend of Mrs. Beauclerk, whom he had first known in Sussex, and that the account of Fitzgerald may well derive not from conversation with Byron but directly from Mrs. Beauclerk. See Medwin's *Shelley*, II, 232-234, and Cline, *Byron, Shelley and their Pisan Circle*, p. 240, note 51.]

"What did you mean," asked I one day, "by that line in 'Don Juan,'—

'Some play the devil, and then write a novel?' "[525]

"I alluded," replied he, "to a novel that had some fame in consequence of its being considered a history of my life and adventures, character and exploits, mixed up with innumerable lies and lampoons upon others. Madame de Staël asked me if the picture was like me,—and the Germans think it is not a caricature. One of my foreign biographers has tacked name, place, and circumstance to the Florence fable, and gives me a principal instead of a subordinate part in a certain tragical history therein narrated.[526] Unfortunately for my biographers, I was never at Florence for more than a few days in my life,[527] and Fiorabella's beautiful flowers are not so quickly plucked or blighted.[528] Hence, however, it has been alleged that murder is my instinct; and to make innocence my victim and my prey, part of my nature. I imagine that this dark hint took its origin from one of my Notes in the 'The Giaour,'[529] in which I said that the countenance of a person dying by stabs retained the character of ferocity, or of the particular passion imprinted on it, at the moment of dissolution. A sage reviewer makes this comment on my remark:—'It must have been the result of personal observation!'

---

[525] [*Don Juan*, II, cci, referring to Lady Caroline Lamb's *Glenarvon* (1816).]

[526] *Goethe in his review of Manfred*: When a bold and enterprising young man, he [Byron] won the affections of a Florentine lady. Her husband discovered the amour, and murdered his wife; but the murderer was the same night found dead in the street, and there was no one on whom any suspicion could be attached. Lord Byron removed from Florence, and these spirits haunted him all his life after. [Moore, *Life*, pp. 448-449. Goethe's review summarizes *Glenarvon*, ii, 83-85, the title character of which he identified with Byron, who forwarded the review to Murray on June 7, 1820.]

[527] [Byron passed through Florence at the end of October, 1821, on his way to Pisa, with Rogers.]

[528] [The preceding clause is supplied from the first edition. Fiorabella is the character who is murdered by her husband, who is in turn murdered by Glenarvon.]

[529] [Byron's note to l. 89.]

"But I am made out a very amiable person in that novel! The only thing belonging to me in it, is part of a letter;[530] but it is mixed up with much fictitious and poetical matter. Shelley told me he was offered, by Hookham the bookseller in Bond Street, no small sum if he would compile the Notes of that book into a story; but that he declined the offer.[531] *   *

*   *   *   *   *   *   *

*   *   *   *   *   *   *

*   *   *   *   *   *   *

*   *   *   *   *   *   *

But if I know the authoress, I have seen letters of hers much better written than any part of that novel. A lady of my acquaintance told me, that when that book was going to the press, she was threatened with cutting a prominent figure in it if ——.[532] But the story would only furnish evidence of the unauthenticity of the nature of the materials, and shew the manner and spirit with which the piece was got up.—Yet I don't know why I have been led to talk about such nonsense, which I paid no more attention to than I have to the continual calumnies and lies that have been unceasingly circulated about me,[533] in public prints, and through anonymous letters. I got a whole heap of them when I was at Venice, and at last found out that I had to thank Mr. Sotheby for the greater share of them.[534] It was under the waspishness produced by this discovery that I made him figure also in my 'Beppo' as an 'antique gentleman of rhyme,' a 'bustling Botherby,' &c. I always thought him the most insufferable of bores, and the curse of the Hampden,[535] as Edgeworth was of *his* club. There was a society formed for the suppression of Edgeworth, and sending him back to Ireland;[536]—but I should have left the other to his

'Snug coterie and literary lady,'[537]

and to his Sister that Rogers pretended to take for an old arm-chair, if he had not made himself an active bore, by dunning me with disagreeable news,—and, what was worse, and more nauseous and indigestible still, with his criticisms and advice.

[530] [Reprinted in *LJ*, ii, 136, note.]

[531] [Hookham published Shelley's *Queen Mab* and the *History of a Six Weeks' Tour*, took the part of Harriet Shelley. There are no notes to any edition of *Glenarvon* which I have seen. A number of the characters are identified in *LJ*, ii, 137, note.]

[532] *Medwin to Edward Bulwer*, September 10, 1825: A lady whose name I am not allowed to mention told Lord Byron that when *Glenarvon* was in the press she received a letter threatening her with cutting a very prominent figure in the novel unless she sent £300 as hush-money. Since his death I have made enquiries of the lady mentioned, who not only confirmed the anecdote but added that the money was paid. [*Captain Medwin*, p. 184.]

[533] *Medwin*: The little impression this libelous novel [*Glenarvon*] made on him was proved by his indifference to its being translated by a Venetian and published. See Moore's *Notices* [*LJ*, iv, 156].

[534] *Harness*: It is true, that Byron was once rash and idle enough to suppose a man of Mr Sotheby's sincere and gentlemanly character, guilty of committing the meanness that the above extract has imputed to him. . . . [*BEM*, xvi, 539 (M). Byron was long convinced that Sotheby was the writer of an anonymous letter received at Rome, telling him that eight out of "ten things" in *The Prisoner of Chillon* were "good for nothing" (*LJ*, iv, 216).]

[535] *Byron in his "Detached Thoughts"*: It [the Alfred Club] was pleasant—a little too sober and literary, and bored with Sotheby . . . I [also] belonged . . . to the Hampden political Club. . . . [*LJ*, v, 424; see also *LJ*, v, 433.]

[536] *Byron in his diary*, January 19, 1821: A paper had been presented for the *recall of Mrs. Siddons to the stage*, . . . to which all men had been called to subscribe. Whereupon Thomas Moore, of profane and poetical memory, did propose that a similar paper

should be *sub*scribed and *circum*scribed "for the recall of Mr. Edgeworth to Ireland." [*LJ*, v, 179.]

[537] *Medwin*: Lydia White, where I have more than once met Sotheby. [The quoted lines from *Beppo* appear in stanzas lxxii, lxxiii, and lxxvi.]

"When Galignani was about to publish a new edition of my works, he applied to Moore to furnish him with some anecdotes of me; and it was suggested that we should get up a series of the most unaccountable and improbable adventures, to gull the Parisian and travelling world with:[538] but I thought afterwards that he had quite enough of the fabulous at command without our inventing any thing new, which indeed would have required ingenuity.

"You tell me that the Baron Lutzerode has been asking you for some authentic particulars of my life, to affix to his translation of 'Cain,'[539] and thus contradict the German stories circulated about me, and which, I understand, even Goethe believes. Why don't you write something for him, Medwin? I believe you know more of me than any one else,—things even that are not in *the book*."[540]

I said, "My friend the Baron is a great enthusiast about you, and I am sure you would like him."

"Taaffe told me the other day," he replied, "a noble trait of him, which perhaps you have not heard, and which makes me highly respect him. An only child of his was dangerously ill of a malignant fever:—it was supposed by the physicians that he might be saved by bleeding; but blood would not follow the lancet, and the Baron breathed the vein with his mouth. The boy died, and the father took the contagion, and was near following his child to the grave."

"Well then," said I, "shall I bring the Baron?"

"I have declined," replied Lord Byron, "going to Court; and as he belongs to it, must also decline his visit. I neither like princes nor their satellites; though the Grand Duke is a very respectable tyrant—a kind of Leopold.[541] I will make my peace with your amiable friend by sending him a 'Cain' and 'Don Juan' as a present, and adding to the first page of the latter an impression of my seal, with the motto *'Elle vous suit partout.'** This will please a German sentimentalist."

* See 'Don Juan,' Canto I. Stanza 198.

---

[538] *Moore*: Mr. Galignani having expressed a wish to be furnished with a short Memoir of Lord Byron, for the purpose of prefixing it to the French edition of his works, I had said jestingly in a preceding letter to his Lordship, that it would be a fair satire on the disposition of the world to "bemonster his features," if he would write for the public, English as well as French, a sort of mock-heroic account of himself, outdoing, in horrors and wonders, all that had yet been related or believed of him, and leaving even Goethe's story of the double murder at Florence far behind. [Moore, *Life*, p. 545, note to Byron's letter of December 12, 1821.]

[539] [An undated letter from the Baron Lutzerode of Dresden to Shelley enclosed a translation of the first act of *Cain* and continued, "Be so kind as to present my best respects to Mrs. Shelley—Beauclerk—Lord Byron—Mr. Medwin and Taaffe. . . ." Shelley, *Letters*, II, 457. See also *LJ*, VI, 74 and note 2, and Medwin's *Shelley*, p. 371.]

[540] *Medwin*: This was said jestingly, not seriously. It was in accordance with what is contained in the Note [Moore's note above, on his suggestion that Byron should "bemonster his features"].

Trelawny: Errata—for Medwin—read Shelley. S[helley] knew B[yron] 12 years [*sic*] Medwin four or 5 months.

Washington Irving to Medwin, no date: Whilst reading your conversations I fancied myself page after page reading his autobiography. [Quoted by Medwin in marginalia on p. 30 of his *Conversations*. Irving had indeed read Byron's burned memoirs.]

[541] [Perhaps Leopold II (1747-1792), whose intelligent reforms greatly increased the material prosperity of the grand duchy. He was the father of Ferdinand III, grand duke of Tuscany when Byron lived at Pisa.]

"There is an acquaintance of mine[542] here," said I, "who has made a translation of a passage in De Lamartine, relating to you, which I will shew you. He compares you to an eagle feeding on human hearts, and lapping their blood, &c."

"Why, we have got a little nest of singing birds here," said he; "I should like to see it. I never met with the '*Méditations Poétiques*:'[543] bring it to-morrow."

The next day I shewed him the lines, which he compared with the original, and said they were admirable, and that he considered them on the whole very complimentary!! "Tell your friend so, and beg him to make my compliments to Mr. De Lamartine, and say that I thank him for his verses."

---

[542] *Medwin*: Mr. Otway Cave.

[543] [By July 13, 1820, Byron had already seen at least an extract from Lamartine's volume and quotes a phrase from "L'Homme —à Lord Byron." See *LJ*, v, 51.]

"Harrow," said he, "has been the nursery of almost all the politicians of the day."

"I wonder," said I, "that you have never had the ambition of being one too."

"I take little interest," replied he, "in the politics at home. I am not made for what you call a politician, and should never have adhered to any party.* I should have taken no part in the petty intrigues of cabinets, or the pettier factions and contests for power among parliamentary men. Among our statesmen, Castlereagh is almost the only one whom I have attacked; the only public character whom I thoroughly detest, and against whom I will never cease to level the shafts of my political hate.

* "The consequence of being of no party,
I shall offend all parties. Never mind!"
Don Juan, Canto IX. Stanza 26.

"I only addressed the House twice, and made little impression. They told me that my manner of speaking was not dignified enough for the Lords, but was more calculated for the Commons. I believe it was a Don Juan kind of speech.[544] The two occasions were, the Catholic Question,* and (I think he said) some Manufacturing affair.[545]

"Perhaps, if I had never travelled,—never left my own country young,—my views would have been more limited. They extend to the good of mankind in general—of the world at large. Perhaps the prostrate situation of Portugal and Spain—the tyranny of the Turks in Greece—the oppressions of the Austrian Government at Venice—the mental debasement of the Papal States, (not to mention Ireland,)—tended to inspire me with a love of liberty.[546] No Italian could have rejoiced more than I, to have seen a Constitution established on this side the Alps. I felt for Romagna as if she had been my own country, and would have risked my life and fortune for her,[547] as I may yet for the Greeks.†[548] I am become a citizen of the world.[549] There is no man I envy so much as Lord Cochrane. His entrance into Lima, which I see announced in to-day's paper, is one of the great events of the day.[550] Mavrocordato, too, (whom you know so well,) is also worthy of the best times of Greece.[551] Patriotism and virtue are not quite extinct."

* A gentleman who was present at his maiden speech, on the Catholic question, says, that the Lords left their seats and gathered round him in a circle; a proof, at least, of the interest which he excited: and that the same style was attempted in the Commons the next day, but failed.

> † "And I will war, at least, in words, (and—should
>   My chance so happen,—deeds) with all who war
> With thought. And of Thought's foes by far most rude
>   Tyrants and sycophants have been and are.
> I know not who may conquer; if I could
>   Have such a prescience, it should be no bar
> To this my plain, sworn, downright detestation
>   Of every despotism in every nation!"
>   *Don Juan*, Canto IX. Stanza 24.

{ 229 }

[544] *Byron to Francis Hodgson*, March 5, 1812: I spoke very violent sentences with a sort of modest impudence, abused every thing and every body. . . . As to my delivery, loud and fluent enough, perhaps a little theatrical. [*LJ*, ii, 105.]

[545] *Medwin*: It was on The Nottingham Frame breaking Bill. Byron spoke also in the House on the presentation of a Petition by, I think, Major Cartwright.

[546] [Portugal, exhausted after the Peninsular War, humiliated at the Congress of Vienna, governed or controlled in large part by the British (in fact, if not in name), achieved independence following a liberal revolution that began in August, 1820, but King John VI did not return from Brazil to Portugal until July, 1821, and did not swear allegiance to the new constitution until the next year. In Spain, the unbelievably cruel and corrupt government of Ferdinand VII had been interrupted by the Revolution of 1820, but the revolutionary liberals quarrelled among themselves, resorted increasingly to violence, and the country sank into a condition of near anarchy. The French intervened in 1823, acting for the Holy Alliance. The Greek War of Independence began in March (or April), 1821. Bonaparte delivered Venice to Austria in 1787. The Papal States, abolished by Bonaparte, were fully restored by the Congress of Vienna in 1815 and placed under Austrian protection. The Irish Parliament had been abolished in 1800.]

[547] [For Byron's involvement in the Carbonari movement at Ravenna, in Romagna, see Iris Origo, *The Last Attachment*, p. 202 *et seq*. The Neapolitan revolt, which the cities of the Romagna had hoped to join, was put down with the aid of Austrian troops in March, 1821.]

[548] *Medwin*: I have heard him often speak disparagingly of the Greeks and the Greek character. I remember his saying, "Greece— it is as easy to raise a corpse as to resurrect her." [Cf. Byron in Medwin's *Shelley*, p. 355.]

[549] [*Le Cosmopolite, ou, le Citoyen du Monde* supplied the motto for *Childe Harold*, I-II.]

[550] [Thomas Cochrane, 10th Earl of Dundonald, disgraced and imprisoned in 1814, assumed command of the infant navy of Chile in 1817, neutralized the powerful Spanish squadron, transported San Martin's army to Peru, and contributed greatly to the capture of Lima in July, 1821. See *LJ*, v, 299.]

[551] *Medwin*: I met Mavrocordato at Pisa in 1821 and passed many an evening with him at Shelley's. At that time the last thing in his thoughts was the Insurrection in Greece, tho' Shelley, with his enthusiasm for that oppressed country, frequently spoke of it prophetically. Mavrocordato spoke French and Italian with great purity and was well acquainted with the politics of Europe. He was also an evident Greek scholar and we read [?] plays of Aeschylus, but Shelley could not . . . admit that a modern Greek was better able than a foreigner to edit the old Masters. [It was on April 1, 1821, that Mavrocordato learned of the Greek declaration of independence, which he had expected for "some weeks" (*Letters of Mary Shelley*, I, 136-137). He sailed for Greece on June 26.]

I told him that I thought the finest lines he had ever written were his "Address to Greece," beginning—

"Land of the unforgotten brave!"[552]

"I should be glad," said he, "to think that I have added a spark to the flame.* I love Greece, and take the strongest interest in her struggle."

"I did not like," said I, "the spirit of Lambrino's ode; it was too desponding."

"That song," replied he, "was written many years ago, though published only yesterday.[553] Times are much changed since then. I have learned to think very differently of the cause,—at least of its success. I look upon the Morea as secure. There is more to be apprehended from friends than foes. Only keep the Vandals out of it; they would be like the Goths here."

"What do you think of the Turkish power," I asked, "and of their mode of fighting?"

"The Turks are not so despicable an enemy as people suppose. They have been carrying on a war with Russia, or rather

---

* But words are things;—and a small drop of ink
  Falling, like dew, upon a thought, produces
That which makes thousands, perhaps millions, think."
            Don Juan, Canto III. Stanza 88.

Russia with them, since Peter the Great's time;—and what have they lost, till lately, of any importance? In 1788 they gained a victory over the Austrians, and were very nearly making the Emperor of Austria prisoner,[554] though his army consisted of 80,000 men.

"They beat us in Egypt, and took one of our generals.[555] Their mode of fighting is not unformidable. Their cavalry falls very little short of ours, and is better mounted—their horses better manèged. Look, for instance, at the Arab the Turkish Prince here rides!—They are divided into parties of sixty, with a flag or standard to each. They come down, discharge their pieces, and are supplied by another party; and so on in succession. When they charge, it is by troops, like our successive squadrons."

[552] [A misquotation from *The Giaour*, l. 103, "Clime of the unforgotten brave."]

[553] *Medwin*: It was written in 1818. Ld. B. began to compose Canto III in 1819 and together with Cantos IV and V came out in August 1821. ["Lambrino's ode" must be "The Isles of Greece" lyric. It seems rather strange that of the six stanzas in Canto III shown to be without revision in Steffan and Pratt's variorum edition of *Don Juan*, four of these six should appear in this lyric (stanzas 7, 10, 11, 16). Did Byron write at least a part of it at some earlier time than 1819?]

[554] *Medwin*: He was saved principally by the courage of some English officers, two of whom I was acquainted with—Sir Edward Parkhoughton [? Parkhington] and Sir William Grant Keir. [In the campaign of 1788 the forces of Joseph II were driven back across the Danube by the Turks, and the command was then transferred to Marshal Loudon.]

[555] [Byron is probably referring to the unfortunate British expedition of 1807, in the course of which British forces were twice decisively defeated. At Rosetta they suffered four hundred casualties, General Wauchope being killed. At Hamad an entire British force, originally numbering 733 men, was captured, after expending all ammunition. It was commanded by a lieutenant-colonel.]

"I reminded you," said I, "the other day of having said, in 'Childe Harold,' that the Greeks would have to fight their own battles,—work out their own emancipation. That was your prophetic age; Voltaire and Alfieri had theirs, and even Goldsmith."

Shelley, who was present, observed:—"Poets are sometimes the echoes of words of which they know not the power,—the trumpet that sounds to battle, and feels not what it inspires."

"In what year was it," I asked, "that you wrote that line,

'Will Frank or Muscovite assist you?—No!' "[556]

"Some time in 1811. The ode was written about the same time. I expressed the same sentiment in one of its stanzas.*

"I will tell you a plan I have in embryo. I have formed a strong wish to join the Greeks.[557] Gamba is anxious to be of the party. I shall not, however, leave Italy without proper authority and full power from the Patriot Government. I mean to write to them, and that will take time;—besides, the Guiccioli!†"

"I have received," said he, "from my sister, a lock of Napoleon's hair, which is of a beautiful black.[558] If Hunt were

---

* The lines to which he alluded were—
    "Trust not for freedom to the Franks;
      They have a king who buys and sells:
    In native swords and native ranks,
      The only hope of freedom dwells!"
            Don Juan, Canto III. Page 51.

† I have heard Lord Byron reproached for leaving the Guiccioli. Her brother's accompanying him to Greece, and his remains to England,[559] prove at least that the family acquitted him of any blame. The disturbed state of the country rendered her embarking with him out of the question; and the confiscation of her father's property[560] made her jointure, and his advanced age her care, necessary to him.—It required all Lord Byron's interest with the British Envoy, as well as his own guarantee, to protect the Gambas at Genoa. But his own house at length ceased to be an asylum for them, and they were banished the Sardinian States[561] a month before he sailed for Leghorn; whence, after laying in the supplies for his voyage, he directed his fatal course to the Morea.

here, we should have half-a-dozen sonnets on it. It is a valuable present; but, according to my Lord Carlisle, I ought not to accept it. I observe, in the newspapers of the day, some lines of his Lordship's, advising Lady Holland not to have any thing to do with the snuff-box left her by Napoleon, for fear that horror and murder should jump out of the lid every time it is opened! It is a most ingenious idea—I give him great credit for it."

He then read me the first stanza, laughing in his usual suppressed way,—

"Lady, reject the gift," &c.

and produced in a few minutes the following parody on it:

"Lady, accept the box a hero wore,
   In spite of all this elegiac stuff:
Let not seven stanzas, written by a bore,
   Prevent your Ladyship from taking snuff!"[562]

---

[556] [Misquoted from *Childe Harold*, II, lxxvi: "Will Gaul or Muscovite redress ye? No!"]

[557] [Conversation about Byron's Greek plans probably took place during Medwin's second period of acquaintance with Byron, in August, 1822. See Byron to Kinnaird on September 12, 1822 (Cline, p. 190) and Mary Shelley to Jane Williams, April 10, 1823 (*HVSV*, p. 358).]

[558] *Hobhouse*: The *lock* of hair sent by Mrs. Leigh was just eight hairs, half an inch long, and all the hairs were either white or of a grisly gray. [*WR*, iii, 31.]

[559] *Hobhouse*: Count Peter Gamba *did not* accompany lord Byron's remains to England. [*WR*, iii, 31. Gamba had originally planned to accompany Byron's remains to England, decided against it for fear of gossip about Teresa, sailed on another ship, but arrived in time to follow Byron's body to London. See Marchand, p. 1235.]

[560] *Teresa Guiccioli*: The Confiscation of the property of the Counts Gamba and the consequences—unfortunately imaginary.

[561] *Hobhouse*: The Counts Gamba were never banished from the

Sardinian states. [*WR*, iii, 31. The Gambas were exiled from Romagna and Tuscany.]

[562] [Byron parodied the first stanza of Carlisle's verses:

> Lady, reject the gift! 'tis tinged with gore!
>   Those crimson spots a dreadful tale relate;
> It has been grasp'd by an infernal Power;
>   And by that hand which seal'd young Enghien's fate.

For other details see *Poetry*, vii, 77, note 2.]

"When will my wise relation leave off verse-inditing?" said he. "I believe, of all manias, authorship is the most inveterate. He might have learned by this time, indeed many years ago, (but people never learn any thing by experience,) that he had mistaken his *forte*. There was an epigram, which had some logic in it, composed on the occasion of his Lordship's doing two things in one day,—subscribing 1000*l.* and publishing a sixpenny pamphlet! It was on the state of the theatre, and dear enough at the money.[563] The epigram I think I can remember:

> 'Carlisle subscribes a thousand pound
>   Out of his rich domains;
> And for a sixpence circles round
>   The produce of his brains.
> 'Tis thus the difference you may hit
> Between his fortune and his wit.'

"A man who means to be a poet should do, and should have done all his life, nothing else but make verses. There's Shelley has more poetry in him than any man living; and if he were not so mystical, and would not write Utopias and set himself up as a Reformer, his right to rank as a poet, and very highly too, could not fail of being acknowledged. I said what I thought of him the other day; and all who are not blinded by bigotry must think the same. The works he wrote at seventeen are much more extraordinary than Chatterton's at the same age."[564]

A question was started, as to which he considered the easiest of all metres in our language.

"Or rather," replied he, "you mean, which is the least difficult? I have spoken of the fatal facility of the octo-syllabic metre. The Spenser stanza is difficult, because it is like a sonnet, and the finishing line must be good. The couplet is more difficult still, because the last line, or one out of two, must be good. But blank-verse is the most difficult of all, because every line must be good."

"You might well say then," I observed, "that no man can be a poet who does any thing else."

[563] *Byron in a note to English Bards*: The Earl of Carlisle has lately published an eighteen-penny pamphlet on the state of the Stage, and offers his plan for building a new theatre. [*Poetry*, I, 355, note 1 (M).]

[564] *Medwin*: This was a mistake. Shelley was 19 when he wrote *Queen Mab*. [Shelley had made a substantial start on *Queen Mab* by August 18, 1812, finished it in March, 1813 (*Letters*, I, 324, 361). He was thus twenty, perhaps, when he began it, twenty-one when he finished it. He had of course written other poems earlier.]

D URING our evening ride the conversation happened to turn upon the rival Reviews. "I know no two men," said he, "who have been so infamously treated, as Shelley and Keats. If I had known that Milman had been the author of that article on 'The Revolt of Islam,' I would never have mentioned 'Fazio' among the plays of the day,—and scarcely know why I paid him the compliment.[565] In consequence of the shameless personality of that and another number of 'The Quarterly,' every one abuses Shelley,—his name is coupled with every thing that is opprobrious: but he is one of the most moral as well as amiable men I know. I have now been intimate with him for years, and every year has added to my regard for him.— Judging from Milman, Christianity would appear a bad religion for a poet, and not a very good one for a man. His 'Siege of Jerusalem' is one *cento* from Milton; and in style and language he is evidently an imitator of the very man whom he most abuses. No one has been puffed like Milman: he owes his extravagant praise to Heber. These Quarterly Reviewers scratch one another's backs at a prodigious rate. Then as to Keats, though I am no admirer of his poetry, I do not envy the man, whoever he was, that attacked and killed him.[566] Except a couplet of Dryden's,

> On his own bed of torture let him lie,
> Fit garbage for the hell-hound infamy,'[567]

[565] [The author of the review of *The Revolt of Islam* in the *Quarterly* for April, 1819, was Sir John Taylor Coleridge; Shelley first believed the reviewer to be Southey, later thought him to be Milman. On Byron's change of mind concerning Milman, see his letter of August 31, 1821 (*LJ*, v, 353). Byron had praised Milman in the Preface to *Marino Faliero*.]

[566] *Byron to Murray*, July 30, 1821: I do not envy the man who wrote the article: your review people have no more right to kill than any other foot pads. [*LJ*, v, 331.]

[567] [*Concordance to the Poetical Works of Dryden* by Guy Montgomery and Lester A. Hubbard contains no reference to these lines, which may be from one of the plays, if indeed they are by Dryden.]

I know no lines more cutting than those in 'Adonais,'* or more feeling than the whole elegy.

"As Keats is now gone, we may speak of him. I am always battling with *the Snake* about Keats, and wonder what he finds to make a god of, in that idol of the Cockneys: besides, I always ask Shelley why he does not follow his style, and make himself one of the school, if he think it so divine. He will, like me, return some day to admire Pope, and think 'The Rape of the Lock' and its sylphs worth fifty 'Endymions,' with their faun and satyr machinery. I remember Keats somewhere says that 'flowers would not blow, leaves bud,' &c. if man and woman did not kiss.[568] How sentimental!"

I remarked that 'Hyperion' was a fine fragment, and a proof of his poetical genius.

" 'Hyperion!' " said he: "why a man might as well pretend to be rich who had one diamond. 'Hyperion' indeed! 'Hyperion' to a satyr![569] Why, there is a fine line in Lord Thurlow (looking to the West that was gloriously golden with the sunset) which I mean to borrow some day:

'And all that gorgeous company of clouds'—

Do you think they will suspect me of taking from Lord Thurlow?"[570]

Speaking to him of 'Lalla Rookh,' he said:
"Moore did not like my saying that I could never attempt to describe the manners or scenery of a country that I had not visited.[571] Without this it is almost impossible to adhere closely

---

* The lines to which he referred were these:
 "Expect no heavier chastisement from me,
 But ever at thy season be thou free
  To spill their venom when thy fangs o'erflow.
 Remorse and self-contempt shall cling to thee;
  Hot shame shall burn upon thy Cain-like brow,
  And like a beaten hound tremble thou shalt as now."
                                                      Adonais.[572]

to costume. Captain Ellis once asked him if he had ever been in Persia. If he had, he would not have made his Parsee guilty of such a profanity. It was an Irishism to make a Gheber die by fire."[573]

"I have been reading," said I, " 'The Lusiad,' and some of Camoens' smaller poems. Why did Lord Strangford call his beautiful Sonnets, &c. translations?"

"Because he wrote," said Lord Byron, "in order to get the situation at the Brazils, and did not know a word of Portuguese when he commenced."[574]

"Moore was suspected of assisting his Lordship," said I. "Was that so?" They are very *Moorish.*

"I am told not," said Lord Byron. "They are great friends; and when Moore got into a difficulty about the Bermuda affair, in which he was so hardly used, Lord Strangford offered to give him 500*l.*; but Moore had too much independence to lay himself under an obligation.[575] I know no man I would go further to serve than Moore.

---

[568] [. . . but who, of men, can tell
 That flowers would bloom, or that green fruit would swell

       . . .

 If human souls did never kiss and greet?
       —*Endymion, I,* 835-836, 842.]

[569] *Medwin:* Meaning as compared with *Endymion,* with its Faun and Satyr machinery.

[570] [Lord Thurlow's *Select Poems* appeared in 1821. See also *HVSV*, pp. 67-68.]

[571] [For this aspect of Byron's thought, see my *Byron: The Record of a Quest,* pp. 95-108.]

[572] [Misquoted from stanza xxxvii.]

[573] [A reference to Moore's "The Fire-Worshippers," a tale of the Ghebers or Persians of the old religion, in *Lalla Rookh* (1817). Hafed, the hero, throws himself on a funeral pyre.]

[574] [Lord Strangford published *Poems from the Portuguese by Luis de Camoens* in 1803, later served in the diplomatic service in Brazil. Byron referred to him in *English Bards*.]

[575] *Moore to Lord Strangford*, April, 1820: I hasten to say what all my life will not be long enough to feel as much, and as strongly as I ought to do, the deep, hearty, genuine gratitude with which my heart is full towards you for the letter you wrote me. I should have preferred waiting till we met, rather than attempt through the cold medium of a letter to tell you half how much I thank you. . . . My dear friend, how delightful to have the companion of one's young days taking the part you have done in the moment of need. . . . [*The Letters of Thomas Moore*, ed. Wilfred S. Dowden (London, 1965), p. 484. It seems clear that Strangford offered pecuniary aid to Moore, who was in great need of it. However, Moore's original debt to the Admiralty of £6,000, the sum misappropriated by his deputy, was reduced by arrangement and paid by Lord Landsdowne, who was shortly repaid by Moore. There were other offers of aid, one of them from Lord John Russell. For Byron's knowledge of many of these details, see *LJ*, v, 399-400, 478.]

" 'The Fudge Family' pleases me as much as any of his works. The letter which he versified at the end was given him by Douglas Kinnaird and myself, and was addressed by the Life-guardsman, after the battle of Waterloo, to Big Ben.[576] Witty as Moore's epistle is, it falls short of the original. 'Doubling up the *Mounseers*[577] in brass,' is not so energetic an expression as was used by our hero,—all the alliteration is lost.

"Moore is one of the few writers who will survive the age in which he so deservedly flourishes. He will live in his 'Irish Melodies;' they will go down to posterity with the music; both will last as long as Ireland, or as music and poetry."[578]

[576] [See Moore's "Epistle from Tom Crib to Big Ben, concerning Some Foul Play in a Late Transaction," purportedly written by the pugilist to the Prince Regent on the transportation of Napoleon to St. Helena. Medwin's "Life-guardsman" appears only in a note identifying "the *Cheesemonger*" of the poem as "A Life Guardsman,

one of *the Fancy*, who distinguished himself, and was killed in the memorable *set-to* at Waterloo." For Byron's knowledge of the poem, see *LJ*, vi, 27.]

[577] *Medwin*: The B------s. [Moore wrote, ll. 28-29, "Oh, shade of the *Cheesemonger*! you, who, alas,/ *Doubled up*, by the dozen, those Mounseers in brass . . ."]

[578] *Medwin*: P. 326 [p. 258, this edition] to come in from "I have finished" down to "four weeks" [p. 260], transposed in Editing the ms. [Inasmuch as the point indicated on p. 260 seems to be an unsatisfactory place to break off (there is a natural transition between *Werner* and Goethe), the pages have been allowed to stand in their original position. Internal evidence suggests that pages 258-262 (through the discussion of Goethe) should be transposed, if any at all.]

I TOOK leave of Lord Byron on the 15th of March,[579] to visit Rome for a few weeks. Shortly after my departure an affray happened at Pisa, the particulars of which were variously stated. The *Courier François* gave the following account of it:

"A superior officer went to Lord Byron a few days ago. A very warm altercation, the reason of which was unknown, occurred between this officer and the English poet. The threats of the officer became so violent, that Lord Byron's servant ran to protect his master. A struggle ensued, in which the officer was struck with a poniard by the servant, and died instantly. The servant fled."

This was one among many reports that were circulated at Rome, to which I was forced one day to give a somewhat flat contradiction. But the real truth of the story cannot be better explained than by the depositions before the Governor of Pisa, the copies of which were sent me,[580] and are in my possession. They state that

"Lord Byron, in company with Count Gamba, Captain Hay, Mr. Trelawney, and Mr. Shelley, was returning from his usual ride, on the 21st March, 1822,[581] and was perhaps a quarter of a mile from the Piaggia gate, when a man on horseback, in a hussar uniform, dashed at full speed through the midst of the party, violently jostling (*urtando*) one of them. Shocked at such ill-breeding, Lord Byron pushed forward, and all the rest followed him, and pulled up their horses on overtaking the hussar. His Lordship then asked him what he meant by the insult? The hussar, for first and only answer, began to abuse him in the grossest manner; on which Lord Byron and one of his companions drew out a card with their names and address, and passed on. The hussar followed, vociferating and threatening, with his hand on his sabre, that he would draw it, as he had often done, effectually. They were now about ten paces from the Piaggia gate. Whilst this altercation was going on, a common soldier of the artillery interfered, and called out to the hussar, 'Why don't you arrest them? Command us to arrest them!' Upon which the hussar gave the word to the guard at the gate, 'Arrest—arrest them!' still continuing the same threatening gestures, and using language, if possible, more offensive and insulting.

"His Lordship, hearing the order given for their arrest, spurred on his horse, and one of the party did the same; and they succeeded in forcing their way through the soldiers, who flew to their muskets and bayonets, whilst the gate was closed on the rest, together with the courier, who was foremost.

"Mr. Trelawney now found his horse seized by the bridle by two soldiers, with their swords drawn, and himself furiously assaulted by the hussar, who made several cuts at him with his sabre, whilst the soldiers struck him about the thighs. He and his companions were all unarmed, and asked this madman the reason of his conduct; but his only reply was blows.

"Mr. Shelley received a sabre-stroke on the head, which threw him off his horse. Captain Hay, endeavouring to parry a blow with a stick that he used as a whip, the edge of the weapon cut it in two, and he received a wound on his nose. The courier also suffered severely from several thrusts he received from the hussar and the rest of the soldiers. After all this, the hussar spurred on his horse, and took the road to the Lung' Arno.

"When his Lordship reached the palace, he gave directions to his secretary to give immediate information to the police of what was going on; and, not seeing his companions come up, turned back towards the gate. On the way he met the hussar, who rode up to him, saying, 'Are you satisfied?' His Lordship, who knew nothing or hardly any thing of the affray that had taken place at the gate, answered, 'No, I am not! Tell me your name!'—'Sergeant-Major Masi,' said he. One of his Lordship's servants came up at the moment, and laid hold of the bridle of the Sergeant's horse. His Lordship commanded him to let it go; when the Sergeant spurred his horse, and rushed through an immense crowd collected before the Lanfranchi palace, where, as he deposes, he was wounded and his *chaco* found, but how or by whom they knew not, seeing that they were either in the rear or in their way home. They had further to depose that Captain Hay was confined to his house by reason of his wound; also that the courier had spit blood from the thrust he received in the breast, as might be proved by the evidence of the surgeons."

There was also another deposition from a Mr. James Crawford. It stated that "the dragoon would have drawn his sabre against Lord Byron, in the Lung' Arno, had it not been for the interposition of the servant; and that Sergeant-Major Masi was knocked off his horse as he galloped past the Lanfranchi palace, Lord Byron and his servants being at a considerable distance therefrom at the time."

It appears that Sergeant-Major Masi was wounded with a pitchfork, and his life was for some time in danger; but it was never known by whom the wound had been given. One of the Countess's servants, and two of Lord Byron's, were arrested and imprisoned. It was suspected by the police that, being Italians and much attached to their master,* they had revenged his quarrel; but no proof was adduced to justify the suspicion.[582]

During the time that the examination was taking place before the police, Lord Byron's house was beset by the dragoons belonging to Sergeant Major Masi's troop, who were on the point of forcing open the doors, but they were too well guarded

---

* Lord Byron was the best of masters, and was perfectly adored by his servants. His kindness was extended even to their children. He liked them to have their families with them: and I remember one day, as we were entering the hall after our ride, meeting a little boy, of three or four years old, of the coachman's, whom he took up in his arms and presented with a ten-paul piece.

within to dread the attack.[583] Lord Byron, however, took his ride as usual two days after.[584]

"It is not the first time," said he, "that my house has been a *Bender*,[585] and may not be the last."

---

[579] [Medwin probably left on March 11, 1822, although it is possible that he lingered until March 15, as he says.]

[580] [Copies of the depositions concerning the Pisan affray, upon which Medwin's account is based, were sent to him on April 12, 1822, by Mary Shelley, at the request of Byron, significantly. Copies were also sent to Kinnaird, Scott, and Hobhouse. For the details of this episode, see Cline, chapters 6 and 7.]

[581] [*I.e.*, March 24, 1822.]

[582] *Medwin*: Some years afterward, when I was at Sienna, a mendicant with a wooden leg, who was begging his way to Rome, his native city, called on me for alms, and when I had given him a trifle, said,—"Do you not remember me? I was Lord Byron's coachman at Pisa, and used to drive you and Signor Shelley every day to the Contadino's." The man was so much changed, that it was some time before I could recognize his features; but at length did so, and after some conversation, he confessed with all the pride of a Guelph or Ghibelline, that he had avenged his master's quarrel. [On Papi and the Pisan affray, see Cline.]

[583] *Hobhouse*: Lord Byron's house at Pisa, on the occasion alluded to, was not beset by dragoons, nor by any soldiers or police-men, and no attempt was made to force his doors. [*WR*, III, 31-32. Medwin seems mistaken, although Byron was quite aware of the possibility of trouble from Masi's troop. Taaffe went so far as to call on Masi's commanding officer to ask for a guarantee of the safety of the English group against any hostile act by the soldiers.]

[584] *Hobhouse*: Lord Byron went out riding one day—not *two* days after. [This is confirmed by E. E. Williams, who noted the "great crowd that surround the door."]

[585] [See *Don Juan*, VIII, cvii, and Pratt's note in the variorum edition.]

All Lord Byron's servants were banished from Pisa, and with them the Counts Gamba, father and son.

Lord Byron was himself advised to leave it; and as the Countess accompanied her father, he soon after joined them at Leghorn, and passed six weeks at Monte Nero. His return to Pisa was occasioned by a new persecution of the Gambas. An order was issued for them to leave the Tuscan States in four days; and on their embarkation for Genoa, the Countess and himself took up their residence (for the first time together) at the Lanfranchi palace,[586] where Leigh Hunt and his family had already arrived.[587]

[586] *Hobhouse*: The counts Gamba did not "embark for Genoa," they rode to Lucca. This opportunity may be taken of stating, that count Peter Gamba, who is now in London, denies the accuracy of the statements respecting his family; and declares that Lord Byron could not have uttered the conversation imputed to him on that subject. [*WR*, III, 32. This account contains more than Medwin's usual number of errors; however, his chief implication is true: the Pisan affray was to have "far-reaching effects on the lives of all of them" involved (Marchand, p. 998). Tita was exiled and went first to Florence, Byron sending Pietro Gamba on ahead to make arrangements for him there. At Leghorn, on July 2, 1822, Pietro Gamba and his father were formally exiled and given four days, as Medwin states, to leave Tuscany. It was this sentence that determined Byron to go to Genoa. Teresa moved into the Lanfranchi palace while the Gambas were in Lucca.]

[587] [The Hunts were settled in the Lanfranchi palace by early July.]

18TH AUGUST, 1822.—On the occasion of Shelley's melancholy fate I revisited Pisa, and on the day of my arrival learnt that Lord Byron was gone to the sea-shore, to assist in performing the last offices to his friend.* We came to a spot

* It is hoped that the following memoir, as it relates to Lord Byron, may not be deemed misplaced here.[588]

Percy Bysshe Shelley, born at Field-place, Sussex, in 1792, was removed at thirteen years of age from a private school, and sent to Eton:—he there shewed a character of great eccentricity, mixed in none of the amusements natural to his age, was of a shy and reserved disposition, fond of solitude, and made few friends. Neither did he distinguish himself much at Eton:—he had a great contempt for modern Latin verses; and directed his attention to Chemistry, and German, instead of the exercises of his class. From an early acquaintance with German authors he perhaps imbibed a romantic turn of mind; for we find him, before he was fifteen, publishing two Rosa-Matilda-like Novels called 'Zastrozzi' and 'The Rosicrusian,' that bore every mark of being the productions of a boy, and were much reprobated as immoral by the journals of the day. He also made great progress in chemistry. He used to say that nothing ever delighted him so much as the discovery that there were no *elements* of fire, air, and water:—but he nearly lost his life by being blown up in one of his experiments, and had for many years discontinued the pursuit. He now turned his active mind to metaphysics, and became infected with the materialism of the French school. He was now sent to University College, Oxford, being only sixteen; and after the second term printed a pamphlet with a most ridiculous title, 'The Necessity of Atheism.' This silly work, which was a recapitulation of some of the arguments of Voltaire, he not only affixed his name to, but circulated it among the Bench of Bishops. The consequence was obvious:—he was soon summoned before the heads of his College; and, refusing to retract his opinion, (which he proposed to argue with the examining masters—a greater madness still,) was expelled the University.

This disgrace little affected Shelley at the time; but it proved fatal to all his hopes of happiness and prospects in life; and was the means of alienating him, for ever, from his family. His father, for some time after it occurred, would not see him; and at length when he received him under his roof, treated him with so much coldness that he soon quitted his home; went to London; and thence eloped to Gretna Green with a Miss Westbrook, their joint ages amounting to thirty-six. This last act exasperated his father to such a degree, that he broke off all communication with Shelley; who, after a residence in Edinburgh of some months, passed over to Ireland: and that country being in a disturbed state, published a pamphlet that had a considerable sale, the object of which was to soothe the minds of the people, telling them that moderation and not rebellion would tend to conciliate their oppressors, and give them their liberties. He also spoke at some of their public meetings with great fluency and eloquence. He was at that time a great admirer of Southey's Works, and before he left England had paid a visit to the Lakes, and passed several days at Keswick.

He now became devoted to poetry; and, after imbuing himself with 'The Age of Reason' and 'The Political Justice,' printed his 'Queen Mab,' and presented it to most of the literary characters of the day— among the rest to Lord Byron, who thought it superior to Chatterton's Works at the same age. Speaking of it in his notes to 'The Two Foscari,' he says, "I shewed it to Mr. Sotheby as a poem of great power and imagination. No one knows better than its real author that his opinions and mine differ radically upon the metaphysical portion of that work: though, in common with all who are not blinded by baseness and bigotry, I highly admire the poetry of that and his other productions."

It is to be remarked that 'Queen Mab' eight years afterwards fell into the hands of a knavish bookseller, and on its prosecution its author disclaimed all desire of publishing the opinions of his youth contained in that juvenile production. His marriage, by which he had two children, soon turned out as might have been expected, an unhappy one; and a separation ensuing in 1814, he went abroad, and passed the summer of that year in Switzerland.

The scenery of that romantic country tended to make Nature a passion and an enjoyment; and there, during a second visit in 1816, he contracted a friendship with Lord Byron that was destined to last for life. Perhaps the perfection of every thing Lord Byron wrote at Geneva (his Third Canto of 'Childe Harold,' his 'Manfred,' and 'Prisoner of Chillon') owe something to the critical judgment which Shelley exercised over his works, and his dosing him (as he said) with Wordsworth.

From Switzerland he was soon called to England by his wife's unhappy fate, which threw a cloud of melancholy over his own. The year subsequent to this event, he married Mary Wolstonecraft Godwin, the daughter of the celebrated Mary Wolstonecraft by William Godwin.

He now took up his abode in Bucks, and published his 'Alastor, or the Spirit of Solitude:' perhaps one of the most perfect specimens of harmony in blank verse that our language possesses; and full of the wild scenery that his imagination had treasured up in his travels. In this poem he deifies Nature much in the same manner that Wordsworth did in his earlier productions.

Inattentive to pecuniary matters, and generous to excess, he soon found himself embarrassed; and not being able to live on his income, and still unforgiven by his family, he came to a resolution of quitting England, and never returning to it.

There was also another thing that tended to disgust him with his native country. His children were taken from him by the Lord Chancellor, in consequence of his atheistical opinions.

He now crossed the Alps; afterwards visiting Venice—where he strengthened his intimacy with Lord Byron. His 'Revolt of Islam,' an allegorical poem in the Spenser stanza, written at Marlow, soon after made its appearance. Spoken of with much commendation in Blackwood's Magazine, it fell under the lash of 'The Quarterly,' which disgraced itself by gross and personal abuse of the author, both openly, in the review of that work, and *insidiously* under the critique of Hunt's 'Foliage.' Perhaps little can be said for the philosophy of the 'Loves of Laon and Cythna.' Like Owen of Lanark, he believed in the perfectibility of human nature; and looked forward to a period when a new golden age would return to earth; when all the different creeds and systems of the world would be amalgamated into one; when crime would disappear, and man be freed from shackles civil and religious.

Wild and visionary, and dangerous, as such a doctrine must be confessed to be, in the present state of society at least, it sprang from a mind enthusiastic in its wishes for the good of his species, and the amelioration of mankind: and however mistaken the means of bringing about this reform or revolt may be considered, the object of his whole life and writings seems to have been to develope them. This is particularly observable in his next work, the 'Prometheus Unbound,' a bold attempt to revive the play of Æschylus. This drama shews an acquaintance with the Greek tragedians, that perhaps no other person possessed in an equal degree; and was written at Rome in the flower-covered ruins of the Baths of Caracalla. Here also he formed into a tragedy the story of 'The Cenci:' which, but for the harrowing nature of the subject, would not have failed to have had the greatest success, both on the stage and in the closet.

After passing several months at Naples, he finally settled in Tuscany, where he passed with an amiable wife the last four years of his life in domestic retirement, and intense application. His acquirements were great. He was perhaps the best classic in Europe. The books he considered as the models of style in prose and poetry were Plato and the Greek dramatists. He made himself equally master of the modern languages: Calderon in Spanish, Petrarch and Dante in Italian, and Goethe in German, were his favourite authors. French poetry he never read; and said he never could understand the beauty of Racine's verses.

Discouraged by the ill success of his writings; persecuted by the malice of reviewers, to which he was indifferent—for the last three years, though he continued to write, he had almost given up publishing. There were only two occasions that induced him to deviate from the resolution. His ardent love of liberty inspired him to write 'Hellas, or the Triumph of Greece,' since translated into Greek, which he dedicated to his friend Prince Mavrocordato:—and his attachment to Keats produced an Elegy, that he entitled 'Adonais.' This is perhaps the most finished and beautiful of all his compositions, and the one he considered his best. I cannot give a fairer specimen of his style and manner, or a better portrait of Shelley, than the one he drew of himself in this poem, and afterwards expunged from it.

> " 'Mid others of less note came one frail form,
>   A phantom among men, companionless
> As the last cloud of an expiring storm,
>   Whose thunder is its knell;—he, as I guess,
> Had gazed on Nature's naked loveliness
>   Actæon-like; and now he fled astray
> With feeble steps o'er the world's wilderness,
>   And his own thoughts along that rugged way
> Pursued, like raging hounds, their father and their prey.
>
> His head was bound with pansies overblown,
>   And faded violets, white and pied and blue,
> And a light spear topp'd with a cypress cone,
>   (Round whose rough stem dark ivy tresses grew,

Yet dripping with the forest's noonday dew,)
   Vibrated as the ever beating heart
Shook the weak hand that grasp'd it;—of that crew
   He came the last, neglected and apart,—
A herd-abandon'd deer, struck by the hunter's dart."

The last eighteen months of his short but eventful life (he used to say he had lived to an hundred) were passed in daily intercourse with Lord Byron, to whom the amiability, gentleness, and elegance of his manners, and great talents and acquirements, had endeared him. Like his friend, he wished to die young, and perished in the 30th year of his age in the Mediterranean, between Leghorn and Lerici, in a storm, from the upsetting of an open boat. The sea had ever been his great delight; and in the following lines, written as early as 1814, he seems to have anticipated that it would prove his grave:—

"To-morrow comes:
Cloud after cloud with dark and deep'ning mass
Roll o'er the blacken'd waters; the deep roar
Of distant thunder mutters awfully;
Tempest unfolds its pinions o'er the gloom,
And shrouds the boiling surge; the pitiless fiend
With all his winds and lightnings tracks his prey;
The torn deep yawns,—the vessel finds a grave
Beneath its jagged jaws."

Well might his disconsolate widow, and the friends by whom he was adored, as he was by all who knew him, add in the words of Lycidas:—

"It was that fatal and perfidious bark,
Built in the eclipse, and rigg'd with curses dark,
That struck so low that sacred head of thine."

For fifteen days after the loss of the vessel, his body remained undiscovered; and when found, was not in a state to be removed.

In order to comply with his wish of being buried in Rome, his corpse was therefore directed to be burned; and Lord Byron, faithful to his trust as an executor, and duty as a friend, superintended the ceremony. The remains of one who had little repose here, now sleep with those of his friend Keats, in the burial-ground near Caius Cestus's tomb;—"a spot so beautiful," said he, "that it would almost reconcile me to death, to lie there!"

Even if Shelley had not set himself up as a reformer, his poetry was never calculated to be popular. His creations were of another world. His metaphysical speculations are clothed in too mystical a language; his allusions are too deep and classical for many minds to comprehend or enjoy them:—but there are some also who will love to place his works on the same shelf with the 'Republic' of Plato, and the 'Utopia' of Sir Thomas More.

marked by an old and withered trunk of a fir-tree;[589] and near it, on the beach, stood a solitary hut covered with reeds. The situation was well calculated for a poet's grave. A few weeks before I had ridden with him and Lord Byron to this very spot,[590] which I afterwards visited more than once. In front was a magnificent extent of the blue and windless Mediterranean, with the Isles of Elba and Gorgona,—Lord Byron's yacht at anchor in the offing: on the other side an almost boundless extent of sandy wilderness, uncultivated and uninhabited, here and there interspersed in tufts with underwood curved by the sea-breeze, and stunted by the barren and dry nature of the soil in which it grew. At equal distances along the coast stood high square towers, for the double purpose of guarding the coast from smuggling, and enforcing the quarantine laws. This view was bounded by an immense extent of the Italian Alps, which are here particularly picturesque from their volcanic and manifold appearances, and which being composed of white marble, give their summits the resemblance of snow.

---

[588] *Medwin*: This Memoir, written for Sir Egerton Brydges in one sitting, is incorrect as to several dates and trifling circumstances. [Medwin intended to delete it, although he made five alterations in it. His chief errors of fact may be briefly summarized. Shelley was sent to Eton at the age of eleven, not thirteen; entered Oxford at the age of eighteen, not sixteen. If the college records may be believed, Shelley was expelled for "contumaciously refusing to answer questions," not for proposing "to argue" his opinions. The combined age of Harriet and Shelley at the time of their marriage was thirty-five, not thirty-two, as Medwin originally wrote, nor thirty-six, as he later wrote in his revision. The summer of 1814 Shelley spent in Switzerland and elsewhere abroad. He did not return to England in 1816 *because of* Harriet's death, which took place after his return, nor did he marry Mary the year following Harriet's death: his second marriage took place on December 30, 1816.]

[589] *Trelawny*: An extract from my letter—written to Mrs. Shelley —Medwin never was at the place of Shelley interment. [As Marchand points out ("Trelawny on the Death of Shelley," *Keats-Shelley Memorial Bulletin*, iv, 33), "Actually Medwin was relying on Trelawny's Narrative 3 (an account of the cremation of Williams!) whole phrases of which he copied verbatim."]

Medwin in The Shelley Papers: I have already, as taken from the mouth of Mr. Trelawny, given a description of the funeral ceremony . . . and have nothing to add to that account. [P. 77.]

Medwin in his Life of Shelley: I arrived at Pisa some hours later than I could have wished, for Lord Byron and Leigh Hunt and Trelawny, had been engaged since the morning in burning Shelley's remains. . . . I say, I arrived at Pisa too late. [Pp. 394-395.]

[590] *Teresa Guiccioli*: A site too distant for a daily ride on horseback.

As a foreground to this picture appeared as extraordinary a group. Lord Byron and Trelawney were seen standing over the burning pile, with some of the soldiers of the guard; and Leigh Hunt, whose feelings and nerves could not carry him through the scene of horror, lying back in the carriage,—the four post-horses ready to drop with the intensity of the noonday sun. The stillness of all around was yet more felt by the shrill scream of a solitary curlew, which, perhaps attracted by the body, wheeled in such narrow circles round the pile that it might have been struck with the hand, and was so fearless that it could not be driven away. Looking at the corpse, Lord Byron said,

"Why, that old black silk handkerchief retains its form better than that human body!"

Scarcely was the ceremony concluded, when Lord Byron, agitated by the spectacle he had witnessed, tried to dissipate, in some degree, the impression of it by his favourite recreation. He took off his clothes therefore, and swam off to his yacht, which was riding at some distance. The heat of the sun and checked perspiration threw him into a fever, which he felt coming on before he left the water, and which became more violent before he reached Pisa.[591] On his return he immediately ordered a warm bath.

"I have been very subject to fevers," said he, "and am not in the least alarmed at this. It will yield to my usual remedy, the bath."

The next morning he was perfectly recovered. When I called, I found him sitting in the garden under the shade of some orange-trees, with the Countess. They are now always together, and he is become quite domestic. He calls her *Piccinina*,[592] and bestows on her all the pretty diminutive epithets that are so sweet in Italian. His kindness and attention to the Guiccioli have been invariable. A three years' constancy proves that he is not altogether so unmanageable by a sensible woman as might be supposed. In fact no man is so easily led: but he is not to be driven. His spirits are good, except when he speaks of Shelley and Williams. He tells me he has not made one voyage in his yacht since their loss, and has taken a disgust to sailing.

[591] *Byron to Moore*, August 27, 1822: The other day at Viareggio, I thought proper to swim off to my schooner (the Bolivar) in the offing, and thence to shore again. . . . The consequence has been a feverish attack, and my whole skin's coming off. . . . But it is over,—and I have got a new skin, and am as glossy as a snake in its new suit. [*LJ*, vi, 107-108.]

[592] [A diminutive form of endearment, *little one*.]

"I have got Hunt with me," said he. "I will tell you how I became acquainted with him.

"One of the first visits I paid to Hunt was in prison. I remember Lady Byron was with me in the carriage, and I made her wait longer than I intended at the gate of the King's Bench.[593]

"When party feeling ran highest against me, Hunt was the only editor of a paper, the only literary man, who dared say a word in my justification.[594] I shall always be grateful to him for the part he took on that occasion. It was manly in him to brave the obloquy of standing alone.

"Shelley and myself furnished some time ago a suite of apartments in my house for him, which he now occupies. I believe I told you of a plan we had in agitation for his benefit. His principal object in coming out was to establish a literary journal, whose name is not yet fixed.[595]

"I have promised to contribute, and shall probably make it a vehicle for some occasional poems;—for instance, I mean to translate Ariosto. I was strongly advised by Tom Moore, long ago, not to have any connection with such a company as Hunt, Shelley, and Co.;[596] but I have pledged myself, and besides could not now, if I had ever so great a disinclination for the scheme, disappoint all Hunt's hopes. He has a large family, has undertaken a long journey, and undergone a long series of persecutions.

"Moore tells me that it was proposed to him to contribute to the new publication, but that he had declined it.[597] You see I cannot get out of the scrape. The name is not yet decided upon,—half-a-dozen have been rejected.

"Hunt would have made a fine writer, for he has a great deal of fancy and feeling, if he had not been spoiled by circumstances. He was brought up at the Blue-coat foundation, and had never till lately been ten miles from St. Paul's.[598] What poetry is to be expected from such a course of education? He has his school, however, and a host of disciples. A friend[599] of mine calls 'Rimini,' *Nimini Pimini*; and 'Foliage,' Follyage.[600] Perhaps he had a tumble in 'climbing trees in the Hesperides!'* But 'Rimini' has a great deal of merit. There never were so many fine things spoiled as in 'Rimini.' "[601]

* The motto to his book entitled 'Foliage,' and a most ridiculous motto it is. It is no bad comment on the book.

---

[593] *Hobhouse*: Hunt was *not* in the K[ing's] B[ench] and had been released from Horsemonger Lane 3d Feb^r 1815, a month be-

fore L. & Lady B. went to London after their wedding.

Leigh Hunt: He [Byron] sat one morning so long [at Hunt's home, in 1815] that Lady Byron sent up twice to let him know she was waiting. [Hunt, *Lord Byron and Some of His Contemporaries*, I, 6.]

[594] *Hobhouse*: The Examiner was not the only paper that defended lord Byron. The Morning Chronicle was a zealous advocate of his lordship; and Mr. Perry, the editor, had a personal altercation with Sir R. Noel on the subject. [*WR*, III, 26.]

[595] [Before the publication of its first issue, *The Liberal* was called the *Hesperides*. For the whole story, see William H. Marshall, *Byron, Shelley, Hunt, and The Liberal* (Philadelphia, 1960), the best and fullest account.]

[596] *Moore to Byron*, January, 1822: *Alone* you may do any thing; but partnerships in fame, like those in trade, make the strongest party answerable for the deficiencies or delinquencies of the rest, and I tremble even for *you* with such a bankrupt *Co.* [Moore, *Life*, p. 553.]

[597] *Byron to Moore*, August 27, 1822: Leigh Hunt is sweating articles for his new Journal; and both he and I think it somewhat shabby in *you* not to contribute. [*LJ*, VI, 109. It was Byron himself who had invited Moore to contribute.]

[598] *Leigh Hunt*: The Captain ought to have known enough of his Lordship's random way of talking, not to take for granted every thing that he chose to report of another. I had never been out of England before; except, when a child, to the coast of France; but I had perhaps seen as much of my native country as most persons educated in town. I have been in various parts of it, from Devonshire to Yorkshire. I merely mention these things to show what idle assertions Lord Byron would repeat, and how gravely the Captain would echo them. [*HVSV*, p. 308.]

[599] *Medwin*: Moore.

[600] *Shelley to Mary Shelley*, August 24, 1818: We talked of . . . Foliage which he [Byron] quizzes immoderately. [*Letters*, II, 37.]

[601] *Byron in his "Second Letter on Bowles's Strictures"*: When he was writing his *Rimini*, I was not the last to discover its beauties . . . but Mr. Hunt is, probably, the only poet who could have had the heart to spoil his own Capo d'Opera. [*LJ*, V, 588; first published 1835.]

"SINCE you left us," said he, "I have had serious thoughts of visiting America; and when the Gambas were ordered out of Tuscany, was on the point of embarkation for the only country which is a sanctuary for liberty.

"Since I have been abroad, I have received many civilities from the Americans[*]; among the rest, I was acquainted with the captain of one of their frigates lying in the Leghorn roads, and used occasionally to dine on board his ship.[602] He offered to take me with him to America.[603] I desired time to consider; but at last declined it, not wishing to relinquish my Grecian project.

"Once landed in that country, perhaps I should not have soon left it;—I might have settled there, for I shall never re-visit England. On Lady Noel's death, I thought I should have been forced to go home (and was for a moment bent on doing so on another occasion, which you know);[604] but I told Hanson that I would rather make any sacrifice.

"The polite attentions of the American sailor were very different from the treatment I met with from the captain of a sloop of war belonging to our Navy, who made the gentleman commanding my yacht haul down my pennant.[605] They

[*] I have been favoured with a sight of a letter addressed by Lord Byron to Mr. Church, one of the American Consuls,[606] in which he thus speaks of his Grecian project a few months after:

"The accounts are so contradictory, as to what mode will be best for supplying the Greeks, that I have deemed it better to take up (with the exception of a few supplies) what cash and credit I can muster, rather than lay them out in articles that might be deemed superfluous or unnecessary. Here we can learn nothing but from some of the refugees, who appear chiefly interested for themselves. My accounts from an agent of the Committee, an English gentleman lately gone up to Greece, are hitherto favourable; but he had not yet reached the seat of the Provisional Government, and I am anxiously expecting further advice.

"An American has a better right than any other to suggest to other nations the mode of obtaining that liberty which is the glory of his own!"

might have respected the name of the great navigator.* In the time of peace, and in a free port, there could have been no plea for such an insult. I wrote to the captain of the vessel rather sharply, and was glad to find that his first lieutenant had acted without his orders, and when he was on shore; but they had been issued, and could not be reversed.

"You see I can't go any where without being persecuted. I am going to Genoa in a few days."[607]

* His grandfather, Admiral Byron. I have heard him more than once speak of Campbell's having named him in 'The Pleasures of Hope.'

---

[602] *Hobhouse*: Lord Byron did not *"dine occasionally"* on board any American ship at Leghorn—he breakfasted once on board the Constitution frigate. [*WR*, III, 32. At the invitation of Commodore Jacob Jones, Byron inspected the *Constitution* on May 21, 1822. On the next day he discussed with George Bancroft his planned American tour (*HVSV*, p. 290).]

[603] *Byron to E. J. Dawkins*, July 4, 1822: Both Captain [Isaac] Chauncey of the American Squadron (which returns in September) and Mr. Bruen an American Merchantman at Leghorn offered me a passage in the handsomest manner. . . . [*Byron, A Self-Portrait*, ed. Peter Quennell (London, 1950), II, 702.]

[604] *Medwin*: To call out Southey.

[605] [The affair of the pennant may be one aspect, perhaps, of Byron's troubles with the Tuscan authorities, who denied his "request that his schooner 'Bolivar' should be allowed to embark and disembark people without hindrance along the coast" (Marchand, p. 1007, note 3).]

[606] [See Paul R. Baker, "Lord Byron and the Americans in Italy," *Keats-Shelley Journal*, XIII (1964), 62, note 7. Byron's letter, June 21, 1823, has been reprinted in *The Autograph Album*, I (June, 1933), 24-25. Edward Church (1779-1845), U.S. consul, built the first steamer to supply regular service on the Lake of Geneva (between Geneva and Lausanne), beginning on June 1, 1823. "He also organized a company and built and operated three steamers on the Rhone river from Lyons to the sea. He offered one of these steamers to Lord Byron for his expedition to Greece to aid the insurrectionists but other arrangements had been made and his

offer was not accepted. He also sought to interest Byron in establishing a steamboat line in Greece but the famous poet replied that the Greeks were 'too ignorant to become interested in such an undertaking'" (*The National Cyclopædia of American Biography*, New York, 1929, xx, 52).]

[607] [Byron arrived in Genoa on October 3, 1822.]

"I have finished," said he, "another play, which I mean to call 'Werner.'[608] The story is taken from Miss Lee's 'Kruitzner.' There are fine things in 'The Canterbury Tales;' but Miss Lee only wrote two of them: the others are the compositions of her sister, and are vastly inferior.[609]

"There is no tale of Scott's finer than 'The German's Tale.'[610] I admired it when I was a boy, and have continued to like what I did then. This tale, I remember, particularly affected me. I could not help thinking of the authoress, who destroyed herself.[611] I was very young when I finished a few scenes of a play founded on that story.[612] I perfectly remember many of the lines as I go on.

" 'Vathek' was another of the tales I had a very early admiration of. You may remember a passage I borrowed from it in 'The Siege of Corinth,' which I almost took verbatim.*[613] No Frenchman will believe that 'Vathek' is the work of a foreigner. It was written at seventeen. What do you think of the Cave of Eblis, and the picture of Eblis himself? There is poetry. I class it in merit with (though it is a different sort

---

* "There is a light cloud by the moon;
'Tis passing, and will pass full soon.
If by the time its vapoury sail
Hath ceased the shaded orb to veil,
Thy heart within thee is not changed,
Then God and man are both avenged,—
Dark will thy doom be—darker still
Thine immortality of ill."

Siege of Corinth.

of thing from) 'Paul and Virginia,' and Mackenzie's 'Man of Feeling,' and 'La Roche' in the 'Mirror.' "[614]

⌒

[608] *Medwin*: January 20th [1822, when *Werner* was completed. Earlier editions have "almost finished . . . 'Werner.'"]

[609] *Medwin*: This is not correct. *The Young Lady's Tale* and *Pembroke* were contributed by the Eldest Sister, *Kruitzner* and all the others by Harriet the youngest. Lord Byron in his Preface to *Werner*, which I had not seen, makes the same mistake.

[610] [Volume IV of *The Canterbury Tales*, by Harriet Lee, was often reprinted as "Kruitzner or the German's Tale."]

[611] *Harness*: It is not more than a year and a half ago, that I had the pleasure of meeting this lady at an evening party; she is, I believe, still at Bath, enjoying the respect and admiration of a large and intellectual circle of acquaintance, and with all the vigour of her talents unimpaired by age, regretted the publication of Lord Byron's *Werner*; because it put a stop to the production of her own dramatic version of the same story. [*BEM*, XVI, 539. Harriet Lee lived until 1851; Sophia Lee died March 13, 1824.]

[612] *Byron in the Preface to Werner*: I had begun a drama upon this tale so far back as 1815, (the first I ever attempted, except one at thirteen years old, called "Ulric and Ilvina," which I had sense enough to burn,) and had nearly completed an act, when I was interrupted by circumstances. [*Poetry*, V, 338 (M). Inasmuch as Ulric also appears in *Werner*, it would appear that Byron had indeed when "very young" begun a play based on *Kruitzner*, as Medwin reports.]

[613] [Byron confessed his debt in a footnote to *The Siege of Corinth*, ll. 643-648.]

[614] [*Paul et Virginie* (1786) by Bernardin de St. Pierre, one of the most sentimental tales ever published, is nearly equalled in sentimentality by Henry Mackenzie's novel, *The Man of Feeling* (1771). Mackenzie's "The Story of La Roche" appeared in three installments (June 19, 22, 26, 1779) in his periodical, *The Mirror*. The title character is an aged Swiss clergyman whose faith sustains him when his daughter dies of heartbreak on the eve of her marriage upon learning that her fiancé had been killed in a duel. There are also commonplaces about the beauty of the Swiss

Alps, able to inspire deep reverence for the Creator. The atheistic philosopher of the tale, who is deeply touched but not converted by La Roche's faith, is an idealized portrait of Mackenzie's friend David Hume. The tale was frequently reprinted in the nineteenth century.]

'Werner' was written in twenty-eight days, and one entire act at a sitting. The MS. had scarcely an alteration in it for pages together.[615] I remember retaining in my memory one passage, which he repeated to me, and which I consider quite Shakspearian.

> "Four
> Five—six hours I have counted, like the guard
> Of outposts, on the never-merry clock,—
> That hollow tongue of time, which, even when
> It sounds for joy, takes something from enjoyment
> With every clang. 'Tis a perpetual knell,
> Though for a marriage-feast it rings: each stroke
> Peals for a hope the less; the funeral note
> Of love deep buried without resurrection
> In the grave of possession; whilst the knoll
> Of long-lived parents finds a jovial echo
> To triple time in the son's ear."[616]

"What can be expected," said I to him, "from a five act play, finished in four weeks?"

"I mean to dedicate 'Werner,'" said he, "to Goethe. I look upon him as the greatest genius that the age has produced. I desired Murray to inscribe his name to a former work; but he pretends my letter containing the order came too late.—It would have been more worthy of him than this."[617]

[615] *Medwin*: He brought it down to us one morning, and I perused it. It was an inspiration, for there was scarcely a word altered in the MSS. He was that day in pretty high spirits. [In an illegible

passage of about 35 words which follows, Medwin seems to be expressing his surprise at the difference between Byron's high spirits and the tragic tone of the play. *Werner* was begun on December 18, 1821, completed on January 20, 1822, according to Byron's notes on Mary Shelley's transcript of the play. She read all or part of *Werner* to Jane Williams on January 16 (Mary's *Journal*, p. 165). Byron's rough draft has disappeared. Did Medwin see this or Mary's copy? If the former, the relative absence of revisions might be explained by the short time of composition and Byron's more than customary dependence on his source.]

[616] [*Werner*, III, iii, 1-12.]

[617] [Murray omitted the dedications of *Sardanapalus* and of *Marino Faliero* to Goethe, although Byron sent a copy of the former dedication to the German poet. See Butler, *Byron and Goethe*, pp. 168-177. *Werner* appeared with a dedication to "the illustrious Goethe."]

"I have a great curiosity about every thing relating to Goethe, and please myself with thinking there is some analogy between our characters and writings. So much interest do I take in him, that I offered to give 100*l*. to any person who would translate his 'Memoirs,' for my own reading.* Shelley has sometimes explained part of them to me. He seems to be very superstitious, and is a believer in astrology,—or rather was, for he was very young when he wrote the first part of his Life.[618] I would give the world to read 'Faust' in the original. I have been urging Shelley to translate it; but he said that the translator of 'Wallenstein' was the only person living who could venture to attempt it;—that he had written to Coleridge, but in vain.[619] For a man to translate it, he must think as *he* does."

"How do you explain," said I, "the first line,—

'The sun thunders through the sky'?"[620]

* An English translation of this interesting work has lately appeared, in 2 vols. 8vo.

"He speaks of the music of the spheres in Heaven," said he, "where, as in Job, the first scene is laid."

618 [Butler, *Byron and Goethe*, p. 121, comments, "Far from being very young when he wrote the first part of *Dichtung und Wahrheit*, Goethe was sixty if a day; and surely even Shelley might have realized that the horoscope of his nativity given in the opening paragraph was meant to be taken symbolically and not literally."]

619 [Coleridge translated the last two parts of Schiller's trilogy.]

620 [From the opening of Goethe's *Faust*, the Prologue in Heaven.]

"Since you left us," said Lord Byron, "I have seen Hobhouse for a few days.621 Hobhouse is the oldest and the best friend I have. What scenes we have witnessed together! Our friendship began at Cambridge. We led the same sort of life in town, and travelled in company a great part of the years 1809, 10, and 11.622 He was present at my marriage, and was with me in 1816, after my separation. We were at Venice, and visited Rome together in 1817. The greater part of my 'Childe Harold' was composed when we were together, and I could do no less in gratitude than dedicate the complete poem to him. The First Canto was inscribed to one of the most beautiful little creatures I ever saw, then a mere child: Lady Charlotte Harley was my Ianthe.

"Hobhouse's Dissertation on Italian literature is much superior to his Notes on 'Childe Harold.'623 Perhaps he understood the antiquities better than Nibbi, or any of the Cicerones; but the knowledge is somewhat misplaced where it is. Shelley went to the opposite extreme, and never made any notes.

"Hobhouse has an excellent heart: he fainted when he heard a false report of my death in Greece,624 and was wonderfully affected at that of Matthews—a much more able man than the *Invalid*. You have often heard me speak of him. The tribute I paid to his memory was a very inadequate one, and ill expressed what I felt at his loss."[625]

[621] *Hobhouse*: It is impossible that lord Byron should have told capt. Medwin that he had seen Mr. Hobhouse at the time alluded to; that is to say, in August, 1822. Mr. Hobhouse did not arrive at Pisa nor see lord Byron until the 15th of September, 1822, after which time capt. Medwin, according to his own statement, never saw lord Byron. . . . So that the whole of this conversation must be a pure fiction, and must have been invented for the sake of making it appear that lord Byron was in the habit of talking confidentially with Mr. Medwin respecting his private friendships. [*WR*, iii, 32-33.]

Medwin: It should have been, "I have heard from Hobhouse, I am to see him." Lord Byron's voice was so low and he mumbled his words so much that the mistake was not extraordinary. But whether he made use of the past or future tense is of little import. It was, however, a nest egg for Hobhouse's viper broth. [Medwin's revised recollection of Byron's words seems a reasonable one. Hobhouse sailed from Dover on July 25 and had made plans well in advance to see Byron, who wrote a letter on September 2, 1822, discussing the proposed visit: "I wrote to you as you requested at Geneva, but you have not apparently received the letter" (*Correspondence*, ii, 227). Thus Byron must have known of Hobhouse's proposed visit at least as early as mid-August, if not long before that time. If so, it is quite possible he mentioned it to Medwin.]

[622] [Hobhouse returned to England in 1810.]

[623] [Hobhouse's *Historical illustrations of the fourth canto of "Childe Harold," containing dissertations on the ruins of Rome and an essay on Italian literature* appeared in 1818. Ugo Foscolo was the author of the essay on modern Italian literature, translated and adapted by Hobhouse. The deception was apparently unknown to Byron.]

[624] *Hobhouse in his diary*, October 25, 1824: The papers this morning full of Captain Medwin's Conversations of Lord Byron [published October 23]—alas, my poor friend! into what society did he fall—but the attaching so much contemptible gossip to his name more than punishes him for that love of low company which I think distinguished him in his latter days. The honorable Cap-

tain has put into Byron's mouth three falsehoods respecting myself.
. . . The third [is] that I fainted when I heard the false report of
Byron's death during his first travels in Greece. I never fainted in
my life.

Some other anecdotes mentioned by Medwin may I think have
come from Byron's mouth—but such anecdotes!! [Unpublished;
from a transcript kindly supplied by Mrs. Doris Langley Moore.]

625 [Charles Skinner Matthews, to whom Byron paid a tribute in
a note to *Childe Harold*, I, xci, drowned in 1811; his brother Henry
was the author of *The Diary of an Invalid*. On Hobhouse's grief
upon the death of Matthews, see Marchand, p. 1244.]

IT may be asked *when* Lord Byron writes. The same question was put to Madame de Staël: *"Vous ne comptez pas sur ma chaise-à-porteurs,"* said she. I am often with him from the time he gets up till two or three o'clock in the morning, and after sitting up so late he must require rest; but he produces, the next morning, proofs that he has not been idle. Sometimes when I call, I find him at his desk; but he either talks as he writes, or lays down his pen to play at billiards till it is time to take his airing. He seems to be able to resume the thread of his subject at all times, and to weave it of an equal texture. Such talent is that of an *improvisatore*. The fairness too of his manuscripts (I do not speak of the handwriting) astonishes no less than the perfection of every thing he writes. He hardly ever alters a word for whole pages, and never corrects a line in subsequent editions. I do not believe that he has ever read his works over since he examined the proof-sheets; and yet he remembers every word of them, and every thing else worth remembering that he has ever known.

I never met with any man who shines so much in conversation.[626] He shines the more, perhaps, for not seeking to shine. His ideas flow without effort, without his having occasion to think. As in his letters, he is not nice about expressions or words;—there are no concealments in him, no injunctions to secresy. He tells every thing that he has thought or done without the least reserve, and as if he wished the whole world to know it; and does not throw the slightest gloss over his errors. Brief himself, he is impatient of diffuseness in others, hates long stories, and seldom repeats his own. If he has heard a story you are telling, he will say, "You told me that," and with good humour sometimes finish it for you himself.

He hates argument, and never argues for victory.[627] He gives every one an opportunity of sharing in the conversation, and has the art of turning it to subjects that may bring out the person with whom he converses. He never shews the author, prides himself most on being a man of the world and of fashion,[628] and his anecdotes of life and living characters are inexhaustible.[629] In spirits, as in every thing else, he is ever in extremes.

Miserly in trifles—about to lavish his whole fortune on the Greeks; to-day diminishing his stud—to-morrow taking a large family under his roof, or giving 1000*l.* for a yacht;* dining for a few Pauls when alone—spending hundreds when he has friends. *"Nil fuit unquam sic impar sibi."*

* He sold it for 300*l.* to Lord Blessington and refused to give the sailors their jackets;[630] and offered once to bet Hay that he would live on 60*l.* a-year.

[628] *Leigh Hunt:* That is to say, Captain Medwin never met with a lord so much the rage. . . . The truth is, as I have before stated, that he had no conversation in the higher sense of the word, owing to these perpetual affectations. . . . [*HVSV*, p. 308.]

[627] [This sentence was deleted by Medwin.]

[628] *Leigh Hunt:* Instead of never showing the author . . . he never forgot it. His sole object was to have an admiring report of himself, as a genius, who could be lord, author, or what he pleased. [*HVSV*, p. 308.]

[629] *Leigh Hunt:* This was true, if you chose to listen to them, and to take everything he said for granted; but every body was not prepared, like the Captain, to be thankful for stories of the noble Lord and all his acquaintances, male and female. [*HVSV*, p. 308.]

[630] *Byron to Trelawny,* November 21, 1822: I have given the boy and one of the men [of the *Bolivar's* crew] their clothes, and if Mr. Beere had been civil, and Frost honest, I should not have been obliged to go so near the wind with them. [*LJ*, vi, 142. The *Bolivar* was sold for 400 guineas, cost £1,000.]

I am sorry to find that he has become more indolent. He has almost discontinued his rides on horseback, and has starved himself into an unnatural thinness; and his digestion is become weaker. In order to keep up the stamina that he requires, he indulges somewhat too freely in wine, and in his favourite beverage, Hollands, of which he now drinks a pint almost every night.

He said to me humourously enough—"Why don't you drink, Medwin? Gin-and-water is the source of all my inspiration. If you were to drink as much as I do, you would write as good verses: depend on it, it is the true Hippocrene."

O N the 28th of August I parted from Lord Byron with increased regret, and a sadness that looked like presentiment. He was preparing for his journey to Genoa, whither he went a few days after my departure.[631] I shall, I hope, be excused in presenting the public with the following sketch of his character, drawn and sent to a friend a few weeks after his death, and to which I adapted the following motto:*

Αστηρ πριν μεν ελαμπες ενι ζωοισιν Εωος,
Νυν δε θανων λαμπεις Ἑσπερος εν φθιμενοις.

" 'Born an aristocrat, I am naturally one by temper,' said Lord Byron.[632] Many of the lines in 'The Hours of Idleness,' particularly the Farewell to Newstead, shew that in early life he prided himself much on his ancestors: but it is their exploits that he celebrates; and when he mentioned his having had his pennant hauled down, he said they might have respected a descendant of the great navigator. Almost from infancy he shewed an independence of character, which a long minority and a maternal education contributed to encourage. His temper was quick, but he never long retained anger. Impatient of control, he was too proud to justify himself when right, or if accused, to own himself wrong; yet no man was more unopinionated, more open to conviction, and more accessible to advice,† when he knew that it proceeded from friendship, or was motivated by affection or regard.

* The following passage in an unpublished life of Alfieri, which I lately met with, might not inaptly be applied to Lord Byron:[633]
"Dès son enfance tous les symptômes d'un caractère fier, indomptable et mélancolique se manifestèrent. Taciturne et tranquille à l'ordinaire, mais quelquefois très babillard, très vif, et presque toujours dans les extrêmes—obstiné et rebelle à la force, très soumis aux avis donnés par amitié; contenu plutôt par la crainte d'être grondé, que par toute autre chose; inflexible quand on voudroit le prendre à rebours;—tel fut-il dans ses jeunes années."
† "Perhaps of all his friends Sir Walter Scott had the most influence over him. The sight of his hand-writing, he said, put him in spirits for the day. Shelley's disapprobation of a poem caused him to destroy it. In compliance with the wishes of the public, he relinquished the drama.

[631] *Medwin*: And here I closed my Journal. [Preceding words either underlined or deleted. It was at this point that Medwin intended to end his own account of Byron, deleting all that followed in the New Edition of 1824 except the translation of Goethe's *Beitrag* on pp. 343-351 in that edition, the Italian depositions of Byron and others concerning the Pisan affair of the dragoon on pp. iii-ix of the Appendix, and Goethe's German on pp. x-xvii of the Appendix. I have omitted the Italian and German documents. On p. xviii of the Appendix, Medwin has written, "In another Edition this appendix [p. xviii-ciii] will be omitted. It was inserted without my Consent—or even knowledge." This confirms the introductory statement at the head of this portion of the Appendix: "In the absence of the Author, who is in Switzerland, the London Editor has ventured to add a few Documents. . . ." I see no reason to omit Medwin's sketch of Byron, "drawn and sent to a friend a few weeks after his death," on pp. 337-343. Although Medwin has deleted each of these pages by drawing a single vertical line down through each one of them, he has also annotated and amended three of them. At the end of the sketch, on p. 343, he has written, "Geneve, 25th July, 1824," which may be the date when Medwin completed copying his manuscript for the printer. On July 10, 1824, he had written to Mary Shelley that he had already "compiled a volume" from notes on Byron's conversation made in Pisa.]

[632] [In the Appendix to *The Two Foscari* (*LJ*, vi, 388): "Born an aristocrat, and naturally one by temper. . . ."]

[633] *Medwin*: Moore has carried out this comparison between Alfieri and Byron. The hint was not lost upon him. [See Moore, *Life*, pp. 9, 268, 644.]

"Though opposed to the foreign policy of England, he was no revolutionist. The best proof of his prizing the constitution of his own country, was that he wished to see it transplanted[634] on the Continent, and over the world; and his first

---

Disown it as he might, he was ambitious of fame, and almost as sensitive as Voltaire or Rousseau: even the gossip of Pisa annoyed him."

Extract from a Letter to a friend, written at Pisa.

and last aspirations were for Greece, her liberty and independence.

"Like Petrarch, disappointed love, perhaps, made him a poet. You know my enthusiasm about him. I consider him in poetry what Michael Angelo was in painting: he aimed at sublimity and effect, rather than the finishing of his pictures; he flatters the vanity of his admirers by leaving them something to fill up. If the eagle flights of his genius cannot always be followed by the eye, it is the fault of our weak vision and limited optics. It requires a mind particularly organized to dive into and sound the depths of his metaphysics. What I admire is the hardihood of his ideas—the sense of power that distinguishes his writings from all others. He told me that, when he wrote, he neither knew nor cared what was coming next.* This is the real inspiration of the poet.

"Which is the finest of his works?—It is a question I have often heard discussed. I have been present when 'Childe Harold,' 'Manfred,' 'Cain,' 'The Corsair,' and even 'Don Juan,' were named;—a proof, at least, of the versatility of his powers, and that he succeeded in many styles of writing. But I do not mean to canvass the merits of these works;—a work on his poetical character and writings is already before the public.†

"Lord Byron's has been called *the Satanic school of poetry.* It is a name that never has stuck, and never will stick,[635] but among a faction.

* ——————— "But, note or text,
I never know the word which will come next."
　　　　Don Juan, Canto IX. Stanza 41.
　† I alluded to Sir E. Brydges' Letters. I lent him my mss Journal of the Conversations to read at Geneva, and without my knowledge he set to work on his Critique. He was perfectly welcome so to do.[636]

[634] [Paraphrased from Byron's Appendix to *The Two Foscari* (*LJ*, VI, 388): "I look upon such as inevitable, though no revolutionist: I wish to see the English constitution restored. . . ."]
[635] *Southey to the Editor of the Courier,* January 5, 1822: His lordship has thought it not unbecoming in him to call me a scribbler of all work. Let the word *scribbler* pass; it is an appellation

which will not stick like that of *the Satanic School.* [*LJ,* VI, 391.]
[636] [See *Captain Medwin,* pp. 163-165.]

"To superficial or prejudiced readers he appeared to con-
found virtue and vice; but if the shafts of his ridicule fell on
mankind in general, they were only *levelled* against the hypo-
critical cant, the petty interests, and despicable cabals and
intrigues of the age. No man respected more the liberty from
which the social virtues emanate. No writings ever tended
more to exalt and ennoble the dignity of man and of human
nature. A generous action, the memory of patriotism, self-
sacrifice, or disinterestedness, inspired him with the sublimest
emotions, and the most glowing thoughts and images to express them; and his indignation at tyranny, vice, or corrup-
tion, fell like a bolt from Heaven on the guilty. We need look
no further for the cause of the hate, private and political, with
which he has been assailed. But 'in defiance of politics,—in
defiance of personality,—his strength rose with oppression;
and laughing his opponents to scorn, he forced the applause
he disdained to solicit.'

"That he was not perfect, who can deny? But how many
men are better?—how few have done more good, less evil, in
their day?[637]

'Bright, brave, and glorious was his young career!'

And on his tomb may be inscribed, as is on that of Raleigh—

> 'Reader! should you reflect on his errors,
> Remember his many virtues,
> And that he was a mortal!' "

The high admiration in which Lord Byron was held in Germany may be appreciated by the following communication,[638]
and tribute to his memory, which I have just received from
the illustrious and venerable Goethe, who, at the advanced
age of seventy-five, retains all the warmth of his feelings, and
fire of his immortal genius.

[637] [Perhaps a recollection of the Appendix to *The Two Foscari* (*LJ*, vi, 389): "I . . . have done more real good in any one given year . . . than Mr. Southey in the whole course of his . . . existence."]

[638] [On the history of Goethe's communication, see Butler, *Byron and Goethe*, pp. 104-108. Goethe's letter was retranslated between Medwin's first edition and "A New Edition."]

Weimar, 16th July, 1824.

"It is thought desirable that I should give some details relative to the intercourse that existed between Lord Noel Byron, alas! now no more! and myself: a few words will suffice for this object.

"Up to the time of my present advanced age, I have habituated myself to weigh with care and impartiality the merit of illustrious persons of my own time generally, as well as of my immediate contemporaries, from the consideration that it would prove a sure means of advancing myself in knowledge. I might well fix my attention on Lord Byron; and, having watched the dawn of his early and great talents, I could hardly fail to follow their progress through his important and uninterrupted career.

"It was easy to observe that the estimate of his poetical talent by the public increased progressively with the advancing perfection of his works, which so rapidly succeeded each other. The interest which they excited had been productive of more unmingled delight to his friends, if self-dissatisfaction and the restlessness of his passions had not in some measure counteracted the power of a most comprehensive and sublime imagination, and thrown a blight over an existence which the nobleness of his nature gave him a more than common capacity for enjoying.

"Not permitting myself to come to a hasty and erroneous conclusion respecting him, I continued to trace, with undiminished attention, a life and a poetical activity alike rare and irreconcileable, which interested me the more forcibly, inasmuch as I could discover no parallel in past ages with which to compare them, and found myself utterly destitute of the elements necessary for calculating the movement of an orb so eccentric in its course.

"In the mean while, neither myself nor my occupations remained unknown or unnoticed by the English poet, who not only furnished unequivocal proofs of an acquaintance with my works, but conveyed to me, through the medium of travellers, more than one friendly salutation.

"Thus I was agreeably surprised by indirectly receiving the original sheet of a dedication of the tragedy of 'Sardanapalus,' conceived in terms the most honourable to me, and accompanied by a request that it might be printed at the head of the work.

"Well knowing myself and my labours, in my old age, I could not but reflect with gratitude and diffidence on the expressions contained in this dedication, nor interpret them but as the generous tribute of a superior genius, no less original in the choice than inexhaustible in the materials of his subjects. I felt no disappointment when, after many delays, 'Sardanapalus' appeared without the preface: for I already thought myself fortunate in possessing a fac-simile in autograph, and attached to it no ordinary value.

"It appeared, however, that the Noble Lord had not renounced his project of shewing his contemporary and companion in letters a striking testimony of his friendly intentions, of which the tragedy of 'Werner' contains precious evidence.

"It might naturally be expected that the aged German poet, after receiving a kindness unhoped for, from so celebrated a person, (proof of a disposition thoroughly generous, and the more to be prized from its rarity in the world,) should also prepare, on his part, to express most clearly and forcibly a sense of the gratitude and esteem with which he was affected.

"But this task was great, and every day seemed to make it

more difficult,—for what could be said of an earthly being whose merit was not to be conceived in thought, or expressed in words?

"But when, in the spring of 1823, Mr. S———,[639] a young man of amiable and engaging manners, brought direct from Genoa to Weimar a few words under the hand of this estimable friend, by way of recommendation, and when shortly after a report was spread that the Noble Lord was about to consecrate his great powers and varied talents to high and perilous enterprize, I had no longer a plea for delay, and addressed to him the following hasty stanzas:[640]

'One friendly word comes fast upon another
    From the warm South, bringing communion sweet,—
Calling us amid noblest thoughts to wander
    Free in our souls, though fetter'd in our feet.

How shall I, who so long his bright path traced,
    Say to him words of love sent from afar?—
To him who with his inmost heart hath struggled,
    Long wont with fate and deepest woes to war?

May he be happy!—*thus* himself esteeming,
    He well might count himself a favour'd one!
By his loved Muses all his sorrows banish'd,
    And he *self-known*,—e'en as to *me* he's known!'

"These lines arrived at Genoa, but found him not. My excellent friend had already sailed; but, being driven back by contrary winds, he landed at Leghorn, where this effusion of my heart reached him. On the eve of his departure, July 23d, 1823, he found time to send me a reply, full of the most beautiful ideas and the noblest sentiments, which will be treasured as an invaluable testimony of worth and friendship among the choicest documents which I possess.

"What emotions of hope and joy did not that paper once excite!—now it has become, by the premature death of the noble writer, an inestimable relic—a source of unspeakable regret; for it increases in me particularly, to no small degree, that mourning and melancholy which pervade the whole moral and poetical world,—in me, who looked forward (after the success of his great efforts) to the prospect of being blessed with the sight of this master-spirit of the age,—this friend so fortunately acquired; and of having to welcome, on his return, the most humane of conquerors.

"Yet I am consoled by the conviction, that his country will instantly *awake*, and shake off, like a troubled dream, the partialities, the prejudices, the injuries, and the calumnies with which he has been assailed,—causing them to subside and sink into oblivion,—that she will at length universally acknowledge that his frailties, whether the consequence of temperament, or the defect of the times in which he lived, (against which even the best of mortals wrestle painfully,) were fleeting and transitory; whilst the imperishable greatness to which he has raised her name now remains, and will for ever remain, boundless in its glory, and incalculable in its consequences. There is no doubt that a nation so justly proud of her many great sons, will place BYRON, all radiant as he is, by the side of those who have conferred on her the highest honour."

<hr />

[639] [On Charles Sterling, son of the British consul at Genoa, see Butler, pp. 86-88.]

[640] *Medwin*: [Translated] by Coleridge. [This translation is not included in E. H. Coleridge's Oxford edition of the *Poems* (1921). The presence of Coleridge's hand is uncertain, witnessed only by Medwin's note. It may be significant that although Goethe's prose was retranslated between the first edition and the New Edition of 1824, his poem was not. Professor Kathleen Coburn, general editor of the forthcoming definitive edition of Coleridge's complete works, informs me that "there are phrases that could be Coleridge's," and she observes that "the sentiments of Goethe's poem are such as to attract Coleridge."]

SELECTIVE BIBLIOGRAPHY
WITH ABBREVIATIONS

BEM—John Galt, "Lord Byron's Conversations," *Blackwood's Edinburgh Magazine*, XVI (November, 1824), 530-535.

BEM—"Harroviensis" [William Harness], "Lord Byron's Conversations," *Blackwood's Edinburgh Magazine*, XVI (November, 1824), 536-540.

Correspondence—*Lord Byron's Correspondence*. Ed. John Murray. London, 1922.

GM—J[ohn] M[urray], "Murray on '*Conversations of Lord Byron*,'" *The Gentleman's Magazine*, CXXXVI (November, 1824), 438-442.

HVSV—*His Very Self and Voice: Collected Conversations of Lord Byron*. Ed. Ernest J. Lovell, Jr. New York, 1954.

Journal—*Maria Gisborne & Edward E. Williams, Shelley's Friends: Their Journals and Letters*. Ed. Frederick L. Jones. Norman, Okla., 1951.

Letters—*The Letters of Percy Bysshe Shelley*. Ed. Frederick L. Jones. London, 1964.

Life—Thomas Moore, *Letters and Journals of Lord Byron: with Notices of His Life*. London, 1892.

LJ—*The Works of Lord Byron. Letters and Journals*. Ed. Rowland E. Prothero. London, 1898-1901.

(M)—Marginalia by Medwin in his annotated copy of his *Conversations of Lord Byron*, transcribed from Moore's *Life* of Byron.

Poetry—*The Works of Lord Byron. Poetry*. Ed. Ernest Hartley Coleridge. London, 1898-1904.

Recollections—John Cam Hobhouse (Lord Broughton), *Recollections of a Long Life*. Ed. Lady Dorchester. London, 1909-1911.

Shelley—Thomas Medwin, *The Life of Percy Bysshe Shelley*. London, 1847. [Distinguished from the 1913 edition, in one volume, ed. H. Buxton Forman, by the use of a Roman numeral to refer to the volume number.]

WR—[John Cam Hobhouse], "Dallas's *Recollections* and Medwin's *Conversations*," *The Westminster Review*, III (January, 1825), 1-35.

OTHER BOOKS

Butler, E. M., *Byron and Goethe: Analysis of a Passion*. London, 1956.

Cline, C. L., *Byron, Shelley and their Pisan Circle*. Cambridge, Mass., 1952.

Elwin, Malcolm, *Lord Byron's Wife*. New York, 1963.

Galt, John, *The Life of Lord Byron*. London, 1830.

Hunt, Leigh, *Lord Byron and Some of his Contemporaries*. London, 1828.

Lovelace, Ralph Milbanke, Earl of, *Astarte*. Ed. Mary, Countess of Lovelace. London, 1921.

Lovell, Ernest J., Jr., *Captain Medwin, Friend of Byron and Shelley*. Austin, 1962.

Marchand, Leslie A., *Byron, A Biography*. New York, 1957.

Mayne, Ethel Colburn, *The Life and Letters of Anne Isabella, Lady Noel Byron*. London, 1929.

Medwin, Thomas, *The Angler in Wales*. London, 1834.

Moore, Doris Langley, *The Late Lord Byron*. Philadelphia, 1961.

Moore, Thomas, *The Letters of Thomas Moore*. Ed. Wilfred S. Dowden. London, 1964.

——, *Memoirs, Journal and Correspondence*. Ed. Lord John Russell. London, 1853-1856.

Origo, Iris, *The Last Attachment*. New York, 1949.

Peck, Louis F., *A Life of Matthew G. Lewis*. Cambridge, Mass., 1961.

Polidori, John William, *The Diary of John William Polidori*. Ed. William Michael Rossetti. London, 1911.

Scott, Sir Walter, *The Letters of Sir Walter Scott*. Ed. H. J. C. Grierson and others. London, 1932-1937.

Shelley, Mary W., *The Letters of Mary W. Shelley*. Ed. Frederick L. Jones. Norman, Okla., 1944.

——, *Mary Shelley's Journal*. Ed. Frederick L. Jones. Norman, Okla., 1947.

Shelley, Percy Bysshe, *The Complete Works of Percy Bysshe Shelley*. Ed. Roger Ingpen and Walter E. Peck. London, 1926-1930.

White, Newman Ivey, *Shelley*. London, 1947.

INDEX

Addison, Joseph, *Cato*, 135
Aeschylus, 231n; *Eumenides*, 156; *Prometheus Bound*, 156, 159n
Agrigentum, 11, 11n
air vessels, 187-88
Albanians, Byron's, 87, 91, 92n
Alfieri, Vittorio, 94, 95, 95n, 97, 97n, 178, 233, 268n
Ali Pasha, 84, 84-86n
Americans, 52, 256, 256n, 257n
Angelina, 75, 76n
Ariosto, 254
Aristotle, 165
Athens, 86
Austrians, 11n, 75-76, 229, 230n

bailiffs, 38
Baillie, D. "Long," 80
Baillie, Joanna, *De Monfort*, 95, 95n
Baillie, Dr. Matthew, 44-45, 45n, 46, 46-47n
Bailly, Jean Sylvain, 139-140n
Bartolini, Lorenzo, 7n, 8n
Battista ("Tita"), *see* Falcieri
Beauclerk, Mrs. Emily, 107, 222n, 227n
Beckford, William, *Vathek*, 218, 258
Benzoni, Countess Marina, 23, 24n, 120
Best, Mr., 19n
billiards, 10, 14, 19, 265
blank verse, 236
Blessington, Lord, 6n, 266n
Boccaccio, *The Decameron*, 53, 53n, 164
Bolivar (Byron's boat), 13, 14n, 252, 253, 253n, 256-57, 257n, 266, 266n
Bonstetten, Charles Victor de, 12
Bosphorus, 11
Boswell, James, xx, xxi
Bowles, Rev. William Lisle, 197-98, 199n
Brougham, Henry, 142, 144-47

Browne, William George, 80, 81n
Brummell, Beau, 72n, 108n, 182, 183n, 214
Brydges, Sir Samuel E., xvi n, 251n, 270n
Burckhardt, John Lewis, 79, 81n
Burdett, Sir Francis, 112, 112n
Burghersh, Lady, 30, 31n
Byron, Allegra (natural daughter of poet), 101, 102n
Byron, Lady (Anne Isabella Milbanke, wife of poet), 20n, 31n, 109, 111, 182, 253, 255n; declines to read Byron's "Memoirs," 31-32, 32n; Byron's first sight of, 32, 33n; appearance of, 33-34; rejects Byron's first proposal, 34; renews correspondence, 34, 34-35n; marries, 34; begins honeymoon, 35n, 36, 37n; wedding ring of, 35, 36n; fortune of, 36; marriage settlement of, 37-38n, 51n; deed of separation of, 37n, 51n; returns to father, 38, 39n; Byron speaks harshly to, 41, 42n, 43n; opens Byron's writing desk, 42, 43-44n; never in love with Byron, 46; wished to reform Byron, 46, 47n; a spoiled child, 46, 47n; analyzes Byron's character, 46; cannot express herself clearly, 48; inconsistent, 48; receives Byron's mistresses, 69, 69n; sends Byron prayer book, 81, 81n; an only child, 101, 102n; separation of, 110; inheritance of, 111-12, 112n; cannot manage Byron, 134n; and de Staël, 184, 185n
Byron, Augusta Ada (daughter of poet and Lady Byron), 32n, 58, 101-104, 111
Byron, Mrs. Catherine Gordon (mother of poet), 9n, 50, 51n,

56-57, 57n, 58n, 59, 91, 92n, 101, 102n, 214, 215n

Byron, Captain George (father of the 7th Lord), 58-59, 59n

Byron, George Anson (cousin of poet, later 7th Lord), 48, 49n

Byron, George Gordon, 6th Lord —traits, habits, possessions, etc., of: affections, xv; alcoholic drink, 19, 266-67; animals, 3, 3n, 4n, 4-5, 10, 10n, 67, 68n; appearance, 7-9, 7-9n; breakfast, 9; carriages, 3, 4n, 19, 38, 38n; conversation, xvi-xvii, 9, 52, 255n, 265-66, 266n; debts, 50; diet, 9-10, 109; digestion, 9, 266; dissipation, 30, 54, 64, 72, 73; exile, 50; extravagance, financial, 38, 72; friendships, 63n, 124, 125n; frivolity of life, 70, 72; furniture, 3; gambling, 70-71, 71n; generosity, 112, 113n, 266; health, 11, 72, 91, 92n, 252-53, 253n, 266; horsemanship, 14, 15n, 72-73, 73n, 266; income, 36, 38n; indolence, 11, 266; insanity, supposed, 45-46, 46-47n; library, 3, 4n; lockets, 61n, 62n; marksmanship, 15, 15n, 16n, 18, 18n, 19, 103, 118n; marriage, 55; mimicry, 136, 136n, 137n; mistresses, 67, 68n, 87-88, 88-89n, 214-19; name, pronunciation of, 35n; nephritic complaint, 19; openness, xvi; ostracism, 48, 49n; parsimony, 109n, 266, 266n; passions, xv, 55, 71, 268; plagiarism, 139-40, 141n; politics, 228, 229, 269-70; prejudices about women, 41, 73; privacy invaded, 11, 52; proposal of marriage, 56n; religion, 77, 78, 80, 82; reputation, 11, 46; restlessness, xv; routine, daily, 19, 265; separation, 146-47, 147n; servants, 3, 5, 244, 244n, 245n, 246; skull cup, 64-65, 66n; sociability, 109;

speeches, parliamentary, 229, 229n, 230n; strangers, dislike of, 3; superstitiousness, 4, 55, 103-104, 104n, 107; swimming prowess, 116-18, 118n, 252, 253n; unhappiness, 110; unpopularity of poems, 123n; vanity, 116n; voice, 132, 133n, 263n

WORKS: *Beppo*, 21n, 23n, 224, 226n; *Cain*, 126-31, 150, 155, 156, 171, 171-73n, 212, 226, 227, 227n; *Childe Harold*, 50n, 54, 64n, 104n, 159, 159n, 160n, 164, 169, 177, 183n, 185, 186n, 194, 214, 233, 262; Italian translation of, 76, 76n, 162, 163n; "Condolatory Address," 219, 219n; *Corsair*, 104n, 123n, 144, 163n, 167n, 206, 207n, 214; *Deformed Transformed*, 153-54, 155n; *Don Juan*, 10n, 25n, 26, 29n, 45n, 50n, 60n, 72n, 77, 101n, 108n, 110, 121n, 139, 140, 161n, 168, 175n, 223, 223n, 227, 229, 231, 231n, 232n; proposed continuation of, 164-65, 165-66n; "Dream," 60n, 64n; *English Bards and Scotch Reviewers*, 144, 145n, 147-48, 168, 170n; "Fare Thee Well," 177, 177n; *Giaour*, 29n, 223, 231, 232n; factual foundations of, 86-88, 88-89n; *Heaven and Earth*, 5, 6n, 142, 155-56, 159n; proposed continuation of, 157-58; *Hebrew Melodies*, 47n; *Hours of Idleness*, 59, 62, 64, 131n, 142, 144, 145n, 268; *Irish Avatar*, 220, 221n; *Lament of Tasso*, 158; *Lara*, 206; "Lines to a Lady Weeping," 219, 219n; *Manfred*, 163n, 169; *Marino Faliero*, 21n, 22, 53n, 98, 119-21, 122n, 125, 134, 135, 139, 139-40n, 141, 175, 175n; *Mazeppa*, 105; "Memoirs," xv, xv n, 30, 30-31n, 31, 49n, 54, 173n, 178, 226; "New Vicar of Bray,"

212, 213n; "Ode on Venice," 169n; *Parisina*, 169n; *Prisoner of Chillon*, 52n, 158, 169; *Prophecy of Dante*, 21, 158-61; "Question and Answer," 209n; "Remember thee," 218; *Sardanapalus*, 171, 171-73n, 273; *Siege of Corinth*, 44, 45n, 163n, 169n, 177, 177n, 258, 258n, 259n; "To Mr. Murray," 174n; *Two Foscari*, 111, 119-20, 148, 151n, 171, 171-73n; *Vision of Judgment*, 150; *Werner*, 123, 123n, 175, 175n, 258, 259n, 260, 260-61n, 273; "Windsor Poetics," 219, 219n

Byron, Admiral John (grandfather of poet), 257, 257n

Byron, John (father of poet), 55-56, 55-56n, 57, 57-58n

Byron, William, 5th Lord, duel of, 58; eccentricity of, 58

Cain, 126, 126n
Calderón de la Barca, Pedro, 123, 133n, 142, 143n
Caligula, 48
Calthorpe, Lord, 63-64, 65n
Cambridge University, 67, 68n, 132, 262
Camelford, Lord, 19n
Campbell, Thomas, 115; "Hohenlinden," 114, 136, 136n
Canning, George, 182
cant, 96, 271
Carbonari, 26, 27n, 28n, 230n. *See also* Constitutionalists
Carlisle, Lord, 234-35, 236n
Carmarthen, Lady (mother of Augusta Leigh), 57, 58n
Casti, Giovanni Battista, *Novelle*, 140, 140n
Castlereagh, Robert Stewart, Viscount, 228
Catherine the Great, 165
Catholicism, Roman, 78, 80, 220, 229, 229n
Cavalier Servente, 22, 23n, 74
Cecil, Lieutenant, 15, 16-17n
Charlemont, Lady, 215n

Charles Albert (prince of Carignano), 26, 27n
Charlment, Mrs., *see* Clermont, Mrs.
Chateaubriand, François, René, 95
Chatterton, Thomas, 235
Chaworth, Mary, 60-62, 64, 66n
Christianity, 77-83, 237
Church, Edward (American consul), 256n, 257n
Churchill, Charles, 126-27
Cibber, Colley, 140
Clare, Lord, 31n, 63, 63n
Clermont, Mrs., 41, 43n
Cochrane, Thomas, Lord, 229, 230n
Cogni, Margarita, 74, 74-75n
Coleridge, Samuel Taylor, 197, 198, 261; *Remorse*, 97; "Ye Clouds! that far above me float," 114, 148; *Christabel*, 156, 177, 203, 204n; *Ancient Mariner*, 177; *Kubla Khan*, 178; *Biographia Literaria*, 178; "Sonnet: To the Autumnal Moon," 178, 179n; translates Goethe's poem on Byron for Medwin, 275n
Constantinople, 11, 164
Constitutional Association, 173, 174n
Constitutionalists, Italian, 24, 26. *See also* Carbonari
Cowper, William, 79, 81n
Crawford, James, 244
Crébillon, Claude, 44n, 206, 207n
Creech, Thomas, 79, 81n
Croker, John Wilson, 169-70n; on personal confidences, xvi n, 40n; asserts Hobhouse's review supports Medwin's veracity, 128n; supports Medwin against Hobhouse, 140n; questions Byron's veracity, 146n, 172n; on Murray's generosity, 167n
Cuvier, Georges, 157

Dacre, Lady (Mrs. Wilmot), 95, 97n, 99

141-42, 143n, 183n, 223, 223n, 226, 227n, 260-62; his contribution to Medwin's *Conversations of Byron*, 272-75
Goths, 11, 65, 231
Grattan (son of Henry Grattan), 218
Grattan, Thomas Colley, xvi n
Gray, Thomas, 12, 114
Greece, 21n, 24, 159, 214, 229, 230n, 231, 233, 233n, 234n, 256, 256n, 257-58n, 266, 270
Grey, Lord, 182
Guiccioli, Count Alessandro, 22, 23n, 24, 24n
Guiccioli, Countess Teresa, 3n, 19-21, 20-21n, 22, 23n, 24, 25n, 150, 164, 233, 233n, 253; vetoes performance of *Othello*, 134; suggests *Prophecy of Dante*, 158; moves into Lanfranchi Palace, 246, 246n
Guilford, Lord, 180, 181n

Hamilton, Anthony, *De Grammont*, 178
Hampden Club, 224, 225n
Hanson, John, 147, 256
Harlow, George Henry, 74, 75n
Harness, William, 6n
Harrow, 5, 60, 62-64, 124-25, 228
Hastings, Warren, 202, 203n
Hawke, Martin, 6n, 166n
Hay, Captain John, 6n, 55, 56n, 72, 72n, 242, 243, 244, 266n
Hayley, William, 178, 179n
Heathcote, Lady, 217n, 218n
Heber, Bishop, 122
Hellespont, Byron swims, 116-17
Henry VIII, 48, 49n
Hentsch, Charles, 10, 10n, 12
Hervey, Mrs. Elizabeth, 12, 12n
Hinduism, 78, 118
Hobhouse, John Cam, 4n, 13, 14n, 15, 16n, 31n, 109, 131n; quarrels with Scrope Davies, 71, 71n; denounces Byron's *Cain*, 126-28; and the story of

the Definite Article, 132, 132-33n; his friendship with Byron, 262, 263n, 264n
Hodgson, Francis, 147n
Hogg, James, 120, 196, 197n
Holland, Lady, 6n, 234
Homer, 164
Hook, Theodore, 136, 137n, 183n
Hookham (the publisher), 224, 225n
Hoppner, Richard B., 158, 159n
Horton, Sir Robert Wilmot, 49n
Hume, David, 79, 81n, 260n
Hunt, John, 150
Hunt, Leigh, 93, 233-34, 252, 252n; *Foliage*, 151, 152n, 254, 255n; moves in with Byron, 246, 246n, 266; acquaintance with Byron, 253-55; *Rimini*, 254, 255n

improvisatores, 136-38
Ireland, 229, 230n
Irving, Washington, xvi n, 227n

Jeffrey, Francis, 20, 144, 145-46n, 147, 158; reviews *Marino Faliero*, 121
Jersey, Lady, 48, 50, 50n, 51n, 214
Job, book of, 142, 143n, 262
Jocelyn, Lord, 124, 125n
Johnson, Dr. Samuel, 79, 81n, 126-27, 130, 164, 198, 199n
Jonson, Ben, 93; *Every Man in his Humour*, 96n
Joseph, son of Jacob, 69

Kant, Immanuel, 178
Kean, Edmund, 95, 97n, 134, 135n
Keats, John, 144, 145n, 237; *Endymion*, 238; *Hyperion*, 238
Kemble, John Philip, 94, 135, 135n, 136, 136n, 137n
Kinnaird, Charles, 8th Lord, 107
Kinnaird, Douglas, 30, 31n, 92, 150, 155, 166

Lake poets, 194-97

Milbanke, Sir Ralph and Lady Judith, *see* Noel

Milman, Henry Hart, 122, 123n; *Fazio*, 97, 98n; *Fall of Jerusalem*, 237

Milton, John, 77-78, 78n, 79n, 122, 126, 129, 130, 162, 164, 198, 237

missionary societies, 78

Moloni (the Pisan bookseller), 179

moon, flight to, 187

Moore, Thomas, xix, xx, xxi, 16n, 32, 33n, 78, 99, 121, 208, 209n, 220, 226, 254; Byron's "Memoirs" given to, 30, 30n, 31n; *Irish Melodies*, 114; on Byron's *Cain*, 128; introduction to Byron, 147, 147n, 148, 149n; writes poem on Southey, 154-55, 155n; *Love of the Angels*, 156, 158, 158n; *Lalla Rookh*, 158, 238, 239; *Life of Sheridan*, 192; *Life of Lord Fitzgerald*, 222n; *The Fudge Family*, 240; "Epistle from Tom Crib to Big Ben," 240, 240-41n

Morat, field of, 67, 68n

More, Hannah, *Cœlebs in Search of a Wife*, 57

Morning Chronicle, The, 50n, 255n

Mulock, Thomas, 81, 81n

Munden, Joseph Shepherd, 94, 96n

Murray, John, xvi n, xix, xx, 30n, 31n, 99, 99n, 128, 150, 155, 156, 200; his relations with Byron, 166-75

Napier, Sir Charles, 85-86n

Naples, 11

Napoleon, 55, 72n, 73, 104, 184-85, 185n, 233-34

Neapolitan revolution, 27n

Nero, 48

Newstead Abbey, 50, 51n, 60; monkish parties at, 64-65, 66n

Noel, Lady Judith, 34, 34n, 35n, 41, 42n, 46, 103n, 120-21; death of, 111, 256

Noel, Sir Ralph, 36, 38, 39n, 40n, 41n, 46, 49n

Nott, Rev. George Frederick, 212-13

novel, 165n

O'Connor family, 222

Old Bailey proceedings, 139, 139n, 140n

O'Neill, Eliza (the actress), 134, 138

opera, 138, 150, 184

Otway, Thomas, 139, 139n

Oxford, Lady, Byron's affair with, 70, 71n

Pæstum, 11

Paine, Thomas, 221, 222n

Papal States, 229, 230n

Papi, Vincenzo, 245n

Patras, 91, 92n

Patterson, Mr., 53n

Pausanias, 123-24, 124n

Peacock, Thomas Love, *Melincourt*, 67, 67n

peasants, 24

Peel, Sir Robert, 92n

Petrarch, 64; *Africa*, 99, 99-100n

Phillips, Thomas, 47n, 102n

phrenology, 58, 58n, 59n

Phrosine, story of, 84, 84-86n, 89n

Pictet, M., 12-13, 13n, 14n

Pio VII, Pope, 24

piracy, 168

Pisa, 10, 18

Plato, 80, 81n

Plautus, *Amphytrion*, 178, 179n

Polidori, Dr. John William, 11, 13, 13n, 14n, 104-07, 214, 215n

politics, 228

Pope, Alexander, 93, 126-27, 198

Portugal, 229, 230n

Potiphar's wife, 69

Powerscourt, Lord, 6n

Priestley, Joseph, 79, 79n

Prince Regent (later George IV),